Appraising *Genji*

Appraising *Genji*

Literary Criticism and Cultural Anxiety in the Age of the Last Samurai

Patrick W. Caddeau

State University of New York Press

Cover print by Tsukioka Yoshitoshi (1839–1892): Ghost of Yūgao in *The Tale of Genji*, from the series *Tsuki Hyakushi*, "One Hundred Aspects of the Moon" (1886). Courtesy of Israel Goldman, London.

Published by

State University of New York Press, Albany

Printed in the United States of America

For information, address State University of New York Press,
194 Washington Avenue, Suite 305, Albany, NY 12210-2384

Production, Laurie Searl
Marketing, Susan Petrie

Library of Congress Cataloging-in-Publication Data

Caddeau, Patrick W., 1965–
Appraising Genji : literary criticism and cultural anxiety in the age of the last samurai / Patrick W. Caddeau.
p. cm.
Includes bibliographical references and index.
ISBN 0-7914-6673-6 (hardcover : alk. paper)
ISBN-13: 978-0-7914-6673-5 (hardcover : alk. paper)
ISBN-13: 978-0-7914-6674-2 (paperback : alk. paper)
1. Murasaki Shikibu, b. 978? Genji monogatari. I. Title.

PL788.4.G
895.6′314–dc22 2005014022

10 9 8 7 6 5 4 3 2 1

CONTENTS

ILLUSTRATIONS

ACKNOWLEDGMENTS

I am indebted to friends and colleagues in the United States and Japan for their advice and comments. Yamazaki Jun patiently guided me through numerous passages of commentary that to me were impenetrable. Yamazaki Katsuaki made it possible for me to gain access to important documents I might never have discovered on my own and helped me better understand Hagiwara Hiromichi as a person and as a scholar. Edwin McClellan's advice, knowledge, and encouragement were of incalculable benefit to me in the early stages of this book. Thomas Harper and Gaye Rowley have been unfailingly kind and generous from the start. This book would not have been possible without their insightful scholarship and felicitous translations. Edward Kamens has been and continues to be my teacher. Tanada Teruyoshi kindly introduced me to the world of *Genji* in *manga*. Ii Haruki gave generously of his time, insight, and vast knowledge. Royall Tyler's new translation of *Genji* and his interpretation of the tale helped guide and inspire me. Haruo Shirane encouraged me to participate in many publications, conferences, and conversations on *Genji*. My debt to him is great beyond words. Wako Tawa and Paola Zamperini have been great colleagues and generous friends during my time in Amherst. I would also like to thank anonymous reviewers for their insightful and constructive comments. Many thanks go to Laurie Searl for her enthusiasm and editorial guidance.

Support for this book was provided by the H. Axel Schupf 1975 fund for Intellectual Life at Amherst College.

This book would not have been completed without the support of family and friends. David Odo, Dawn Lawson, and John Urda provided the friendship and advice that kept me going. Above all, I wish to thank my wife, Meg. I dedicate this book to her and to my children, Jacob and Isabella, who have made it possible for me to understand the wonder of life that Murasaki Shikibu captured with such eloquence.

CHRONOLOGY AND CONVENTIONS IN THIS BOOK

MAJOR HISTORICAL PERIODS

Nara	710–794
Heian	794–1185
Kamakura	1185–1333
North and South Courts	1337–1392
Muromachi	1333–1568
Warring States	1477–1573
Edo/Tokugawa	1600–1868
Meiji	1868–1912
Taishō	1912–1926
Shōwa	1926–1989
Heisei	1989–

DATES

Dates in reference to events before the Meiji period are based on the lunar calendar. For this reason the number of the month is provided rather than the Western month name associated with the solar calendar. Numbered months according to the lunar calendar are roughly equivalent to the following Western conventions:

First through third month: spring—February to April
Fourth through sixth month: summer—May to July
Seventh through ninth month: fall—August to October
Tenth through twelfth month: winter—November to January

ROMANIZATION

Japanese words are romanized according to the Hepburn system—as found in *Kenkyūsha's New Japanese-English Dictionary*. Words frequently found in English-language sources, such as Shinto and Tokyo, are romanized without macrons.

Unless otherwise indicated, modern orthography in romanized format is used for the transcription of classical Japanese. Chinese words are romanized according to the *pinyin* system, and a Japanese reading is provided when the term would have been familiar to contemporary readers in Japan. Because many premodern names, titles, and terms can only be found in Chinese and Japanese language reference texts a character glossary for these terms is included in the notes.

NAMES

Japanese names appear with the family or surname first, followed by the given, personal, or artistic name. This book also follows the convention in Japanese scholarship of referring to premodern figures solely by their given, personal, or artistic name after the first occurrence of the full name. Figures who lived during the modern period but are closely associated with premodern or early modern culture are often referred to according to the convention of premodern names. For example, Tsubouchi Shōyō (1859–1935) was most active during the Meiji and Taishō periods but is commonly referred to in Japanese publications as *Shōyō*. Modern figures are normally referred to solely by their surnames following the first appearance of their full names.

TERMINOLOGY

A few Japanese terms central to the themes of this book do not lend themselves to a single equivalent in English translation because they have crossed the boundary that often divides scholarship on premodern and modern Japan. *Kokugaku* (lit. "scholarship of the country") refers to the study of Japanese texts with particular reference to texts from antiquity that were not originally composed in classical Chinese. At the end of the Edo period and during the early years of the Meiji period, the meaning of *kokugaku* took on additional connotations as the study of texts from Europe and the United States also came to play a role in scholarship. During this period *kokugaku* came to stand for scholarship focused on Japanese texts as opposed to both Chinese and Western texts. The term *kokugaku* is often translated as *nativism*. This book follows that convention but also acknowledges conventions of Western scholarship by referring to the ideology promoted by the *kokugaku* school as *nationalism*, following Japan's rise as a modern nation-state in 1868. This is not meant to suggest that *kokugaku* thought in the Edo period is somehow discontinuous with *kokugaku* thought in the Meiji period. This book emphasizes the continuity of ideas across the divide that separates Edo from Meiji.

In the Edo period, works of didactic vernacular fiction imported from China came to be widely read and emulated in Japan. These works were sometimes referred to using the Japanese reading, *shōsetsu*, of the Chinese characters for the literary genre from which they originally came, *xiao shuo*. The late-Edo critic Hagiwara Hiromichi (1815–1863) sought to read *The Tale of Genji* (*Genji monogatari*) as if it were a work of popular fiction. He applied critical terms associated with the interpretation of Chinese fiction to read *Genji* as if it were a *shōsetsu*. In the Meiji period, the critic Tsubouchi Shōyō applied the Edo-period term *shōsetsu* to translate the word *novel* into modern Japanese. In this light, the Western convention of labeling *Genji* as a *novel* and Hiromichi's practice in the Edo period of interpreting *Genji* as if it were a *shōsetsu* intersect in significant ways. This book deliberately tries to avoid conflating terminology on this important point. For this reason, *The Tale of Genji* is most often referred to simply as *Genji*, or as a work belonging to the broader literary genre of narrative prose, most commonly referred to in Japanese as the *monogatari* (tale, lit. "narrative"). The *shōsetsu* is referred to in terms of its status as *popular fiction*. The term *novel* is reserved for cases where these two distinct notions intersect in meaningful ways.

ABBREVIATIONS

Refer to the bibliography for the full citation of the following abbreviations:

GMH: See Muromatsu Iwao, ed., *Genji monogatari hyōshaku*.
KMZS: See Akiyama Ken, ed., *Kamo no Mabuchi zenshū*.
MNZS: See Ōno Susumu, ed., *Motoori Norinaga zenshū*.
Shikashichiron: See Taira Shigemichi and Abe Akio, eds., *Shikashichiron*.
NKBDJ: See Iwanami Shoten, *Nihon koten bungaku daijiten*.
NKBZS: See Abe Akio, et al., eds., *Nihon koten bungaku zenshū*.
SNKBT: See Yanai Shigeshi, et al., eds., *Shin Nihon koten bungaku taikei*.

INTRODUCTION

Many renowned thinkers have praised *The Tale of Genji* since its composition in the early eleventh century. Undaunted by the efforts of his predecessors, the poet and scholar Hagiwara Hiromichi (1815–1863) chose deliberately simple language to turn the world of *Genji* commentary and criticism on its head. In explaining *Genji*'s status as a monument of prose fiction, he wrote:

> The more one reads *Genji* the more difficult it becomes to express how exceptional it is. . . . The text is remarkably detailed and complete. Put simply, it is written in a way that allows one to scratch in all the places that itch.[1]

Hiromichi's approach was direct and unpretentious. He focused on prose style and structure to substantiate his claim that the tale was a literary masterpiece. This analysis led him to the conclusion that the internal consistency of textual detail and the unvarnished depiction of human feeling and behavior give the reader a sense that he or she has encountered a fictional world as real and compelling as life itself. He equated this sense of realism (*kotogara no makotomekite*) with a theatrical production's power to capture the imagination of its audience by seamlessly integrating scenery, staging, acting, and script. To guide inexperienced readers and allow them to appreciate *Genji* with the same sense of engagement and satisfaction he had discovered after devoting his life to its study, he abandoned the interpretive traditions he found ineffective and devised new ones of his own.

The benefits of close textual analysis based on nothing more than internal evidence may seem obvious to modern readers. However, this approach challenged the dominant conventions of the Edo period (1600–1868). Hiromichi's immediate predecessors were deeply invested in establishing *Genji*'s importance in relation to Buddhism, Confucianism, and, ultimately, the superiority of Japan's indigenous culture over traditions imported from the Asian continent. These interpretive schemes tied the evaluation of *Genji* to particular moral, ideological, or cultural values. Hiromichi emphasized the tale's internal consistency and literary style in ways that avoided such imperatives. He sought to make the language of a literary masterpiece from antiquity available to a wider readership and to capitalize on the voracious appetite for popular fiction that had come to transcend distinctions of class in late-Edo Japan.

The first two installments of his commentary, *Appraisal of Genji* (*Genji monogatari hyōshaku*, published in 1854 and 1861), were well received and widely reprinted. This initial success was soon cut short. After battling illness to see the opening volumes of his greatest work to print, Hiromichi died in 1863. Five years after his death, the Tokugawa Shogunate collapsed and centuries of cultural isolation came to an end. Politicians and intellectuals eager to bring the attributes of modern "civilization and enlightenment" (*bunmei kaika*) to Japan embraced Western culture in the early years of the Meiji period (1868–1912). Readers were also anxious to increase their knowledge of the world beyond East Asia. Domestic literary favorites soon faced stiff competition from adaptations and translations from abroad. Hiromichi's work stands at the apex of Edo-period scholarship on *Genji*. The subtle analysis he sets forth in his *Appraisal of Genji* also establishes him as one of the most perceptive readers of the tale in its thousand-year history. The innovations he made to the format and annotation of *Genji* foreshadow the reconfiguration of the text in modern editions and vernacular translations. All the same, these remarkable achievements were no match for the flood of literary models and ideals from the West.

Excessive Westernization soon led to a more conservative response that stressed national pride and native culture in the effort to modernize. The Imperial Rescript on Education (*Kyōiku Chokugo*) issued in the name of Emperor Meiji (1852–1912) in 1890 emphasized the unique historical bond between Japan's divine ruler and his subjects. To demonstrate their patriotism, citizens of the modernizing nation were urged to pursue moral education and the cultivation of traditional virtues. Scholars of Japanese literature turned to classical texts such as *Genji* to promote the vitality of values and aesthetics associated with antiquity. However, they rarely cited Hiromichi's *Appraisal of Genji* because it invalidated the claims of cultural superiority that were the order of the day. Ironically, Hiromichi's enlightened approach to literary criticism was unappealing to Japan's early modernizers. To this day his work remains in the shadow of interpretations that promote *Genji* as an icon of refined native sensibility. More than a century after it was first published, Hiromichi's *Appraisal of Genji* continues to be a surprisingly fresh source of critical ideas linking our understanding of the tale today with the way it was read in premodern times.

Hiromichi's work is particularly valuable because its absence from much of the discourse on *Genji* for the last century reveals the place of cultural identity in the critical assessment of one of Japan's oldest canonical texts. The tale is set in a world associated with the imperial court and the highest ranks of the aristocracy. For this reason authority and identity have always played a part in its interpretation and reception. In the seventeenth century, economic, political, and technological factors converged to forever transform the analysis of *Genji* and its connection to cultural identity. The Tokugawa Shogunate imposed a level of order and stability that led to far-reaching economic development and commercial growth. However, by the eighteenth century, cycles of prosperity and famine had begun to undermine the social and political order that had served as the basis of unified samurai rule. Scholars turned to the analysis of texts from antiquity to provide a more compelling rationale for this increasingly complex social structure. Confucianists focused on historical texts written in classical Chinese, while nativist scholars (*kokugakusha*) expanded the scope of their analysis to include works of poetry and prose in Japanese from the nation's remote past. Owing to its antiquity and longstanding prominence as a sourcebook for poetic composition and aristocratic culture, *Genji* was one of the first works of prose to which nativist scholars turned their attention.

As a consequence of these converging economic and political forces, a significant number of Edo-period intellectuals began to read and interpret *Genji* with a new intensity. By the late 1700s, some of the most influential thinkers of the day were engaged in critical discourse on *Genji*. In 1796, the nativist scholar Motoori Norinaga (1730–1801) refined a long-standing connection between *Genji* and cultural identity and transformed it into a powerful and persuasive treatise on literature entitled *Genji monogatari tama no ogushi* ("A Fine Jeweled Comb for *The Tale of Genji*"). Norinaga advanced nativist ideology by arguing that readers deeply moved by reading *Genji* were appreciating it as the author intended for it to be read in the Heian period (794–1185). Norinaga's argument was based on the assumption that *Genji* was a sacred repository of Japanese culture. To favorably appraise *Genji* was to demonstrate one had inherited certain values and attitudes, unique to the Japanese race, from the ancestors of the country's shared culture. This theory of emotional, cultural, and aesthetic sensitivity, often referred to as Norinaga's theory of *mono no aware*, argued against the dominance of non-native ideologies. Specifically, Norinaga claimed that Confucianism and Buddhism stifled the pure expression of the Japanese spirit by imposing ethical and moral values derived from foreign traditions. According to Norinaga, those who failed to respond emotionally to *Genji* revealed how deeply their own feelings had become corrupted by foreign ideology. Norinaga's argument found a wide audience because it offered compelling answers to some rather complex and vexing questions: To those who sought guidance in reading and appreciating *Genji*, his *mono no aware* theory offered a simple principle to be followed. To those who sought a sense of belonging, this theory made *Genji* a means of connection with the most admired aspects of national culture. To those who sought to legitimize the authority of the state and political ideology, this theory emphasized *Genji*'s antiquity, making it a sacred storehouse to which one could turn in seeking knowledge and guidance. Norinaga clearly and persuasively integrated notions that had evolved over the centuries with concerns specific to the nativist agenda. His work forcefully linked *Genji* with a sense of Japanese identity rooted in nostalgia.

Advances in printing technology and the subsequent growth of commercial publishing during the Edo period also contributed to an unprecedented distribution of text, commentary, and interpretive theory on *Genji*. Prosperity, particularly among the merchant class, supported the proliferation of "book-lenders" (*kashihon'ya*) and other goods and services associated with leisure and entertainment. By the eighteenth century, *Genji* had become the subject or source of inspiration for works of prose, poetry, drama, visual art, and even the erotic that extended well beyond the exclusive domain of aristocrats, clergy, and scholars to include the world of merchants, artisans, commoners, and prostitutes.

This fascination with *Genji* survived the influx of foreign influences and the rush to embrace the West. In 1912, the author and critic Kōda Rohan (1867–1947) argued that the persistence of *Genji*'s popularity into the Meiji period was due mainly to the success of Ryūtei Tanehiko's *Genji* parody *Phony Murasaki and Rural Genji* (*Nise murasaki inaka Genji*, 1829–1842). He notes:

> Illustrations from *Rural Genji* have inspired everything from garden decorations to trinkets and fashion accessories designed to capture the fancy of young girls. These items can be found in the homes of the well to do and even in businesses where merchants attempt to capitalize on the commercial success of the *Genji* parody by marketing products such as "*Genji* oil, *Genji* rice crackers, *Genji* sushi, and *Genji* soba noodles" to entice their customers.[2]

Genji as both cultural icon and masterpiece of prose fiction played an important role in establishing the place of classical literature in the definition of national culture as Japan entered the modern era. The overwhelming task of reinventing national identity in the face of enormous cultural and ideological change further enhanced the appeal of Norinaga's approach to *Genji*. One of the most influential literary critics of the early Meiji period, Tsubouchi Shōyō (1859–1935), actively promoted Norinaga's stature in the modern era.[3] In his seminal treatise *The Essence of the Novel* (*Shōsetsu shinzui*, 1885–1886), Shōyō argued that Norinaga's views on *Genji* were a source of inspiration for his own conception of how the modern Japanese novel should evolve.

In the decades that followed, scholars continued to turn to Norinaga's theories in their search for the roots of Japanese culture. Kobayashi Hideo (1902–1983), one of Japan's most prominent literary critics in the twentieth century, published an extensive study of Norinaga's life and work between 1965 and 1976. Kobayashi begins his book, titled simply *Motoori Norinaga*, by recalling his interest in the record of Japan's divine origins and ancient chronicles, the *Kojiki* (Record of Ancient Matters, 712), during the period of intense nationalism leading up to the war. This introduction explains that an initial interest in Japan's foundation myths led him to Norinaga's annotated study of the *Kojiki*, the *Kojikiden* (1764). While immersed in reading Norinaga he visited the eminent scholar of Japanese literature and folklore Orikuchi Shinobu (1887–1953). Orikuchi's major work of the prewar era closely followed Norinaga's scholarship in promoting the study of antiquity to reveal the unique nature of Japanese culture. Kobayashi notes that after Orikuchi patiently responded to many questions on the *Kojikiden* his final words of advice were, "Kobayashi-san, after all is said and done, Norinaga-san is really about *Genji*."[4] Kobayashi's recollection of this exchange illustrates how discourse on nationalist sentiment and the reception of *Genji* were transformed by the war. Scholars of the post-war era were pressured to disassociate themselves from militarism and any vestiges of the nationalistic system of State Shinto. In this context, Kobayashi's prefatory remarks serve as an apology for Norinaga's association with ultranationalism. This deliberate reframing of Orikuchi's remarks assures readers that the wartime association of Norinaga's ideas with the dangers of nationalism was an aberration. Linking the essence of Norinaga's teachings to *Genji* rather than the *Kojiki* makes it easier for scholars to continue to rely on texts from antiquity to explore the unique nature of Japanese culture while avoiding the taint of fascism.

Scholarship focused on *Genji* in modern Japan betrays a similar allegiance to Norinaga and the nativist ideas he championed. The departments of Japanese and classical literature (*kokubungaku*) established in the Meiji period were founded by academics who saw themselves as stewards of Japan's literary heritage, advocating national pride through the study of native poetry and prose. Consequently, the majority of research on *Genji* from the Meiji, Taishō (1912–1926) and even early Shōwa (1926–1989) periods is informed in profound ways by the ideology Norinaga championed. The place of his *mono no aware* theory in promoting ultranationalist ideology in modern Japan has long been acknowledged in intellectual circles, but the link Norinaga was instrumental in forging between cultural identity and nostalgia to interpret *Genji* remains largely intact. Norinaga's thought is so resilient that Takahashi Tōru, a leading member of the academic society devoted to the study of Heian literature (*Monogatari Kenkyūkai*) takes pains in the preface to his 1982 study *Genji monogatari taiihō* (Polyphony in the *Tale of Genji*) to point out:

> We lose sight of too much of what *Genji* is about when we seek to represent all fifty-four chapters in such *monophonic* terms as *mono no aware* and *courtly elegance* (*miyabi*). In addition, there is the heavy burden of the ways in which this view of *Genji* has been used in the past to sustain the fantasy that Japan is a country of a homogeneous race and a unified culture. At present, with many readers of *Genji* both in Japan and abroad, the dangers of such an approach are twice as great.[5]

Within the academic community advances continue to be made in our appreciation of the complexity and sophistication of *Genji* as a work of narrative fiction. However, the tale's status as an emblem of national culture is slow to change. In this book, Chapter 1 illustrates how the persistence of Norinaga's interpretive legacy becomes increasingly apparent as one moves from scholarly publications to popular reception of the tale in contemporary Japan. Chapter 6 relies on diary entries, newspaper accounts, and literary essays by influential politicians and respected authors to show how challenges to the validity of nationalist ideology met with fierce resistance in the modern era. Combined, these two chapters shed light on the revival of Edo-period nativist ideology in modern Japan. In concrete terms, these chapters explain how Edo fascination with *Genji* survived the nation's traumatic and abrupt encounter with the forces of Westernization and modernization.

Norinaga's position of prominence in the study of *Genji* and the broader sphere of Japanese intellectual history is well deserved and eloquently described elsewhere.[6] However, ideas that challenged Norinaga's work in fundamental ways also deserve to be heard if we are to seriously undertake the examination of Edo-period commentary and the reception of *Genji* into the modern era. This is not always a simple undertaking. Norinaga's approach to the text is an essential part of what *Genji* has become. To distinguish between Norinaga's interpretation of the text and the meaning of the text itself it is necessary to read both *Genji* and the scholarship underlying its modern presentation with a critical eye. This is a cumbersome process at times, but the modern appraisal of *Genji* stands to benefit from a clearer understanding of how the tale's cultural status survived the tumultuous transition from the Edo to Meiji periods while so many other texts did not.

The core of this book rests upon Hagiwara Hiromichi's *Appraisal of Genji* and the challenge it presented to Norinaga's legacy. Hiromichi sought to prevent cultural identity and nostalgia from dominating *Genji* commentary in the final years of the Edo period. Chapter 2, Hiromichi's biography, tells the story of a gifted young poet who actively sought to understand the teachings of the most prominent thinkers of his time. While eager to increase his knowledge of literature, criticism, and philosophy, he resisted the practice of maintaining a permanent affiliation with a single school or master. Born into the family of a low-ranking samurai, he left the domain of his feudal lord to more actively pursue an interest in literature. In doing so, he became one of the many masterless samurai (*rōnin*) of his era. Poverty and personal turmoil forced Hiromichi to establish himself in various literary genres. As a masterless samurai he struggled to support himself as a poet, author, teacher, translator, and critic. His familiarity with diverse intellectual fields of inquiry and the freedom he enjoyed by not carrying an obligation of loyalty to his feudal lord or any single school of thought allowed him to pursue innovative methods of interpretation. His greatest ambition was to transform the way people read *Genji* by publishing an introduction and revised version of the annotated text for all fifty-four chapters of *Genji*. Each page of his *Appraisal of Genji* draws the reader's attention to the beauty of the tale's language and structure.

Chapter 3 examines the notions that Hiromichi's *Appraisal of Genji* challenged. Hiromichi's predecessors in *Genji* commentary employed various methods to establish the text's compatibility with cultural values dominant at the time. As a result, much of the commentary on *Genji* adopts a tone of moral or didactic argument. Norinaga forcefully articulated how and why these strategies were inappropriate to the interpretation of fiction but ultimately succeeded only in replacing old ideological agendas with new ones. Chapters 4 and 5 cover the innovations Hiromichi introduced to the reading of *Genji* in surmounting the ideological obstacles associated with Norinaga's dogmatic approach to literary interpretation. His foremost concern was to persuade readers to appreciate the aesthetic and literary sophistication with which the text was composed. For Hiromichi, *Genji*'s importance was derived from internal, textual evidence rather than concerns outside the text. His emphasis on literary analysis before ideology inspired him to draw from diverse fields of study in seeking critical methods that facilitated a more effective reading of *Genji*. He integrated interpretive techniques culled from Chinese vernacular fiction, Confucian textual analysis, and nativist studies to elevate the place of literary style and structure in the evaluation of prose fiction. The innovations he introduced were designed to allow readers to approach *Genji* in the same way they might appreciate a contemporary novel or immerse themselves in a theatrical production. As such, Hiromichi emphasized that it was possible to be entertained and inspired by *Genji* but also to learn about life and human nature by engaging with the fictional world inhabited by its characters.

Among these important critical innovations his most daring move was to introduce the same level of critical objectivity that his contemporaries were applying to literature imported from China to a work with canonical status among native texts. This approach was directly at odds with Norinaga's theory that *Genji* should be understood as embodying sacred qualities unique to Japan's "ways of the past" (*inishie no michi*). Norinaga taught that *Genji* should be ennobling and enlightening by rejecting centuries of moral criticism. However, when consistently applied, this approach forces readers to lose sight of *Genji*'s most valuable assets, its insight into the human condition and the beauty with which this tale of extraordinary talent and individual weakness is told. Hiromichi gently, patiently reminds readers of those aspects of the text that Norinaga urged them to overlook.

Hiromichi's *Appraisal of Genji* did not receive widespread recognition in the Meiji period, but to the careful observer scattered hints remain that, in fact, this work played an important role in helping modern critics translate premodern literary ideals into the goals of the modern novel in Japan. A particularly compelling example of Hiromichi's relevance to modern literary theory emerges from an examination of critical discourse on the supernatural in fiction. Meiji thinkers were eager to purge modern culture of seemingly irrational, and thus unenlightened and anti-modern, beliefs and attitudes. Writers and scholars of this period often sought to distance their own work from any trace of Edo-period influence. Hiromichi's *Appraisal of Genji* explicitly addresses the function of the supernatural in the tale. However, academics promoting *Genji* as a source of national pride perceived the prominent place of spirit possession in parts of the text as problematic. The deliberate simplification and avoidance of commentary addressing scenes of spirit possession in a popular Meiji edition of *Genji* provide concrete evidence of the much larger ideological forces at work in the rejection of Hiromichi's scholarship. Anxieties concerning *Genji*'s status as a literary masterpiece also shed light on the complexities faced by writers at the time. Many Meiji authors felt compelled to avoid any vestige of Edo literary aesthetics, in which *Genji* and the supernatural both played significant roles, in crafting a literary language that conveyed a sense of realism for the modern novel in Japan. Chapter 6 concludes with an examination of Tsubouchi Shōyō's account of his own struggle with these issues. Shōyō's emphasis on Norinaga's *mono no aware* theory, compounded by his deliberate avoidance of any reference to the work of Hiromichi in his influential treatise *The Essence of the Novel*, indicates the profound level on which Hiromichi challenged dominant cultural values at the time.

Chapter 1 sets the stage for this study of Hiromichi. Various adaptations and retellings of *Genji* produced in connection with the millennial anniversary of its composition reveal the enduring place of nationalism in the modern appraisal of *Genji*. These examples of *Genji*'s promotion as an object of national pride and Japan's contribution to the canon of world literature offer tangible evidence of Norinaga's commanding legacy. Together the individual chapters of this book all point to the fact that *Genji* is far too rich an exploration of humanity to simply be used in explaining what sets Japan apart from the world. This book is about the enduring power of fiction and the determined efforts of a masterless samurai to transcend nationalism and nostalgia in the final years of the Tokugawa Shogunate.

Chapter One

HEIAN FANTASIES: NATIONALISM AND NOSTALGIA IN THE READING OF *GENJI*

In 2000, *The Tale of Genji* was adapted for the stage of the Takarazuka Theater in a production titled "*Myūjikaru roman Genji monogatari: Asaki yumemishi*" (*The Tale of Genji* Lived in a Dream: A Musical Romance). This modern retelling of *Genji* provides several valuable signposts that will help guide our examination of nativism, a precursor to nationalism, and nostalgia in the transmission of *Genji* over the last thousand years.

Since its establishment in 1913, the Takarazuka Revue has grown to become a major theatrical institution with a nationwide following. Takarazuka has a well-earned reputation for exacting standards in music and choreography. However, the most enduring element of Takarazuka's success is its all-female cast. Takarazuka's particular brand of entertainment makes it possible for actresses portraying leading men to depict a romanticized ideal of masculinity while failing to provoke the anxiety some female members of the audience may have toward men. This allows members of the audience who perceive men as the "other" or as sexual predators to participate more fully in the romantic fantasy on stage. Nearly a century after its founding, the revue boasts two large, successful theaters, in Takarazuka and Tokyo, a devoted following nationwide, and an abiding presence in advertising and popular culture in Japan. Women remain the most loyal fans of the theater's signature style that combines passion, romance, and fantasy.[1]

In keeping with the theater's emphasis on the fantastic, most productions are set in locations deemed exotic and are populated by characters who live tragic lives of legendary proportions. Elaborate musical dance numbers, stunning orchestration, and dazzling costumes are part of every Takarazuka show. Perennial favorites include *The Rose of Versailles* (*Berusaiyu no bara*) and *Gone With the Wind* (*Kaze to tomo ni sarinu*). The goal of Takarazuka is to offer entertainment that helps the audience momentarily leave behind the troubles of daily life. For this reason, the stage is rarely set to reflect life in contemporary Japan. However, *The Tale of Genji* is sufficiently remote in time and exotic in reputation to offer a glimpse of reality as different and compelling as revolutionary Paris or a war-torn plantation in Georgia. The theater's first *Genji* production, an operatic interpretation of the "Sakaki" chapter (chapter 10: "The Sacred Tree"), was staged in July 1919, the month after Japan participated in the signing of the Treaty of Versailles following the end of World War I. Since World War II *Genji* has been adapted for the Takarazuka stage four times. The two most recent adaptations followed in close succession during an extended period of economic malaise that plagued the Japanese economy for more than two decades. The coincidence of Takarazuka's retelling of *Genji* with events of broad national significance speaks to the enduring connection *Genji* has with a sense of pride and pain that register on a national level.

The emphasis Takarazuka places on fantasy will be particularly helpful in illuminating the function nostalgia has come to serve in linking *Genji* to idealized notions of nationalism. However, it should be noted that this association is not limited to Takarazuka. The first major adaptation of *Genji* on film was released in 1951 and directed by Yoshimura Kōsaburō.[2] Heavily promoted by Daiei studios as a feature film commemorating the studio's tenth anniversary, Yoshimura's *Genji* met with enormous popular success and became the top-grossing film in Japan on record at the time.[3] When this first *Genji* film was released, Japan had begun to recover from defeat in World War II, and the allied occupation was coming to an end. The success of Yoshimura's *Genji* came in response not only to the film's cinematic merits but also its ability to evoke a romanticized sense of nostalgia for the nation's imperial household in a less-troubled time.

The construction of a scene in Yoshimura's blockbuster corresponding to events in the eighth chapter of the original tale provides a particularly compelling example of how *Genji* has been used to address the concerns of contemporary culture. The eighth chapter, titled "Hana no En" (Under the Cherry Blossoms), has long played a prominent role in the history of *Genji* reception. "Hana no En" depicts the tale's protagonist, Genji, in a way that defines many of the emotional and cultural complexities underlying his character. The opening chapters recount the details of Genji's birth and the formative experiences of his youth. As the tale begins, readers are told of Genji's mother, Kiritsubo. She became the object of intense jealousy among the intimate attendants of the emperor because she inspired the emperor's most intense passion. Kiritsubo did not come from a family that entitled her to high rank and political protection. The other women serving the emperor took advantage of Kiritsubo's social standing to vent their rage against her. In the first chapter, Kiritsubo dies as a result of the overwhelming pressures of life at court. Later in the chapter, her son is passed over for recognition as an heir apparent or prince by his father. Because he lacks the political support on his mother's side to succeed as a potential heir to the throne, the emperor gives him the surname of a child of imperial parentage, but of common rank: Genji. Despite his status as a commoner, Genji comes to be particularly admired at court because of his physical beauty and his ability to win the favor of both men and women by his sophisticated command of etiquette and romance. The eighth chapter begins with Genji, now twenty years old, exhibiting his cultural prowess in the prime of youth. The emperor has just held a party to celebrate the blossoming of cherry trees in the spring. During the celebration, the heir apparent, Genji's older half-brother, invites Genji to participate in the ceremonial dancing. The elegance of Genji's performance is so overwhelming that it causes one of the most powerful ministers at court to weep. Genji is then called upon to participate in the composition and recitation of poetry. His poems are so extraordinary that everyone hearing them is filled with admiration for his talents. Word seems to have circulated that even the Empress Fujitsubo was inspired by Genji's performance and his physical beauty to express her devotion to him. After the empress has retired for the night, Genji, his confidence emboldened both by the success of his performance and by too much to drink, makes his way secretly to the Fujitsubo chambers. He has been drawn to Fujitsubo since she first came to court as an imperial consort when he was a child. At the age of eighteen, he managed to consummate this enduring romantic interest in Fujitsubo by visiting her while she was away from the imperial court. Fujitsubo became pregnant from this secret union and gave birth to a son. In chapter 7, the emperor named this child a crown prince, designating that he follow the heir apparent in succession to the title of emperor. At the same time, the emperor elevated Fujitsubo to the title of empress. It is an act of unimaginable daring for Genji, now only one chapter later in the tale, to seek the companionship of the woman the emperor has just named his empress. Genji's boldness becomes even more extraordinary when considering, as only Genji, Fujitsubo, and the reader know, that his previous liaison with Fujitsubo resulted in the birth of a son destined to become emperor. In the text, Genji's audacity continues unchecked. He makes his way to the passage leading to Fujitsubo's chambers, only to find it locked. Finding the empress inaccessible, he heads in the direction of the quarters associated with the mother of the heir apparent, Kokiden, the emperor's highest-ranking consort and Genji's greatest antagonist at court. Genji enters Kokiden's chambers to discover a young woman of high rank alone. He immediately forces himself upon her, well aware of the fact that she is probably a younger sister of the Kokiden consort. The rape of this young woman takes place by the light of a misty moon, giving her character the name Oborozukiyo ("Night of a Misty Moon"). In subsequent chapters, this new sexual conquest becomes a particularly blatant offense to his rivals at court. The gravity of Genji's offense is compounded by the fact that Oborozukiyo is to become the consort to the heir apparent. Thus Genji has defiled not only the current emperor's empress but also the woman selected to serve as the principal wife to the next emperor. By the twelfth chapter, the consequences of Genji's hubris become inescapable, and he is forced into exile from the capital. Chapter 8 is short but reveals the tale's hero at his most talented and his most morally corrupt.

In Yoshimura's adaptation of scenes from "Hana no En," Genji dances under the cherry blossoms and captures the attention of everyone in attendance. However, his reckless pursuit of Fujitsubo is not alluded to, and his seduction of Oborozukiyo is omitted altogether.[4] In its place, Oborozukiyo pursues Genji. She is depicted in the film as being drawn to his dashing figure with such intensity that her desire becomes increasingly difficult for her to control each time she sees him. In the scene where one familiar with the text would expect *Genji* to secretly venture first to the chambers of Fujitsubo and then into the imperial consort's chambers, Oborozukiyo takes Genji by surprise. As Genji lounges innocently under the light of a misty moon, she appears seductively before him. Later she reaches from behind a curtain to catch Genji's robes as he passes through an adjoining corridor. She stops him and urges him to visit her again that evening. This slight change of elements in the story renders Genji, who ultimately ascends to the position of honorary emperor, in a light that implies less culpability and moral corruption than one might infer from the original tale. It is not surprising that such a change would have been welcomed by audiences painfully aware of the discussion concerning both national and imperial responsibility for the horrors associated with World War II. A portrayal of Genji, symbolically associated with the ideals of the Heian period and the imperial line, was far more appealing with the taint of scandal and moral corruption minimized where possible. As we will see in this chapter, Yoshimura's strategy of altering and omitting textual details is surprisingly consistent with the way in which scholars seeking to promote the didactic or ideological value of the tale had sought to overlook the complex portrayal of Genji in this chapter for centuries.

The popularity and critical acclaim associated with Yoshimura's *Genji* led Daiei to place the innovative actor and director Kinugasa Teinosuke in charge of another cinematic version of the tale in 1957. Kinugasa's *Genji* focused on the events of the final chapters of the tale and their tragic heroine, Ukifune. The popular Kabuki actor Hasegawa Kazuo, who had so effectively played the part of Genji in Yoshimura's adaptation, was cast as the lead, Kaoru, in Kinugasa's film. Kaoru is Genji's reputed son and central character of the final chapters in the tale. As in Yoshimura's film, Hasegawa plays a kind, sensitive, and vulnerable hero. The 1950s' versions of Genji and Kaoru on the screen are decidedly lacking in malice or ambition. They are young men of exceptional promise who endure deep pain and turmoil. The commercial success of these films suggests that audiences of the time were drawn to stories that allowed them to connect their own experience of the war with characters associated with cultural ideals.

The production of new versions of *Genji* tapered off as Japan emerged from the atmosphere of post-World War II trauma into the 1960s and 1970s. Major studios in this period lost interest in additional *Genji* adaptations. Takarazuka was not to produce its *Genji* revues until the mid-1980s. At the time, Japan was enjoying a robust economy and a general sense of prosperity and optimism. Additionally, widespread social change associated with the 1960s diverted popular attention away from a sense of national identity to the rights of individual groups within society. In the 1990s, this sense of optimism was gradually called into question.

Takarazuka's 2000 *Genji* adaptation was inspired by the overwhelming success of the illustrated comic book series of the same title, "*Genji monogatari asaki yumemishi*" (*The Tale of Genji* Lived in a Dream, 1993). The phrase "lived in a dream" refers to the closing lines of chapter 40 (*Minori*: "The Rites") in which Genji must come to terms with the death of the greatest love of his life, Murasaki. At the end of the chapter, Genji sits before a Buddhist altar in prayer:

> Genji thought he and Murasaki might have a thousand years together. The realization that their inevitable separation had come left him in a state of shock. . . . He now felt as though he were living in a dream.[5]

Genji is so overwhelmed by Murasaki's death that he is not capable of organizing the rites to be performed in her memory. The following chapter (*Maboroshi*: "The Seer") is the last in which Genji appears before his own death. The Takarazuka production features a character referred to as the "Time Spirit" who appears before Genji when he is in the state of despondent reverie that overwhelms him in these chapters. The Time Spirit permits Genji to revisit memorable scenes of his greatest romantic loves and losses. This review helps Genji see how much Murasaki means to him. The production ends with Genji renouncing all ties to this world so that he can join Murasaki in the next life. This retelling of *Genji* takes even greater liberties with the original text than did the cinematic adaptations of the 1950s. Fifty years later, *Genji* is retold in a way that emphasizes coming to terms with loss. This notion was particularly compelling for audiences at the time. After more than a decade of economic slowdown, accompanied by a series of terrorist acts and national political scandals, there was a sense that the era of growth and prosperity that had been building since the post–World War II era had finally come to an end.

The commercial success inspired by this adaptation suggests that Genji's quest to accept the loss of his greatest love resonated deeply with audiences who perceived that an era of affluence had passed from their own lives and was not soon to return. Building on Takarazuka's sensational retelling of *Genji*, Toei studios released a cinematic adaptation of its own the following year under the title, "*Sen' nen no koi: Hikaru Genji monogatari*" (A Thousand Years' Love: The Tale of Shining Genji). The film was heavily promoted as the capstone of the studio's celebration of fifty years in business. Not wanting to stray too far from the Takarazuka formula, Toei cast an actress famous for her portrayal of romantic heroes on the Takarazuka stage, Amami Yuki, in the title role of the romantic hero.

With Takarazuka and Toei saturating the stage and screen markets with *Genji* transformations one might expect the trend to have peaked. However, this was not to be the case. The following year, the comic magazine "Ultra Jump" began serialization of its own version of *Genji*, illustrated by the comicbook author Egawa Tatsuya. While previous adaptations catered to the interest of female consumers, Egawa's version of *Genji* was published in a magazine marketed with the male consumer in mind. Not surprisingly, Egawa's *Genji* is far more masculine in appearance and behavior. His illustrations stand out from previous adaptations of *Genji* to appear since the 1980s, precisely because they amplify the aggressive, almost predatory, aspects of *Genji*'s character that had been carefully downplayed by his predecessors.[6]

These multiple attempts to market *Genji* all met with commercial and popular success. This is particularly remarkable when one considers that they are all based on a work of classical prose fiction nearly a thousand years old. This unusual phenomenon can be attributed to the powerful link that has been forged between *Genji* and cultural identity in Japan. The power of this connection can be seen more clearly by turning to the program guide for the 2000 Takarazuka production "*The Tale of Genji* Lived in a Dream: A Musical Romance." Along with photos and interviews with the actors, this guide features a short essay by the author Tanabe Seiko titled *Eien no Genji eien no Takarazuka* (Eternal *Genji*, Eternal Takarazuka). Tanabe, noted for her own adaptation of *Genji* as a modern novel, *Shin Genji monogatari* (A New *Tale of Genji*, 1977–1990), remarks that Takarazuka is a particularly appropriate venue for the staging of *Genji*. By way of explanation she quotes a line in classical Japanese from the tale describing the splendor of Genji in his youth, looking so beautiful "one might have wished he were a woman" (*onna ni mo mitate matsuramahoshi*). For this reason she argues that there can be no better place to realize the beauty of *Genji* than the Takarazuka stage, where the hero is in fact played by a woman. Her enthusiastic introduction continues:

> They say there's a "*Genji* boom" going on these days, but I wonder if that's really the case. It seems to me that many people have acquired a smattering of knowledge about *Genji*. Based on superficial explanations they have formulated biased opinions. I've even heard people complaining that: "The government is printing two thousand yen notes with the author of that story about the scandalous playboy Genji on them. Can you imagine!" We show no respect at home for this great novel yet it is admired the world over. This lack of esteem comes despite the fact that *Genji* is said to be the first "fictional romance" (*ai no monogatari*) in human history, written some three hundred years before Dante and five hundred years before Shakespeare. . . .
>
> *Genji* is a tale from the Heian period, yet it speaks directly to our lives. This is because the truth of life and humanity is something that does not change in a thousand years.[7]

The tone of Tanabe's essay is pure Takarazuka. But what is most stunning about this rhetorical *tour de force* is the way she artfully translates issues concerning cultural identity and nostalgia, the hallmarks of the nativist school (*kokugaku*) interpretation of *Genji* more than two centuries earlier, into the language that speaks to the concerns of her audience. The quotation she provides in classical Japanese signals her familiarity with *Genji*'s original language. By implication, her engagement with the text on this level gives her the authority to convey to readers the "essence" and the "truths" to be found within the tale.

Having established *Genji*'s importance as a cultural icon in terms of its appearance on national currency and its stature as a classic of world literature, she goes on in brief terms to explain how those unfamiliar with *Genji* can grasp its essence as she has.[8] She argues that *Genji* is a tale of romance and sorrow profound enough to transcend great differences in history and culture in the same way the tenets of Buddhist philosophy address issues of universal concern. Such reasoning does little to improve one's grasp of the tale. In fact, it is based on a selective reading of *Genji* no more precise or comprehensive than the charge that Genji himself is but a scandalous playboy. However, it connects Takarazuka's adaptation back to *Genji* and the Heian period in an important way. Tanabe emphasizes that the essence of *Genji* is infinitely profound yet easily perceived and timeless in nature. By implication, audiences who find themselves moved by the beauty, tragedy, and romance of the Takarazuka production can claim a greater familiarity with *The Tale of Genji* and, by association, an understanding of the essence of a better age.

The most influential nativist scholar of *Genji* in the Edo period, Motoori Norinaga, offered a similar rationale to his contemporaries. Norinaga's argument concerning *Genji*'s essence began with a careful philological analysis of the text. He believed that his sophisticated understanding of *Genji*'s language permitted him to perceive the deeper meaning of the Heian-period author's intentions. Based on his intimate understanding of the text he sought to refute moral criticism of *Genji*. Tanabe's essay suggests that such moral concerns remain alive and well in her own time. Just as Norinaga did in the Edo period, she relies on *Genji*'s association with a romanticized view of Heian society to defend the tale from criticism. Taking Norinaga's technique a step further, Tanabe argues that there is a deeper level of authenticity afforded by Takarazuka's all-female cast in its retelling of *Genji*. Norinaga and Tanabe both urge their audiences to accept Genji's moral lapses by placing his behavior within the larger cultural and aesthetic framework that only one who truly knows the "essence" of the tale can perceive. This strategy is particularly appealing because it offers the individual a sense of reassurance and belonging. It is reassuring because it reminds the audience that failure, moral or otherwise, does exist, but that those who truly understand the essence of Japanese culture are able to accept or overlook such flaws in the individual. Tanabe implies that those who enjoy Takarazuka's production, as she does, demonstrate their appreciation for the eternal cultural values embodied in *Genji*.

Takarazuka provides a dramatic example of *Genji*'s association with the essence, or spirit, of Heian culture. In modern Japan, invoking the Heian period and things associated with it signals one's admiration for a time when aesthetic sophistication dominated all other concerns in the most powerful circles of Japanese society. As such, *Genji* serves as an emblem for shared literary and cultural ideals rooted in a sense of nostalgia. Nostalgia, the longing for a home that has been lost, enables *Genji* to serve as a beacon attracting those in search of both cultural identity and fantasy. In 1796, Motoori Norinaga elevated nostalgia to the level of compelling ideology in his treatise *Genji monogatari tama no ogushi*. The theory he promoted forcefully linked *Genji* and nostalgia with a sense of Japanese identity. As the example of Takarazuka illustrates, Norinaga's legacy continues to thrive.

Norinaga's dogmatic approach to interpreting *Genji* helped refine notions of nostalgia and identity associated with *Genji*, but such notions existed long before his time. His stature looms large because he effectively integrated existing perceptions of *Genji* with nativist concerns particular to the late Edo period that were the precursors to modern-day nationalism. Tracing the roots of cultural identity and nostalgia in the reception of *Genji* to their origins leads us back to the time of the tale's composition and the culture in which it was first read.

The Tale of Genji was composed at a point in the Heian period when the stature of the aristocracy had begun to decline. Genji himself embodies a sense of loss that can be associated with the realization that an era is coming to an end. In the opening chapter of the tale, Genji experiences profound personal loss. His mother dies when he is three. Genji is too young to fully comprehend the loss, but his father, the emperor, deeply mourns the death of Genji's mother and his favorite consort, Kiritsubo. Following her death, he comes to see Genji as a reminder of his departed lover. Genji's grandmother weakens at the shock of losing Kiritsubo and dies when Genji is six. From an early age, Genji is the embodiment of lost traditions as well as personal loss. He excels in the performance of traditional arts such as music, dance, and poetry. His mastery sets him apart from his contemporaries and makes his elders recall fond memories of a better age.

This sense of loss, as both painful and precious, resonates throughout the tale. Genji is drawn to Fujitsubo, the woman who replaces his mother as the emperor's favorite consort, because she closely resembles his mother. Once he comes of age, he continues to pursue Fujitsubo but also seeks other women to replace her as she becomes increasingly inaccessible to him. Genji's abiding interest in Fujitsubo, and his pursuit of women to replace her, leads to some of the most intense and emotionally complex relationships in the story. Genji initially begins his pursuit of the woman who will become his greatest companion in the tale, Murasaki, because a glimpse of her from a distance reminds him of Fujitsubo. When he learns of the death of Murasaki's mother he is even more powerfully drawn to her, because her experience reminds him of his own loss in childhood. At the close of the forty-first chapter, Genji is overwhelmed by the loss of Murasaki and becomes frail and confused. The sense of loss associated with his death is so profound that it is not even described in the text. The remaining chapters of the tale can be seen as an exploration of Genji's life and his legacy in the generation that succeeds him. In this sense, they can be understood as a reflection on loss as well.

In the Heian period, *Genji*'s association was not primarily with such solemn ideas. The accounts still available to us from *Genji*'s first readers suggest that they saw the tale as something akin to gossip. Readers were drawn to the engaging way in which the intense emotions and complex relationships in *Genji* lent themselves to evocative poetic exchanges and scandalous behavior.[9] Serious prose at the time was written in the language acquired through formal education, classical Chinese. A text written in vernacular prose, such as *Genji*, was deemed appropriate for entertainment but not serious reflection. In the tale, characters refer to this style as women's writing (*onnade*) and acknowledge that it was seen as a form of amusement for the idle in general and women in particular.

As good gossip so often does, *Genji* attracted much attention. Accounts of the tale being read and reread with great interest and intensity stretch back to the time when the author was still in service to the imperial court. The author, Murasaki Shikibu, mentions in her diary an incident in which scrolls containing a draft of the tale disappeared from her quarters while she was away at court. She surmises that a minister had the scrolls taken from her quarters and delivered to his fifteen-year-old daughter for her to read—or perhaps have read to her.[10] This incident suggests that *Genji* was highly sought after even before the final chapters were completed.

A slightly later diary provides further evidence of *Genji*'s popularity among readers who were contemporaries of the author. The daughter of Sugawara no Takasue, in recounting events less than a decade after the author's death, mentions that she had read parts of the tale and told her aunt how much she longed to read the entire work from beginning to end. Her diary, *The Sarashina Diary* (*Sarashina nikki*, ca. 1059), recounts the joy she felt when her aunt presented her with a copy of *Genji* as a gift.

However pleasurable, closely engaging with *Genji* simply as a work of prose fiction was not to be wholly recommended. Takasue's daughter immediately follows her account of the pleasure she finds in reading *Genji* by noting that this indulgence prevented her from devoting herself to the reading of more serious texts such as Buddhist sutras. As a result, she comes to dream of a Buddhist priest issuing an ominous warning for her to perform pious acts without delay. The illicit pleasure and danger associated with reading *Genji* recounted by Takasue's daughter, which will become a recurring theme of its reception in the centuries that follow, is examined in more detail in chapter 6.

In part, this theme remains so persistent because prose was closely associated with didacticism. Prose fiction, in particular, was looked down upon as a source of entertainment and diversion that could be harshly criticized if it was perceived as lacking in moral or ethical value. Confucian and Buddhist precepts that pointed to the fabrications and immoral acts depicted in prose fiction were chiefly responsible for this bias. The prevalence of this prejudice at the time of *Genji*'s composition can be seen in the way the status of prose fiction is treated in *Genji*. In the "Hotaru" chapter (chapter 25), Genji discusses both the allure and dangers of fictional literature with a young woman named Tamakazura. Honesty and moral conduct are particularly powerful notions in this chapter, because readers are aware of the fact that Genji is raising Tamakazura under the false pretense that she is his long-lost daughter. At the same time, Genji's interest in Tamakazura is threatening to break the bounds of paternal propriety by becoming sexual in nature. In this chapter, Genji initially faults the fictional tales that Tamakazura is reading due to their presentation of falsehoods. He is clearly articulating the dominant view of prose fiction at the time. Tamakazura protests by suggesting that perhaps Genji is too quick to perceive deception in others because he is all too familiar with it himself. In response, Genji changes his position to argue that fictional tales are capable of presenting the realities of life with more depth than historical chronicles and with no greater departure from reality than the parables found in Buddhist scripture. In explaining to Tamakazura why he believes fictional literature is about more than simply the moral concerns of historical chronicles, Genji states:

> These works are not based on specific people exactly as they existed. Rather, the feeling that events and people in this world are infinitely interesting compels the author to write. Whether these details are good or bad, the author feels such things should be passed on to later generations. Unable to keep such feelings to himself, the author takes things he knows from experience and uses them as the starting point for his fictional work.[11]

Genji's brief argument is insightful and well reasoned. It is particularly remarkable to consider such an interpretive stance in this age if we take this as the author's defense of prose fiction against the distortions inherent in an overly didactic reading. However insightful these remarks praising the art of fiction may be, they are promptly undermined by the narrative of the tale. Immediately following the aforementioned passage, Genji shifts from championing the status of fictional prose to pursuing his sexual interest in Tamakazura. Having placated Tamakazura by retracting his earlier critique of fictional literature, he attempts to capitalize on this conciliatory tone by drawing her into an amorous mood. Tamakazura rebuffs Genji's advances, and the scene comes to a close. The narration then moves to a scene in which Genji advises Murasaki not to expose his daughter, the Akashi Princess, to certain types of fictional tales because they might prove damaging to her young mind. Ultimately, Genji's open mistrust of fiction is more prominent than the defense of its merits he articulates privately to Tamakazura.

While prose was viewed as the source of gossip and trouble, poetry was considered worthy of exacting analysis, critical discussion, and interpretive terminology independent of moral or didactic concerns. Buddhist, Confucian, or Taoist terminology might be used to add depth or symbolic imagery to a poem composed in Japanese (*waka*), but moral or didactic meaning was rarely a factor in determining its critical reception. As a result, poetry was associated with a strong critical tradition while at the same time remaining relatively free from moral concerns.[12]

Precisely because of its privileged status over prose fiction, poetry ends up becoming an important factor in the sustained interest in *Genji*. Annotation of *Genji* flourished as generations of scholars continued to mine the tale for poetic topics and compiled increasingly elaborate commentaries to improve their ability to compose and appreciate *waka*.[13] *Genji* continued to retain the interest of poets because it was associated with such qualities as courtly elegance, nostalgia, and exceptional literary style. The moral and psychological predicaments associated with events in *Genji* may have offended Buddhist and Confucian sensibilities, but to the poet interested in the sincere expression of emotion, this same material proved a valuable source of inspiration. Poetry and poetics thus firmly anchored *Genji* to serious literary scholarship despite its less than secure status as prose fiction.

Fujiwara no Toshinari (also known as Fujiwara Shunzei, 1114–1204) was a leading arbiter of poetry of his age. During his lifetime, he witnessed the marked increase in factional infighting and military upheavals associated with the collapse of the Heian period. By the end of the Heian period, these struggles led to significant changes in the economic and political stature of the aristocracy. These changes culminated in the establishment of a warrior government in Kamakura in 1191. In the Kamakura period (1185–1333), aristocratic culture and its political stature ebbed, but poetry continued to play a significant role in establishing and maintaining political status among the aristocracy. In 1193, when Toshinari's reputation as the leading poet and critic of his time was beyond dispute, he was asked to serve as one of the judges at the poetry competition in 600 rounds (*Roppyakuban utaawase*). In the thirteenth round of the competition, poets from the left and right were given the assignment to compose a poem on the topic "a desolate field" (*kareno*). The poet of the left team composed a poem that relied upon an expression associated with a key moment in the "Hana no En" chapter. As mentioned earlier, this is the chapter in which Genji first seduces Oborozukiyo. Having made love to her against her wishes, he now begins making inquiries as to the young woman's name before departing her chambers in secret. She resists giving her name and replies to his insistent requests with a poem filled with images of desolation and death:

> Were I to perish in this unfortunate state without you knowing my name,
> I wonder if you would truly come in search of my remains on the
> "plains of grass" (*kusa no hara*).[14]

Fujiwara no Yoshitsune (1169–1206), the organizer of the competition writing for the team of the left under the pseudonym "A woman of high rank,"[15] built upon this passage to develop a poem in response to the topic of "a desolate field" as follows:

> What will remain from the autumn views of the grassy plain (*kusa no hara*)
> Is the scene of a burial pyre I saw there
>
> The right team offered the following critique of Yoshitune's poem:
>
> The expression grassy plain (*kusa no hara*) lacks poetic precedence.
>
> To which Toshinari replied:
>
>> The right's critique that the expression "grassy plain" is flawed is gravely wrong. The expression does indeed have a precedent. Murasaki Shikibu is even more commendable for her written style than she is for her poetry. Her chapter "*Hana no en*" is particularly deserving of praise. It is deplorable for anyone to compose poems without having read *The Tale of Genji.*
>
> The poem composed by the left team was judged superior.[16]

Toshinari's advice was heeded. In the next major imperial poetic anthology, *A New Collection of Poems in Japanese from Ancient and Modern Times* (*Shinkokinshū*, 1205), the number of allusions and critical references to *Genji* markedly increased.[17] His comments also provided poets with a tangible reason to brush up on *Genji*. While Toshinari attests to the merits of Murasaki Shikibu's written style, what concerns him most is that poets demonstrate a familiarity with the cultural and aesthetic ethos embodied in *Genji* rather than the meaning of the prose itself. His pronouncement that "it is deplorable for anyone to compose poems without having read *The Tale of Genji*" firmly establishes the notion that *Genji* should be read to capture the essence of a world that has been lost.[18]

A commentary titled the *Kakaishō*, compiled circa 1363 by Yotsutsuji Yoshinari, is one of the earliest works to move beyond the identification of poetic allusion to bring a broader interpretive perspective to *Genji* through the vehicle of textual commentary.[19] In the *Kakaishō*, Yoshinari theorized that the life of Minamoto no Takaakira (914–982), the son of Emperor Daigo (897–930) and an imperial consort, served as the model for certain details in the description of the fictional Genji. Minamoto no Takaakira and Genji were both born to emperors. Both received the surname of a commoner associated with parentage of royal standing. (The first Chinese character used to write the name *Genji* is read as *Minamoto* in isolation.) After marrying the daughter of a powerful member of the Fujiwara clan, Takaakira's political fortunes rose steadily until he was appointed Minister of the Left. However, Takaakira's story took a turn for the worse when he was banished from the capital for taking part in a scandal to compromise the reputation of the crown prince. This incident came to be known as the An'na disturbance (*An'na no hen*) of 969.[20]

Yoshinari's commentary points to similarities between the historical evidence surrounding the An'na disturbance and the description of Genji's life to suggest that Murasaki Shikibu must have based her story of Genji's rise and fall on the life of Takaakira. He believed that this use of allegorical narrative (*gūgen*) was similar to the didactic function performed by works from the Chinese classics that combined fiction allegory, and mythology such as the *Zhuangzi*.[21] Previous commentaries had provided annotation pointing to historical facts underlying the fictional details of the text, but Yoshinari's comments indicate a growing interest in legitimizing *Genji*'s place among venerated works of prose literature. This aspect of his commentary reminded readers that beyond the didactic or poetic issues relevant to *Genji*, it was still important to read the text for the story it tells.

Fujiwara no Toshinari's promotion of *Genji* as a memento of Heian culture remained largely unchallenged by subsequent generations and continued to play an important role in the composition and evaluation of poetry. Over the centuries, *Genji*'s function as a source of poetic inspiration translated to other areas of artistic creation. In the Muromachi period (1333–1568), *Genji* became one of the richest sources of reference in Noh drama. In a treatise on the composition of Noh drama, the leading Noh actor, playwright, and critic of the premodern era, Zeami Motokiyo (1363–1443), observed that plays featuring women must convey the greatest sense of grace and refinement. The examples he cites for models of female characters are all women who appear in *Genji*: Aoi, Yūgao, and Ukifune. He argues that it is the pinnacle of the Noh actor's art to be able to convey the grace and refinement of such women.[22] In characterizing the corpus of Noh plays based on *Genji*, Janet Goff has observed the following:

> Although the *Genji* has never failed to delight readers, its appeal as a source of inspiration and allusion was perhaps greatest during the middle ages, that is, from the late twelfth to the sixteenth century, when the court was in an advanced state of decline. Writers and critics living in a chaotic world cherished the *Genji* because, to them, it epitomized the ideal, aristocratic way of life for which they yearned.[23]

Throughout the medieval period *Genji*'s connection to poetry and idealized notions of aristocratic culture continued to evolve. However, a cultural bias against the genre of prose fiction that we observed in the earliest accounts of reading *Genji* saw little change. Scholars continued to search for a didactic message in *Genji*.

THE EDO PERIOD AND THE RISE OF NATIVISM

As neo-Confucian thought came to play a larger role in the cultural and scholarly activity of early Tokugawa Japan emphasis on the didactic nature of *Genji* took on even greater prominence. The exacting analysis and reevaluation of ancient texts promoted by neo-Confucianists also led to advances in philology that made more reliable and consistent reading of the text possible. The rise of commercial publishing led to a much wider circulation of both text and commentary. In concert, these developments produced a more informed and persuasive analysis of the tale's literary and stylistic qualities.

In the early Edo period, an influential neo-Confucian scholar, Kumazawa Banzan (1619–1691), seized upon the moralistic aspect of medieval commentary to portray *Genji* as a virtual storehouse of Confucian virtue. In his *Genji gaiden* (ca. 1673), Banzan focused on the wealth of court ritual recorded in the text to suggest that *Genji* should be read as a didactic work of literature disguised in the language of a romance.[24] He believed that such a reading would provide moral benefits similar to those derived from studying classical Chinese texts that depicted the idealized past of ancient China. Banzan eschewed annotation that touched upon immoral acts depicted in *Genji*, believing that such a reading was contrary to the author's intended goal in composing the work.[25] This emphasis on certain passages at the expense of others was justified because Banzan envisioned an overall meaning that transcended individual details of the work. *Genji gaiden* provides us with a clear picture of Banzan's understanding of Confucianism at the time but leaves us with a highly subjective view of *Genji*. However, interpretation of *Genji* ultimately benefited from this biased interpretation because it promoted the notion that commentary could go beyond the identification of poetic allusion and historical detail to approach *Genji* from a much broader perspective.[26]

At about the same time Banzan was composing *Genji gaiden*, the poet and scholar of classical literature, Kitamura Kigin (1624–1705), was compiling a massive commentary on *Genji* that not only provided extensive annotation but also a reproduction of the entire text. Kigin's *Kogetsushō* (1673) consisted of an introductory section in six fascicles that contained various short entries devoted to fundamental issues concerning *Genji*, such as its authorship, praise for the work and its author, genealogy of characters, and historical sources for characters and events that appear in the work. This was followed by a reproduction of the complete text with introductory material, interlineal glosses, and notes for each chapter. The *Kogetsushō* combined detailed annotation culled from lectures and commentaries with broader comments in keeping with Buddhist thought and Confucian didacticism to provide what must have seemed in its day to be a comprehensive and highly authoritative edition of *Genji*. The *Kogetsushō* contained numerous textual errors and few original insights, yet its combination of annotation and main text made the tale easier to read and comprehend. These factors contributed to an extensive distribution of *Genji* during the second century of the Edo period.[27] Kigin's integration of extant scholarship and commentary with the complete text of *Genji* into a widely available edition had an enormous impact on the reception of the tale. Appreciating *Genji* as prose fiction remained beyond the ability of most readers, but the availability of *Genji* in the format of the *Kogetsushō* made the powerful statement, if only symbolically, that *Genji* and its essence could be owned by anyone with the means necessary for its acquisition. The private or "secret" versions of the text so closely guarded by aristocratic families up to this point were rendered inferior because they relied upon only a limited portion of the commentary and scholarship available in the integrated format of the *Kogetsushō*. Widespread publication of the *Kogetsushō* established it as the edition most often referred to by scholars of *Genji* for the remaining two centuries of the Tokugawa period. Even scholars highly critical of the interpretation promoted by the *Kogetsushō* continued to rely on it as their point of textual reference in composing their own treatises on *Genji*.[28]

In addition to bringing a broader interpretive approach to *Genji*, a new wave of Confucian ideology brought greater openness to the tradition of scholarly commentary in the Tokugawa period. During the medieval period information contained in commentaries was viewed as a valuable asset to be handed down in secrecy from master to disciple within a specific lineage. As a result, the transmission and preservation of commentary had come to be associated not only with serious scholarship but also with aristocratic prestige. Neo-Confucian thought in the tradition of the Yangming School (J: *Yōmeigaku*) advocated that all men should be engaged in the investigation of the true nature of things to promote an orderly and humane society. In their zeal to apply neo-Confucian principles to all areas of knowledge, scholars were persuaded to break with the tradition of secret transmission of *Genji* commentary. Banzan's *Genji gaiden* and Kigin's *Kogetsushō* both reflect this rejection of the esoteric transmission of knowledge. Due to the open exchange of information, the value of commentary as a sacred possession, which could confer aristocratic status on its owners, was lost. In its place, scholars would now be forced to reevaluate commentary in terms of its utility in explaining the text. In this reevaluation they would discover that much of the material, which had been transposed so conscientiously from one commentary to the next for centuries, no longer made sense or contributed to an understanding of *Genji*.

In 1682, Tokugawa Mitsukuni (1628–1700), *daimyō* of the Mito domain, commissioned the Buddhist priest Keichū (1640–1701) to complete an authoritative edition of Japan's earliest poetry anthology, *A Collection of Ten Thousand Leaves* (*Man'yōshū*, late eighth century). Mitsukuni was interested in realizing the benefits of Confucian ideology more directly by producing great historical documents on Japanese history to rival those imported from China. In 1657, Mitsukuni had undertaken the composition of the *History of Great Japan* (*Dai Nihonshi*) to produce a work equal in stature to the *Records of the Historian* (*Shiji*, J: *Shiki*) by Sima Qian (b. 145 B.C.). Mitsukuni hoped an authoritative edition of the *Man'yōshū* would serve as a fitting companion to the *History of Great Japan* and that it might count as Japan's equivalent of China's *Book of Songs* (*Shijing*, J: *Shikyō*).[29] The compilation of an authoritative edition of the *Man'yōshū* was a daunting task, the success of which relied heavily upon Keichū's philological training in the reading of Buddhist scripture and an extensive knowledge of ancient Japanese poetry. Despite the fact that scholars previously commissioned by Mitsukuni had already spent nine years on the project, the process of comparing variant manuscripts and evaluating archaic language took Keichū eight years to complete. Keichū's successful compilation of the *Man'yōshū* and his exacting commentary demonstrated that textual analysis directed toward native Japanese texts could produce scholarship comparable with works produced by Confucian academies that analyzed texts from Chinese antiquity.

Motivated by his interest in the poetry and poetics of ancient Japan, Keichū moved on from the *Man'yōshū* to apply his philological analysis to the *Tales of Ise* (*Ise monogatari*, mid-tenth-century) and *Genji*. He completed a commentary on *Genji*, the *Genchū shūi*, in 1696. The *Genchū shūi* contained seven fascicles of corrections to errors Keichū found in the annotation of the *Kogetsushō*.[30] His corrections were based on an extensive reading of ancient and Heian-period texts such as *The Chronicles of Japan* (*Nihongi*, 720), *Man'yōshū*, and *The Pillow Book* (*Makura no sōshi*, ca. 996–1012), as well as on his knowledge of Chinese classics and Buddhist scripture. For Keichū, the correction of previous annotation was both a philological and an ideological exercise. He rejected annotation derived from aristocratic commentary if it neither clarified the meaning of the text nor could be justified in terms of language found in other texts from antiquity. He also rejected didactic interpretation because he believed such an approach was inconsistent with the nature of the text itself. His reading of *Genji* led him to conclude that the text reflected life in Heian Japan and realistically depicted individuals in their capacity to act in both good and bad ways. Confucian ideology dictated that good people act morally, and evil people act immorally, which made for fine didactic prose but not realistic fiction. It made no sense to Keichū to impose moral didacticism on a story, such as *Genji*, that operated beyond such concerns.[31] Keichū's work marks the beginning of what is considered the era of "new commentary" (*shinchū*) on *Genji*. His philological analysis managed to penetrate centuries of moralistic rationalization and aristocratic tradition to once again focus on the poetry and prose of *Genji*.

Another scholar commissioned by Tokugawa Mitsukuni was Andō Tameakira (1659–1716). Tameakira contributed to Mitsukuni's work on the *History of Great Japan* and served as his envoy in arranging for Keichū to work on the *Man'yōshū*.[32] The different texts Tameakira and Keichū worked on under Mitsukuni reflect the different perspectives from which they analyzed *Genji*. Tameakira shared Keichū's interest in the texts from Japan's past and their application to the analysis of *Genji*, but he failed to completely reject what Keichū saw as the Confucian conceit of imposing didactic values on fictional prose. Instead, he pursued an agenda similar to Mitsukuni's in attempting to establish Japanese equivalents for the great works of literature from China. In his *Shikashichiron* (Seven Essays on Murasaki Shikibu, 1703), Tameakira draws on material from Murasaki Shikibu's diary and passages from *Genji* to argue that Murasaki Shikibu is comparable in talent and moral virtue to the authors of great historical works from China. While he does not argue for the medieval practice of evaluating individual details of *Genji* in terms of

Buddhist thought or Confucian morality, he does assert that the author's aim in composing *Genji* was no less virtuous than the intention behind great works from China. Unlike Kumazawa Banzan, Tameakira did not simply ignore details of the text that alluded to any impropriety. Instead, he constructed a comprehensive theory that accounted for depictions of immorality. Moving one step back from the details of the text, Tameakira argued that the author's overall goal was to inspire virtuous behavior by depicting vice and its consequences in the form of an engaging narrative.

Tameakira based his interpretive theory on the assumption that Murasaki Shikibu was a virtuous woman whose intentions in composing *Genji* should only be understood as embodying a search for truth and instructing readers in moral behavior. His reading of *Genji* was more sophisticated than the literal application of Confucian ideology pursued by medieval commentators, but it still maintained Confucianism as its central point of reference. By focusing on Murasaki Shikibu rather than on the text of *Genji*, Tameakira was able to develop a convincing argument in favor of her talent as an author and *Genji*'s place as a great work of literature. However, such an approach held little appeal for readers uninterested in Confucian ideology.

Scholars in the second century of the Tokugawa period who advocated Keichū's emphasis on the poetry and poetics of ancient Japan applied what was to become known as "nativist scholarship" or "national learning" (*kokugaku*) to *Genji*. Rather than following Tameakira in trying to establish Japanese counterparts for great works of Chinese literature, nativist scholars argued that Japanese works of literature were inherently superior and did not need to be judged in terms of non-native ideology. Motoori Norinaga was the most notable nativist scholar to apply such theories to *Genji*. His *Genji monogatari tama no ogushi* is widely regarded as the seminal treatise on the tale to arise from the nativist tradition. In *Tama no ogushi*, as well as earlier works, Norinaga rejects all attempts to evaluate *Genji* in terms of Buddhist or Confucian ideology. Instead, he develops an interpretive approach based on traditional Japanese poetics, which he applies to *Genji* in much the same manner that Tameakira applied his theory of the virtuous intentions of the author. In short, Norinaga equated the artistic intentions and aesthetic sensibilities of the author with the literary qualities of the work. Rather than evaluating the work in terms of the moral or religious message to be found in particular passages, he argued that the entire work should be appreciated in terms of its expression of the "poignancy of things" (*mono no aware*).[33] For Norinaga, it is the author's sensitivity to the poignant nature of things and her expression of this sensitivity through the text that provide a true measure of her genius and the tale's worth.

Norinaga's approach to *Genji* clearly had its advantages. His insights into reading classical Japanese texts, particularly *Genji*, are hailed as some of the most significant interpretive achievements of the premodern era. A talented poet, critic, translator, and author of popular fiction, Hagiwara Hiromichi (1815–1863), was among Norinaga's greatest admirers to publish an interpretation of *Genji* in the final years of the Edo period. Hiromichi systematically applied Norinaga's scholarship on *Genji* in constructing his own guide to the text. In building the argument for this own treatise, he came to discover significant inconsistencies in Norinaga's central theory of *mono no aware.* Hiromichi went on to develop an interpretive strategy of his own, which he believed would liberate *Genji* commentary and criticism from the didactic interpretive issues that had distracted previous scholars, including Norinaga. Hiromichi's treatise on *Genji* illustrates that despite the relative merits of the *mono no aware* theory, it ultimately fails to provide a means of appraising *Genji* in terms of its merits as a work of prose fiction.

In spite of these interpretive shortcomings, Norinaga's approach continued to have enormous appeal well into the modern era. Nativist scholars found the theory of *mono no aware* particularly compelling because it helped legitimize arguments for the superiority of Japanese culture. The dogmatic nature of the *mono no aware* theory was simple to convey, thus providing a persuasive explanation as to how *Genji* was distinct from, while also being superior to, other works of literature.

As we will see in the following chapters, Hiromichi's greatest challenge would be to transcend many of the cultural assumptions surrounding *Genji* that had accumulated over seven centuries. His goal was to appraise *Genji* in a way that made its cultural relevance clear while also allowing readers to appreciate the original text as much as they delighted in works of popular fiction and drama from the Edo period.

Chapter Two

HAGIWARA HIROMICHI: MASTERLESS SAMURAI AND ICONOCLASTIC SCHOLAR

Hagiwara Hiromichi was born in 1815 and died in 1863, less than five years before the fall of the Tokugawa Shogunate and the beginning of Japan's modern era in 1868. His contributions to the literary arts of premodern Japan are extraordinary in many ways, but the failure of the modern literary establishment to embrace his greatest achievement makes the story of his life's work all the more compelling. His approach to literature exemplifies the dynamic spirit of a period in which intellectual, social, and commercial interests converged to transform and transcend century-old traditions. His commentary on *The Tale of Genji* draws upon a variety of disciplines and interpretive traditions to deliver this complex classical text, once a sacred treasure of the aristocracy, into the hands of an avid and sophisticated popular readership. He was not the first to use commentary and criticism to promote *Genji*'s importance as a work of narrative fiction, but he was the first to clearly articulate and consistently implement such a goal with a broader readership in mind. To appreciate the significance of Hiromichi's accomplishments, we must begin with a brief examination of the social and intellectual milieu from which he came.

The Edo or Tokugawa period (1600–1868) is commonly associated with economic, social, and cultural developments resulting from an extended period of stability, urban growth, and commercial expansion. Improvements in literacy rates and standards of living generally accompanied these changes. The inhabitants of major urban centers benefited most directly from the economic and social gains of the Edo period. For those fortunate enough to live in major urban centers, the most concentrated site of this cultural dynamism, many traditional distinctions of class and social hierarchy lost the sense of sanctity they had held in earlier periods. Art, entertainment, and intellectual inquiry became much more pluralistic in nature as a result. However, these gains did not come without a price. Tokugawa rule was established through military domination. For over 250 years, fifteen successive heads of the Tokugawa clan vigilantly guarded the title of Shogun through absolute control. Loyalty to the Shogun, and by extension obedience to one's social superiors, was highly valued under a *pax Tokugawa* that rested precariously on the unstable

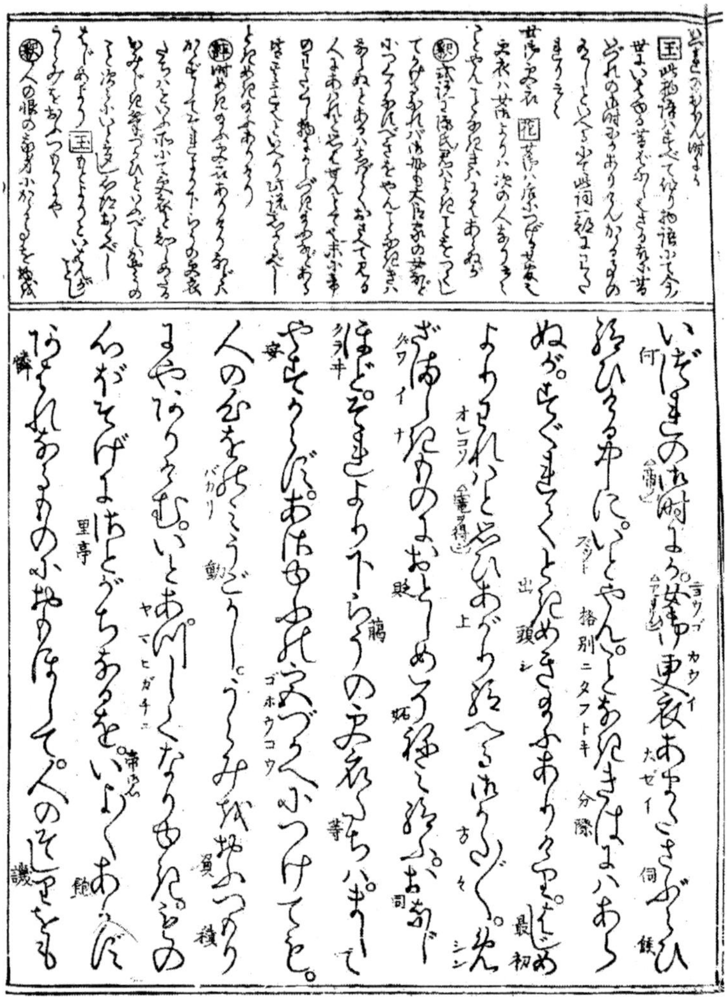

FIGURE 1

Genji monogatari hyōshaku

1854

First page of the "Kiritsubo" chapter

foundation of military dominance and political paranoia. Beginning in 1635, domainal lords were required to alternate residence between their local domains and the capital on a regular basis under a system called *sankinkōtai*. The alternate attendance system not only forced domainal lords to spend a significant portion of their time under the watchful eye of the Shogun but also generated the kind of traffic that created a pressing need for the expansion and standardization of trade, transportation, legislation, and commerce on a nationwide level. During the Kyōhō era (1716–1736), under the rule of Tokugawa Yoshimune, currency, legislation, and arbitration all underwent national standardization to facilitate administration by centralized Shogunal governance.[1] Reforms promulgated during this era also prohibited the publication of "works containing obscene or unorthodox material, erotica,... works in which the true name of the author and publisher are not clearly indicated, and those depicting the Shogunate."[2] The promulgation of censorship laws designed to shield the Shogunate from unflattering portrayals in print is a testament not only to the length to which the Shogunate was willing to go to protect itself from possible criticism but also to increases in literacy and the consumption of literature across various social classes in Japan at the time.

The merchant class benefited most from these developments as samurai interests turned from military dominance to the cultivation of cultural sophistication and material comforts. Domestic stability and the emergence of an economy that integrated all of the major commercial sectors of the nation combined to produce a flood of cultural and artistic accomplishments and innovations by the Genroku era (1688–1704). Not all segments of Japanese society were buoyed aloft by the tides of change. Members of the warrior and aristocratic classes were bound by codes of honor and Confucian ethics prohibiting their direct participation in commerce. As they clung to social status and failed to capitalize on emerging economic developments, their financial base shrank relative to the rest of the economy. Peasants often paid the price for such rigidity, as the ruling classes increased taxation in an attempt to boost income and avoid being eclipsed by merchants and townsmen in material wealth. As these social and economic forces evolved, those engaged in the commercial growth of urban centers became increasingly literate, culturally sophisticated, and financially capable of patronizing the arts. Increased travel and transportation dispersed the culture of major urban centers to outlying castle towns and the advances of one city to the next.

At the same time, many samurai were forced to survive on stipends that often seemed small in comparison to the newfound wealth of merchants and townsmen. Some abandoned or compromised their elite standing to support themselves. Under such circumstances Confucian ideals of social order and hierarchy, dividing those who sought truth and ruled by fiat from those who produced and traded goods, gave way to more practical concerns. As a result, the gulf that once separated the ideals of the literate and culturally sophisticated dilettante from the practical concerns of the professional artist or craftsman became less pronounced. Scholarship and artistry benefited, as abstraction, intuition, and idealism were invigorated and tempered by their counterparts of empiricism, experimentation, and pragmatism. This led to revolutionary breakthroughs in the study of texts from Japan's past.

In 1720, the Shogunate eased restrictions, rigidly enforced for nearly a century, on the importation of Western books. Prohibitions remained in place on the importation of books related to Christianity, but Western language texts on the natural sciences, medicine, and military technology were now widely sought and studied. As a result, Japan's antiquity and contemporary knowledge from the West came to be studied in close proximity and with equal fervor. Despite the proximity in time and place of scholarship on ancient texts and Western learning, discourse between the two fields of knowledge was not the norm. Scholars studying ancient Japanese texts employed many of the philological and rhetorical techniques developed for the interpretation of ancient Confucian texts from China (*kogaku*) but took pains to establish the primacy of native Japanese documents and sentiments over those that were foreign in origin. Western learning (*yōgaku*), first known as Dutch studies (*rangaku*), focused on the challenges of mastering the language and background knowledge on which foreign books were based. For students of Dutch studies and Western learning, the concerns of nativist and Confucian scholars seemed out of date in the face of so much unexplored knowledge from the West.

PROFOUND LOSS IN AN AGE OF ENLIGHTENMENT

During his most successful and prolific period, in his late thirties, Hagiwara Hiromichi began to prepare material for an autobiography.[3] Sadly, the autobiography was never completed. Most of the information we have of Hiromichi's early life must be extracted from the notes that remain describing his life before the age of fourteen. Over several decades, scholars Morikawa Akira and Yamazaki Katsuaki have scrupulously collected documents allowing us to reconstruct an informative, if somewhat obscured, picture of his life.

Hiromichi's father, Kaneko Eizaburō, was born in 1781 and lived in the castle town of Okayama, the center of the Ikeda clan's domain. The Okayama domain, comprised of Bizen province and parts of Bitchū province at the time, had long been an important commercial and cultural center of Japan's central region, the Chūgoku. Okayama is located on a fertile basin facing the inland sea, a midpoint between the modern cities of Osaka and Hiroshima. During Japan's middle ages, the province of Bizen was renowned for its production of swords and ceramics. However, it is the Okayama domain's association with education and scholarship during the second half of the Edo period that plays the most influential role in Hiromichi's biography.

Ikeda Mitsumasa (1609–1682), who assumed control of the Okayama domain in 1632 and ruled for forty years, embraced the tenets of neo-Confucianism with unusual zeal. His interest in putting Confucian ideals into practice made Okayama a forerunner in the effort to promote Confucian education among samurai and increase literacy rates among commoners. In 1650, he elevated the Confucian scholar Kumazawa Banzan to the rank of captain of guards (*bangashira*) with a large stipend of 3,000 koku. The promotion of a Confucian scholar to such a high rank and stipend within domainal hierarchy was without precedent at the time. In his role as confidant and advisor to the daimyō, Banzan promoted the study of neo-Confucianism among samurai and was associated with the founding of what is believed to be the first domain school (*hankō*), the Hanabata Kyōjō (Flower Garden

School), and other associations to promote Confucian learning among samurai.[4] Near the end of his rule Mitsumasa also attempted to establish a system of elementary schools to promote literacy among peasant children. Mitsumasa's successor abandoned the costly plan to establish over 120 elementary schools in the domain, but Okayama continued to play a prominent role in the establishment of educational institutions and promotion of scholarship throughout the Edo period.

The following century, Nishiyama Sessai (1735–1798) expanded upon the educational precedent established by Mitsumasa and Banzan. The precocious son of an Okayama physician, Sessai moved to Osaka at the age of sixteen to study medicine. After establishing his reputation as a poet and scholar of neo-Confucian studies in Osaka and Kyoto, he returned to Okayama in his late thirties. In 1773, he opened Kinjuku, a private academy for neo-Confucian studies, which drew a large number of students. The success of Kinjuku in Okayama provides evidence that private educational institutions had begun to flourish in areas beyond the major urban centers of Osaka, Kyoto, and Edo well before the end of the eighteenth century.

This emphasis on education and scholarship beyond direct administrative control of the domainal government was not limited to the study of Confucianism. Okayama produced a number of influential scholars of nativist studies (*kokugaku*), Dutch learning (*rangaku*), and Western learning (*yōgaku*) as well. One of the most prominent scholars of national learning associated with Okayama is Fujii Takanao (1764–1840). Coming from a family of Shinto officiates, Takanao began studying national learning under Kodera Kiyosaki (1748–1827) from an early age. In 1793, Takanao traveled to the town of Matsuzaka to study national learning under the leading scholar of his day, Motoori Norinaga. He was so taken with Norinaga's work that even after returning to Okayama he continued an active correspondence and a scholarly dialogue with Norinaga. It is a testament to the acuity of Takanao's scholarship, and perhaps his rhetorical skill, that in Norinaga's later years he asked Takanao to write the preface for what would become his greatest work of criticism on *The Tale of Genji*, his *Genji monogatari tama no ogushi*.[5]

Among the number of scholars of Dutch and Western learning associated with Okayama, the most prominent figure is surely Ogata Kōan (1810–1863). At the age of seventeen, Kōan, the son of a samurai family, was assigned by his domain to a post in Osaka. While stationed in Osaka, he began learning Western science through the study of Dutch texts. He continued his studies in Edo and Nagasaki, returning briefly to Okayama in 1836 before establishing a school for Dutch studies and Western Learning, Tekijuku, in Osaka in 1838. Tekijuku's reputation as the leading school for Dutch language and Western science of its day spread rapidly. Students from around the country flocked to study under Kōan, living together while immersing themselves in the memorization of Dutch terms and interpretation of scientific texts. The adherence to Confucian ideals, emphasizing distinctions in social rank and between moral cultivation and pragmatic concerns, had become increasingly flexible in most areas of education, scholarship, and the arts as the Edo period progressed, but Tekijuku was particularly progressive in this regard. It was known as a commoner's school, where admission and promotion were determined by a sincere desire for knowledge and proficiency in reading foreign texts rather than seniority or prestigious background. Records from the years 1844 through 1864 include the names of nearly 650 students registered at Tekijuku.[6] If one factors in the number of unregistered students who studied at the school but lived in the surrounding area, the figure would be even higher. One student, Fukuzawa Yukichi (1834–1902), enrolled in Teikijuku in 1855. He studied there until 1858, when he was summoned by his domain to promote Western learning in Edo. He went on to become one of the most prominent scholars of the West and Western Learning in the early Meiji period. The success of Kōan's medical studies was such that he was named physician to the Shogun and director of the Shogunate's school of Western medicine.

Okayama's ties with progressive scholarship and education were both long-standing and profound in nature. While only two of the aforementioned scholars can be linked directly to Hiromichi, all of their accomplishments were to inform the intellectual course he charted.

Hiromichi's father, Kaneko Eizaburō, was born into a family that had fallen victim to inhospitable economic circumstance. Eizaburō's position as the third son of a low-ranking samurai family in service to the Ikeda daimyō entitled him to an education, but little else. When Eizaburō was in his early twenties, his father died, leaving the Kaneko family in financial ruin. Eizaburō moved to an outlying village, where he made ends meet as an instructor in a small temple school (*terakoya*). When the master of the temple school died, a family in need of a male heir and only slightly more financially stable than his own adopted him in 1804. This adoption allowed him to take on the prestigious surname of Fujiwara and anticipate that someday he might become head of his own household. Around this time he also managed to obtain a position as a low-ranking retainer, a footman of sorts, in service to the Ikeda clan. By the start of the Bunka era (1804–1817) Eizaburō's future seemed to hold more promise. He married, but his first wife died before the couple had any children. Before long he married again, this time taking the stepdaughter of Murakami Hanzaemon, a well-established samurai, as his wife. No record remains as to what thwarted this rise in Eizaburō's fortunes, but by the fall of 1814 there were signs that things were no longer going well. Ill and unable to support a household, Eizaburō went to live with his eldest brother, Kaneko Tokumasa. It was customary for a wife to return to her parents' home in preparation for the birth of her first child. The custom may have provided a convenient excuse at the time for Eizaburō to recuperate under the care of his family while his wife went to live with her family. However, after his wife returned to the comforts of her parents' home, an official samurai residence on the outskirts of Okayama, she continued to live with various members of her family following the birth of their son late in the winter of 1815. There is no record of Eizaburō ever again establishing a permanent residence of his own with his second wife.

Hiromichi's name at birth was Fujiwara Shūzō. It was not until he separated from the ranks of the Okayama daimyō and established himself in literary circles of the Osaka and Kyoto area that he adopted the surname Hagiwara followed by the pen-name Hiromichi. However, in keeping with source materials, Fujiwara Shūzō will be referred to using the name by which he was best known and with which he signed the prefaces to his most famous works of commentary and criticism: Hagiwara Hiromichi.

The year following Hiromichi's birth, Eizaburō's health did not improve. Pleading illness, he requested that he be relieved of his duties in service to the Ikeda clan in 1817. As a result, his stipend from the daimyō was reduced. Forced to seek gainful employment, he quickly accepted a minor post as caretaker and part-time instructor at a local school. Either the position provided such meager accommodations that Eizaburō was unable to permanently house his family or he lived apart from his wife and son for most of the year by choice. In either case, Hiromichi's early childhood was spent mostly in the company of his mother, his young aunt, Tami, and his maternal grandmother. One of the earliest details of Hiromichi's childhood comes to us from a story related to him by his mother and grandmother. Around the time he turned one year old, he began to imitate what adults around him were saying. To keep him out of trouble, his mother and grandmother took to reciting poems from Fujiwara Teika's collection the *Ogura Hyakunin isshu* (Single Poems by One Hundred Poets) in his presence. By the time he was two, he was able to astonish adults by flawlessly reciting the entire collection of 100 poems from beginning to end.[7] This flattering narrative, constructed from memories of childhood, is a testament of precocious intelligence and love of language, but it is even more telling when seen from the perspective of Hiromichi's life and his life's work. A child prodigy, thriving under the care of his mother, aunt, and grandmother, Hiromichi also recalls that he began to take writing lessons at the age of three. Whether or not one can believe that a child of so young an age could master such feats of memorization and linguistic competence, it is important to note that Hiromichi looked back on this period of his life with particular nostalgia. He associated the years spent in the company of his mother and her family with a sense of comfort and promise that was never to be regained.

Of the trauma that was to follow, he recalls: "My stepgrandmother, a woman who had treated me as dearly as her own child since I was in swaddling clothes and who had held me and constantly cared for me, took ill and died when I was five years old."[8] The following summer Tami died at the age of fifteen. Only two months later, family tragedy compounded even more deeply when Hiromichi's mother died. He writes of her death:

> I was just six years old at the time so I was probably looking in at things I should not have seen. I was told I was in the way and that I should go stay with my uncle Kaneko. . . . That night there was a storm and the wind came in strong gusts. My cousin came to fetch me and take me back to my home, talking about this and that along

> the way to cheer me up. When we got to my house everything looked different. I encountered a large group of people from the neighborhood, looked at them in bewilderment and began to sob endlessly. Various people did what they could to soothe me as I sat though the funeral rites.[9]

This sense of loss and bewilderment was never to fade completely from Hiromichi's life. Following his mother's death, he was placed under his father's care, living temporarily in the home of his maternal grandfather. His grandfather, despondent over the loss of his wife and two daughters in the span of only a few years, allowed the household to fall into disrepair. Twice widowed, Eizaburō was equally despondent. Hiromichi recalls that his father began to drink in the morning, around breakfast time. When Hiromichi was nine, Eizaburō was given a teaching post at a domain school. Hiromichi began his education in the four Confucian classics and the five books at the same school. He notes that when he returned home no one was there to encourage his studies, but he diligently made his way through the assigned lessons on his own. The most vivid recollections he has of this time come from the kindness shown to him by an old married couple living nearby and the precarious nature of his family fortunes. Hiromichi recalls that the income on which his father supported the family was barely enough to provide food for one person.[10] In 1825, Eizaburō remarried yet again. The following year Hiromichi became gravely ill with smallpox. In the notes for his autobiography Hiromichi fondly mentions the care with which his stepmother nursed him back to health. The following year she left Hiromichi and his father, never to return. No mention is made as to why she left, but one can readily surmise that living conditions in the Fujiwara household were difficult at best.

Throughout his life, Hiromichi remained unable to distance himself from the profound loss and economic hardship that defined his childhood. Even in his late thirties, when his reputation as one of the finest poets and scholars of the Osaka-Kyoto (*kamigata*) area of his generation was well established, Hiromichi's correspondence continues to contain references to having barely enough rice to feed himself.[11] Not surprisingly, his biography is punctuated by extended bouts with serious illness and periods when he is confined to bed for months at a time.[12] Anecdotal evidence suggests that in his final years his health declined as a result of excessive drinking and the long-term effects of syphilitic infection. Extant manuscripts from this period graphically support complaints he makes in letters to friends that he suffered from such advanced palsy that he was sometimes forced to write with his left hand. There is evidence to suggest that he married once but no clear indication that he ever had children, nor of how long his wife remained with him. The tragic nature of Hiromichi's final years is reflected in the fact that most of what we know of his life comes from the letters and manuscripts he sent to others. Word of his day-to-day existence comes to us mainly in the writings left by his more fortunate contemporaries. Aside from the remarkable works he prepared for publication, few documents in his possession were preserved. His published works, the manuscripts he circulated in hopes of finding a publisher, and the prefaces he wrote for the published works of others serve as the most reliable guide to his life and accomplishments. The paucity of documentation concerning his career and the lack of an heir or a disciple to preserve and promote his accomplishments may be one factor contributing to the surprising lack of scholarly attention his work has received in Japan.

FROM POETRY TO POETICS

Hiromichi continued to pursue his childhood interest in poetry and was well on his way to becoming a man of letters from an early age. When he was thirteen a friend introduced him to Hiraga Motoyoshi (1800–1865). Motoyoshi, then in his late twenties, had developed a reputation as a poet and an avid student of nativist studies. In 1813, Motoyoshi had attended lectures on Shinto by another Okayama native, Kurozumi Munetada (1780–1850). The following year he frequented lectures given in Okayama by Fujii Takanao's disciple in nativist studies, Nariai Ōe (1791–1851). He emerged from these lectures with a passionate interest in the analysis of ancient Japanese texts by the great nativist scholar Kamo no Mabuchi (1697–1769). Throughout his career Motoyoshi continued to integrate Mabuchi's nativist ideology with his eclectic interests in ancient literature, martial arts, and Shinto. Despite his admiration for Mabuchi's work in *kokugaku*, he never developed a strong affiliation with a single school or master.[13]

After securing an introduction to Motoyoshi, Hiromichi eagerly submitted 450 of his own *waka* to him, asking for corrections and advice. Motoyoshi responded enthusiastically to Hiromichi's poems, and the two developed a lasting friendship.[14] Contact with Motoyoshi had a formative influence on Hiromichi's career. Hiromichi's extant poems bear little trace of a *Man'yōshū* style, but like Motoyoshi, he expressed deep admiration for the work of the leading nativist scholars of his age without ever becoming closely affiliated with any single school or master. Just as Motoyoshi professed his greatest admiration for a scholar who flourished a century before his own time (Kamo no Mabuchi), Hiromichi refers most passionately to Motoori Norinaga, who died fourteen years before he was born, as his true master. The draft of Hiromichi's autobiography ends abruptly with the account of his decision to submit 450 of his own waka to Motoyoshi.[15]

Few details concerning his life from this point on until his early twenties remain accessible to us. The Tempo famine (1833–1836) reached its climax during this period, and it is not hard to imagine that his already precarious situation was made more difficult by this widespread natural catastrophe. Some years later there is a fleeting reference in a letter he sent to a fellow poet of having received instruction in philology from Ōkuni Takamasa (1792–1871), one of Hirata Atsutane's leading disciples in nativist studies who had developed a nationwide reputation at the time. This brief contact must have come when

Ōkuni was invited to lecture in the Bizen area in 1836.[16] Following the pattern he had established with Motoyoshi, Hiromichi readily applied what he learned from Ōkuni without becoming a permanent disciple or taking up the particulars of Ōkuni's school of thought. Hiromichi's relationship with his mentors is also consonant with the view Ōkuni espoused, that *kokugaku*, unlike the disciplines of Buddhism and Confucianism, thrived on innovation and each successive generation of scholars improving upon the developments of previous generations rather than simply replicating previous knowledge.[17]

In 1838, when Hiromichi was twenty-three, his father, Eizaburō, died. Hiromichi inherited his father's stipend and title within the Okayama domain. He also inherited many of his father's strategies for survival, supplementing his meager stipend by lecturing and teaching. His late teens and early twenties were a period of extended hardship but also of fantastic intellectual growth. He emerged from this dark period with a heightened awareness of some of the most sophisticated and influential interpretive theories of his age. While he resisted the opportunity to become permanently aligned with a single school or master, we can only assume that he took full advantage of the concentration of influential poets and scholars active in the Okayama area.

The first tangible sign of Hiromichi's intellectual maturation comes in 1840, when he was invited to lecture on the favorite text of his childhood, Teika's *Ogura Hyakunin isshu*. The same year he produced a manuscript in which he outlined the major points of a popular annotated edition of the *Hyakunin isshu* by Kagawa Kageki (1768–1843). Kageki's work represents an important turning point in the development of poetry and poetic criticism during the late Edo period. In the late seventeenth and early eighteenth centuries, Keichū and Mabuchi revolutionized interpretation of the *Hyakunin isshu* by applying detailed philological analysis to resolve errors and contradictions found in previous scholarship. Their conclusions challenged the dominance of "hidden" or "secret" commentary that had been passed down from one aristocratic generation to the next. By the end of the eighteenth century, the superiority of their analysis had become so firmly established that scholars were content to overlook both traditional commentary and its philological refutation. Efforts were soon underway to move beyond the rejection of failed commentary to make the poems and the archaic worldview they represented more accessible to the average reader. For example, *A New Commentary on the Hyakunin isshu* (*Hyakunin isshu shin shō*), compiled in 1804, argues that "Both Keichū's *Rectified Commentary* (*Kaikanshō*, 1688) and Kamo no Mabuchi's *First Lessons* (*Uimanabi*, 1765) are generally helpful, but Keichū's explanations are excessively high minded and Mabuchi's are so detailed as to be troublesome." Editions in this style promised to sort through vexing details and present the reader with the most salient points of commentary.[18] Kageki took this process one step further. His reading of the poems, while informed by the philological analysis of Keichū and Mabuchi, dispensed completely with their nativist ideology and valorization of the archaic. In his commentary he chose to reject archaic interpretation and focus on what he characterized as the "euphony" (*shirabe*) and "intensity of language" (*gosei*) of the poems. He later explained his rejection of the overly formalistic interpretation of poetry by arguing, "It is euphony, not reason, that makes a poem" (*uta ha shiraberu mono nari, kotowaru mono ni arazu*).[19] His annotated commentary on the *Hyakushu iken* (Divergent Views on the *Hyakunin isshu*, 1815) immediately distinguished itself from previous scholarship but was treated as ideological heresy by strict adherents of the nativist school.

A related work in which Kageki specifically rejected the influence of Mabuchi's interpretation of poems in the *Hyakunin isshu* (*Nimanabi iken*, Differing Views on Mabuchi's *First Lessons*, 1811) also attracted the ire of nativist scholars. Among the irate was Nariai Ōe, whose 1819 treatise refuting Kageki's position, titled *Nimanabi iken ben* (A Discourse on the Differing Views of Mabuchi's *First Lessons*), remains one of his best-known works.[20] Through his association with Motoyoshi, Hiromichi was no doubt aware of Nariai's dismissal of Kageki's interpretive strategy. Hiromichi outlined his own views on this contentious topic in his *Hyakushu iken tekihyō* (An Outline and Appraisal of the *Hyakushu iken*, 1840).[21] Hiromichi's intellectual maturity and independence can be seen in his bold decision to embrace the interpretive advances made by Kageki rather than simply following the nativist ideology of his mentors. Even more remarkable is the way he chose to step back from the ideological focus of the debate to gain insight into the fundamental nature of commentary itself. He writes:

> Because all things are destined to make themselves manifest [in their perfect form] over time it stands to reason that commentary, the last thing to be created [in the literary process], can achieve a state of perfection through moderation.[22]

In reaching this conclusion Hiromichi conveys a surprisingly nonpartisan appreciation for the greater significance of Kageki's rejection of nativist ideology in his appraisal of the *Hyakunin isshu*. This early appreciation for the value of interpretation that illuminates the meaning of the text over ideological rhetoric will come to play an important role in Hiromichi's later approach to reading *Genji*. His conclusion also betrays a lack of concern for perpetuating factional rhetoric. This is a testament to his independence from an obligation to support the position of a particular school of thought or interpretation.

In 1841, while on an outing to Ōeyama, a mountain in what is now Kyoto Prefecture, Hiromichi was forced to return to Okayama due to a severe case of beriberi.[23] His disappointment over being thwarted in his efforts to reach Ōeyama must have been tempered with a sense of poetic irony. From early childhood he had internalized the reference in the *Hyakunin isshu* to "Ōeyama and the road to Ikuno, so distant that I have not yet set foot there."[24] The fatigue and paralysis of beriberi are often associated with poor diet and chronic alcoholism. What little we know of Hiromichi's life up to this point suggests that both problems are likely to have contributed to his declining health at this time.

In 1843, he completed two more manuscripts in which he outlined his views on various topics related to literature: *Tamazasa sōshi* (Jeweled Bamboo Essays), a collection of miscellaneous writings, and *Man'yōshū ryakugehoi*, which provides supplemental notes and a rough guide to the *Man'yōshū*. *Tamazasa* includes short entries on a variety of literary topics, ranging from classical texts, philology, and poetics to popular literature in Chinese and Japanese. Of his interest in popular literature he writes:

> Among the numerous writers of popular literature in Edo these days, Takizawa Bakin's works stand out as the only ones to skillfully adapt material from Chinese historical literature. They are overwhelmingly fun to read. In them one can see how he has paid close attention to the structure of language (*tenowoha*) and attends carefully to the fullest expression of human emotion (*ninjō no omomuki wo tsukushite*) and exchange of feelings between characters. What's more, he clearly shows an understanding of the principles of Buddhism and Confucianism. I find the style of his writing (*fumidura*) to be outstanding.[25]

He signed both of these works with the pen name Taira Hiromichi, using the first character from Hiraga Motoyoshi's surname, *hira*, which can also be read as *taira*.[26] Hiromichi's request for guidance from Motoyoshi and the friendship that developed between them marks the beginning of Hiromichi's career as a scholar of nativist studies. This contact with Motoyoshi seems to have inspired Hiromichi to cultivate his interest in poetry within a larger intellectual framework. Thus we begin to see his activities expanding from the narrow focus on the popular poetry of the *Hyakunin Isshu* to the earliest anthology of imperial poetry, the *Man'yōshū*. The expansion of Hiromichi's interest from the narrow field of classical poetry in Japanese to major texts and anthologies of the classical Japanese canon is consistent with the trajectory of intellectual development associated with nativist scholarship during the Edo period. As philological analysis allowed scholars to read individual texts from the classical corpus with greater internal consistency, they were able to develop critical theories that addressed a broader literary context. The broader scope of literary inquiry, integrated with the nativist agenda to establish the superiority of Japan's indigenous culture, led to the development of interpretive and cultural theories that addressed the corpus of classical literature written in Japanese as a whole.

OSAKA: ENCOUNTERS WITH HETERODOX LEARNING

In the spring of 1845, Hiromichi left Okayama, making his way eastward through Himeji and on to Osaka. The immediate cause for his departure from Okayama was the need to free himself of the obligations to his domainal lord.

Upon arriving in Osaka he wrote to an acquaintance from Okayama that his poor health had made it difficult to fulfill his obligations to the domain.[27] In leaving Okayama without permission from the daimyō, he joined the growing ranks of masterless samurai, *rōnin*, of the Edo period. This departure from official status as a warrior in service to his domain to a man of letters is marked symbolically by his use of the surname Hagiwara in many of the manuscripts he produced following his arrival in Osaka. Hiromichi left Okayama a frail samurai but seems to have arrived in Osaka a mature and an impressive poet and scholar of nativist studies.

Soon after arriving in Osaka he made the acquaintance of nativist scholars Ajiro Hironori (1784–1856) and Nishida Naokai (1793–1865). Hiromichi favorably impressed these established intellectuals, and within months of arriving in Osaka, he was asked to contribute his remarks to the publication of Naokai's collected works.[28] In the fall of the same year, Fujii Takatsune (1819–1863) traveled to Osaka from Okayama, visiting Hiromichi while he was in the area. Takatsune's grandfather was the famous Okayama scholar of nativist studies and disciple of Motoori Norinaga, Fujii Takanao. As fellow students of Norinaga's work in nativist studies, Hiromichi and Takatsune had probably become acquaintances in Okayama. An impoverished samurai like Hiromichi stood to benefit enormously from such a friendship. Due no doubt to the well-stocked personal library of the Fujii family and to the generosity of his friend Takatsune, he must have been able to borrow and study the texts required to develop a command of previous scholarship in the field of nativist studies. Hiromichi lacked a close affiliation with an established school or master, so it would be hard to account otherwise for his mastery of essential texts in the *Kokugaku* lineage.

Takatsune's friendship was to have an even greater impact on Hiromichi's work. On finding his friend in poor health, he introduced Hiromichi to his uncle, the renowned scholar of Dutch studies and Western medicine, Ogata Kōan. Kōan's school for Western Learning, Tekijuku, was located only a few minute's walk to the north of Hiromichi's first residence in Osaka. Ironically the young student of ancient studies and the established scholar of Western Learning seemed to have many interests in common. A lasting friendship between Hiromichi and Kōan was born from this meeting.

The area of Osaka in which both Kōan and Hiromichi settled (now the Yodoyabashi and Kitahama area of Osaka) had attracted scholars in pursuit of independent thought since the early eighteenth century. Osaka had become the central hub in a nationwide commercial transportation system and rose to prominence as a city of merchants. Its population dominated by affluent financiers, entrepreneurs, and tradesmen, Osaka became a particularly diverse and intellectually stimulating environment during the Edo period. Osaka's culture embraced the openness and independence that were the pillars of commercial success. Despite the upheavals of the Edo period, Osaka's inland neighbor, the ancient capital of Kyoto, had preserved a largely aristocratic and tradition-bound culture. In 1724, a group of successful merchants received permission from Shogun Tokugawa Yoshimune to establish a school to provide commoners with an education in neo-Confucian studies. It seems only natural that they established an academy of trade, commerce, and Confucian studies, known as the Kaitokudō, in the commercial heart of the city.[29] The Kaitokudō's reputation as a center for scholarship, placing the pursuit of knowledge before concerns of political patronage or the perpetuation of tradition, had been a factor in attracting Kōan to found his Tekijuku in this area.[30] Kōan wisely situated his school for Western Learning not far from the harbor that welcomed Dutch envoys transporting their goods between ports to the south, including Nagasaki, and the capital city of Edo.[31] Hiromichi, too, must have been drawn to the reputation of this sector of the merchant's capital in making his own transition from a rural samurai to an independent man of letters. Kōan took advantage of Hiromichi's skills as a poet, submitting poems to him for correction and advice. Several years later, in 1851, Kōan was to reciprocate by inviting Hiromichi to give a series of lectures on *Genji monogatari* to a small group of friends and colleagues in the study of Western medicine.[32]

Not long after his arrival in Osaka, another member of Kōan's circle, Naka Tamaki (1808?–1860), loaned Hiromichi several translations of texts from Western languages. Hiromichi was drawn to the transcription of Western terminology in these texts. He found the methods of transcription fascinating, but problematic and confusing. In response to his reading of these translations, and probably consultations with scholars engaged in the translation of Western texts, Hiromichi produced a treatise on the transcription of Western terminology into Japanese (*Seijū on'yakujiron*, Essay on the Transliteration of Western Weaponry Texts, 1845). Hiromichi's preface begins with his concern that current methods of transcription in texts translated from Western languages are overly complicated and inaccessible to the average reader:

> In the fall of 1845 I was in Osaka recuperating from an illness. To assuage the tedium of bedrest I borrowed several translations of texts from far off Western nations from an acquaintance named Naka. While it is indeed difficult to understand the language of such distant lands I found it strange that these texts had all been translated into Chinese based on Han, Six Dynasties, and Tang period character readings used by Japanese scholars of classical Chinese. Phonetic Japanese kana running along the side of the Chinese characters were included. All of this made reading extremely difficult and annoying. . . . I asked my friend why these texts had been translated using this useless system of classical Chinese readings. I also asked him if he didn't think it would be more practical in terms of disseminating such information to use the phonetic kana of our own language which even young children are able to understand. He replied that this was true, but that most of the translators are scholars of Confucianism and Medicine. They rely upon methods they are already familiar with

> in translating. By translating these texts into classical Chinese they are also trying to promote their own discipline. Since many people wish to learn about Western scholarship, scholars of Chinese think they can humiliate people who are not good at classical Chinese by translating things into classical Chinese. He said he'd heard that it was expressly for this purpose that some Chinese scholars were producing such things as translations of Western texts. I told him I found this to be deplorable.[33]

In the essay, Hiromichi goes on to criticize the practice of using a system of writing that is over a thousand years old to translate Western texts when it should be possible to use the phonetic system of *kana*, which is preferable not only because it translates the foreign into purely native Japanese language but also because it is easily comprehensible to most readers. In the essay, he expresses concern over the inherent difficulty of translating Western languages into the limited phonology of Japanese. He then draws upon his own training as a scholar of ancient texts to outline the various ways in which the Japanese have treated texts written in Chinese over the centuries. He illustrates his point by referring to the complications that scholars of Buddhism encountered when trying to translate and transcribe texts written in Sanskrit and the unusual orthography devised to record ancient Shinto prayers (*norito*). He then makes the argument that distinctions between phonetic-based orthography and the use of ideographs have persisted in Japan for many centuries. In particular, he points to the prestige of formal composition in classical Chinese traditionally used by men (*karabumi* or *kanbun*) over the colloquial and phonetic script associated with women's writing (*kana moji*). The prejudice against phonetic-based writing is based, he implies, in the notion that it is somehow best suited to gossip.[34] Such prejudices influenced the way Western language texts were translated and foreign terminology transcribed. As a result, Hiromichi complains that those not intimately familiar with the language of the text being translated would find it difficult, if not impossible, to comprehend.

Hiromichi's treatise is fascinating on many levels. Throughout the essay he is careful not to limit his discussion to the transcription of a specific Western language. He is most concerned with avoiding the rigid adherence to familiar patterns when they detract from the comprehensibility of the text being translated.[35] He notes that such an approach is "important not only for those studying Western nations, but also for scholars of Confucianism and Buddhism alike."[36] He claims no expertise in Western Learning but finds it regrettable that anyone should limit himself to the study of ancient texts from China and Japan and dismiss what contemporary Western Learning has to offer.[37] What is most striking about this approach is his emphasis on the pursuit of knowledge and its implications within a variety of disciplines. Hiromichi was clearly interested in seeing how Western Learning might shape one's view not only of the world beyond Japan's borders but also the familiar world within its borders. While scholars devoted to Western science and medicine shared this perspective at the time, it was not a view commonly held by those deeply invested in the study of Japan's past.

Hiromichi continued to integrate his interest in things Western with his views on the study of native texts well beyond this treastise. In 1851, about the same time that his lectures on *Genji* were taking place at Tekijuku, Hiromichi composed a letter to a fellow poet, Suzuki Kōrai (1812–1860), in which he mentions his decision to publish a commentary on *Genji*. A passing reference he makes in the 1854 preface to his *Appraisal of Genji* suggests that the lectures he gave on *Genji* at Kōan's school of Dutch Learning and Western Medicine were the same lectures that played a formative role in his decision to publish the *Hyōshaku*:

> Close acquaintances urged me to consolidate my comments [on *Genji*] and put them to print. I waved them off, saying such things as, "How could I be so presumptuous as to do such a thing?" But they earnestly persisted and at last, unable to refuse any longer, I wrote the slipshod text you have before you.[38]

It is tempting to speculate here as to the nature of Hiromichi's lectures at Tekijuku, for they must have had a significant impact on the form of his later scholarship. The fact that his lectures were given at a school of Dutch Learning and attended by prominent scholars of Dutch Learning and Western medicine, foremost among them Ogata Kōan, suggests that they differed significantly in nature from lectures on *Genji* given by nativist scholars in the past. Motoori Norinaga, Hiromichi's intellectual predecessor and the era's most influential scholar of nativism, lectured regularly to a devoted audience of nativist students a century earlier. Norinaga's writings on *Genji* clearly adopt a polemic tone, arguing in the strongest terms against Confucian and Buddhist bias in one's reading of the tale. His lectures were equally polemical in nature and were meant to address the interests and concerns of a like-minded audience. On the other hand, Hiromichi's lectures must have established a very different tone. The men in attendance were physicians and students of Western Learning rather than scholars and students of nativism. As such, Hiromichi's lectures must have been more practical and persuasive in tone. His audience assembled with the goal of becoming familiar with an important Japanese work of literature, but Hiromichi knew that they were also well versed in works such as *General Pathology* and *Principles of Cholera* (both works translated from the Dutch into Japanese by Kōan). The emphasis on consistency and the practical application of his theories to the text of *Genji* that characterize his argument in the *Hyōshaku* may in fact owe a debt to the intellectual temperament of the audiences to whom he lectured. The decidedly anti-polemic tone he adopts in his *Appraisal of Genji* may also have developed in response to the nonspecialist audience he encountered at Tekijuku.

In addition to his association with Kōan's Tekijuku, and noted scholars of nativist studies, Hiromichi appears to have quickly become an active participant in the literary circles of Osaka. Within two years of Hiromichi's arrival in Osaka, a physician, Watanabe Akira, was to write an account of his travels departing from Kyushu and traversing the nation. Of his stay in Osaka, Watanabe remarks that, among the poets and scholars of nativist studies in the Osaka area, Hagiwara Hiromichi is considered the finest. Watanabe justified his view, stating that other prominent local scholars, such as "Ōkuni Takamasa, espoused the more bizarre theories of Hirata Atsutane, . . . while others were limited to their skills in poetic composition."[39]

Within three years of his arrival, Hiromichi had completed numerous works that he intended to submit for publication. Among them were a collection of comic verse, *Ashi no ha wake*; a treatise on methods of transliterating Western weaponry manuals, *Seijū on'yakujiron*; a collection of miscellaneous theories concerning the relationship between Japan's religious traditions and national learning, *Hongaku taigai*; and three treatises on classical grammar, *Te-ni-wo-ha ryakuzukai*, *Te-ni-o-ha keijiben*, and *Kogen yakkai*. While the manuscripts on comic verse, translation of Western weaponry manuals, and miscellaneous theories on religion were never published, they serve as a testament to Hiromichi's eclectic interests during this period. His grammatical treatises met with greater success. He managed to have two of them published, and they are now considered among the most influential works on the study of post-position particles (*joshi*) in the development of early modern philology in Japan.[40] During this time, he also served as a judge in a prominent poetic competition of the Kamigata region, and his prefaces can be found in the published works of several fellow poets from the Osaka area.[41]

Hongaku taigai, which Hiromichi completed in 1845, points to a connection he made with Osaka's most prominent school of Confucian studies, Kaitokudō. In this manuscript Hiromichi refers to an iconoclastic scholar who received his training in Confucian studies at Kaitokudō, Tominaga Nakamoto (1715–1746). Hiromichi's reference to Nakamoto is very brief, but its potential impact on his discussion of the history of *Genji* commentary in the *Hyōshaku* is enormous. In the second volume of *Hongaku taigai*, where he discusses the three main religious traditions in Japan, Hiromichi makes a passing reference to Nakamoto's theories concerning the evolution of ideas. Based on an analysis of the history of Confucianism, Buddhism, and Shinto, Nakamoto concluded that religious and philosophical systems and teachings develop in response to ideological difference. Based on this theory, it is possible to argue that religious and moral values change over time. Therefore, it is illogical to assume that teachings found in ancient religious or philosophical texts should be applied to contemporary circumstances. Nakamoto used this theory to argue against what he perceived to be the literal-minded and conservative tendency of scholarship related to Confucian, Buddhist, and Shinto thought in his day.[42] This theory effectively challenges the legitimizing function that nostalgia had come to occupy in the interpretation of texts from antiquity. The threat this position represented to the ideological goals of Confucian studies at the time can be seen in the fact that Nakamoto was asked to leave the Kaitokudō for espousing such notions.[43] In his later work, Hiromichi comes to express a similar notion in his evaluation of previous *Genji* criticism. The fact that Hiromichi integrated Nakamoto's theories into his own work as early as 1845 shows that he was inclined to identify ideological conflict and seek to transcend its limitations well before he began to compose the *Hyōshaku*.

TAKIZAWA BAKIN AND THE EDO "NOVEL"

In addition to his work in classical Japanese literature and poetry, Hiromichi also worked closely with vernacular fiction imported from China. In 1848, the highly successful author Takizawa (Kyokutei) Bakin (1767–1848) died, leaving his serialized publication *Daring Adventures of Chivalrous Men* (*Kaikan kyōki kyōkakuden*, 1832–1835) closely based on a fictional work in vernacular Chinese, complete up to only the fourth volume. Shortly after Bakin's death, Hiromichi was approached by Bakin's publisher and asked to compose an additional volume to continue the successful series.[44] Hiromichi's perceptive reading of Bakin's literary style is put to such good effect in his continuation of the original that later scholars have often praised Hiromichi's style as being almost indistinguishable from the text written by Bakin himself.[45] In fact, Hiromichi's style in the final volume is so compatible with Bakin's earlier volumes that as late as the 1890s its authorship was not widely attributed to Hiromichi as a separate author.[46] In 1911, influential author and literary critic Kōda Rohan observed that Bakin's *Daring Adventures*, including the final volume, rivals his most famous work, *Legend of the Eight Dog Warriors* (*Nansō Satomi Hakkenden*, 1814–1842?), in quality, and one might easily find knowledgeable opinion divided as to which work is superior. He argues that Hiromichi's completion of the novel is so compatible with Bakin's style in the previous volumes that it serves as a true testament to "the acuity of Hiromichi's command of language and style."[47]

Rohan's admiration for Hiromichi's command of literary language and style stems largely from the fact that Hiromichi not only completed the main text of Bakin's novel but also carried on Bakin's practice of parenthetically interjecting authorial commentary along with the main text. Hiromichi also includes a postscript in which he provides the reader with helpful points of literary interpretation and analysis concerning the main text. In this postscript Hiromichi addresses the structure of the previous four volumes and how they relate to the fifth and final volume. He signals his admiration for Bakin and the enormity of the task undertaken by referring to the author of the previous volumes as the reputed "master of the contemporary novel" (*kindai shōsetsu no meika*). Such being the case, he feels compelled "to somehow try to match the conventions followed by the author in the previous volumes." He specifically mentions that he has attempted to "bring to fruition in the fifth volume events foreshadowed in earlier volumes."[48] His analysis elaborates on interpretive comments by Bakin in connection with previous volumes and illustrates how the final volume can be appreciated as consistent with the work as a whole in terms of a larger interpretive framework.

Analyzing Bakin's original prose to produce a sequel of equivalent literary merit seems to have pushed Hiromichi toward new interpretive insights that were to have great significance in his later work on *Genji*. By way of preparation Hiromichi studied Bakin's works and the vernacular novel in Chinese (*Haoqiuji* J: *Kōkyūji*) that served as Bakin's model for the previous volumes. For the continuation of *Daring Adventures* Hiromichi drafted a translation into Japanese of the chapters from the Chinese text that follow the chapters used by Bakin.[49] By the time Hiromichi completed the final chapter of Bakin's novel his command not only of Bakin's style but also the literary and critical conventions associated with Chinese vernacular fiction upon which it was based had reached a level of evident sophistication. Hiromichi's postscript to the final chapter of *Daring Adventures* picks up on Bakin's use of interpretive terminology derived from analysis found in works of Chinese vernacular fiction. Bakin continued to apply Chinese critical terms in the postscripts for various volumes of *Hakkenden*, which he went on to complete before his death while neglecting to finish *Daring Adventures*. His continued use of Chinese critical terms from *Daring Adventures* to *Hakkenden* led to a simplification of terminology and its application. On the other hand, Hiromichi's application of the same terms for the final volume of *Daring Adventures* is more complex, nuanced, and insightful. Bakin followed the conventions afforded by interpretive commentary associated with Chinese vernacular fiction. In *Hakkenden* he continued to follow similar conventions but began to simplify and consolidate his applications of certain critical terms. In his continuation of *Daring Adventures*, Hiromichi, however, explored the nuances and broader implications of this interpretive terminology and chose to expand and elaborate upon the potential provided by such an interpretive system. Where Bakin simply applied the critical apparatus associated with Chinese vernacular fiction to his own Japanese adaptations, Hiromichi saw much greater interpretive potential. In particular, he focused on the function of critical terms related to major and minor characters to provide a compelling analysis of the function of a main character in terms of the overall structure of Bakin's novel. As we will see in the following chapters of this book, Hiromichi applied and elaborated upon Chinese critical terminology in new literary contexts. His innovative application of this interpretive system to the works of Bakin, and ultimately to *Genji*, helped bridge an important gap between the analysis of popular fiction and classical literature. Hiromichi's insights influenced the writings of Tsubouchi Shōyō in his attempts to come to terms with the depiction of realism and narrative perspective in the development of the modern novel. Shōyō's use of the term *shōsetsu*, which Hiromichi was instrumental in applying to the works of Bakin, provides an important link connecting the evaluation of Edo popular fiction and the development of theories of the novel in Meiji Japan.

MARKETING A NEW WAY TO READ *GENJI*

One final work that should be mentioned in relation to the diverse nature of Hiromichi's intellectual achievements is an incomplete, unpublished manuscript that he titled *San'yōdō meisho* (A Guide to Famous Places Along the San'yō Highway). In this work Hiromichi demonstrates his interest in regional culture and botany. In 1850 he toured the *San'yō* region of central Japan with the intention of gathering materials for a travel guide. An increasingly prosperous merchant class in search of new diversions had made travel and tourism into a significant leisure activity of the masses in Hiromichi's time. His detailed publication notes indicate that he hoped to capitalize on this potentially lucrative market by publishing a guide to the scenic areas of his native province. This manuscript also reflects Hiromichi's perception that as a masterless samurai familiar with literature and the world of commercial publishing he might be able to support himself by catering to the interests of a popular readership with increasingly sophisticated literary tastes.

Hiromichi had precisely this in mind when he set out to publish a new edition of *Genji* that would be easier to read and appreciate than earlier editions. In the summer of 1851, he sent a letter to fellow poet Suzuki Kōrai in which he described his plans to publish a new commentary on *The Tale of Genji*. In part, he wrote:

> For some years now I have intended to publish a commentary on *Genji*. I envision that it will consist of headnotes with material from the commentaries of Keichū, Andō Tameakira, and Motoori Norinaga combined with a few of the critical notes that predate the *Kogetsushō*. I plan to include *kanji* and colloquial equivalents [of Heian language] alongside the original text so that even an amateur [*shirōto*] will be able to read *Genji* without trouble. In addition to this, I will add critical comments and introduce a theory of my own that explains [*hyō*] why *Genji* has received such praise ["explains why the text is as famous as it is"]. I intend to call this theory the "principles of composition" [*bunpō no soku*]. I have my doubts as to how good the theory is, but if I can just get this work published, I believe it will surpass the *Kogetsushō*.[50]

Hiromichi planned to raise enough capital to cover the cost of carving the woodblocks needed to print his new commentary by taking advance orders. For this reason he goes on in the letter to request that Kōrai "solicit orders from nearby acquaintances who might be interested in reading *Genji*" (*kinpen nite Genji demo yomisō naru hitobito*). The implication of Hiromichi's letter is that he imagined there was a constituency of consumers likely to be interested in reading *Genji* in the original that remained as yet untapped. He suggests to Kōrai that this new edition of *Genji* will interest a large enough readership and generate enough sales to not only recoup any investment but also to surpass the edition of *Genji* that had dominated the publishing world for more than a century, Kitamura Kigin's *Kogetsushō*. Kōrai's response must have been favorable, because a letter from Hiromichi dated two months later includes a few sample pages from his proposed manuscript. It also states that work is progressing well, and that he intends to publish it under the title *Genji monogatari hyōshaku*.[51]

This brief exchange between Hiromichi and Kōrai gives us a glimpse of Hiromichi's conception of the *Hyōshaku* while he was still in the process of compiling it. He saw his commentary as fulfilling two functions: to provide informative annotation (*chūshaku*) that would clarify the meaning of the text and to present an interpretive explanation (*hyō*) that would help the reader appreciate the literary quality of the work. While Hiromichi was closely associated with the intellectual elite of his age, this introduction to the work would have us believe that his intended audience was not his peers in the literary world or aristocratic patrons of literature but rather the amateur reader. This sentiment is echoed in the preface to the first edition of the *Hyōshaku*, where Hiromichi writes that he fears his own comments, imperfect as they are, may mislead the reader, and that the vernacular glosses he provides may fail to communicate the beauty of the author's original language:

> I realize that I cannot escape blame for such sins, but my only intention is to provide guidance to women and children who are eager to become versed [*kokoroemahoshiku suru ōna warawabe domo*] in *Genji*. Dear reader, please keep this in mind and do not judge my efforts too harshly.[52]

These references to the reader of the *Hyōshaku* suggest that Hiromichi was seeking to address a new audience for *Genji*. He was appealing to people who lacked the education and literary cultivation necessary to read and appreciate *Genji* in its original form, had no intention of devoting a lifetime to poring over old commentaries, and yet were at least captivated enough by the idea of discovering for themselves what a remarkable work of literature *Genji* was to purchase their own copies of the text. His experience with the flourishing industry of commercial publishing, which catered to an increasingly literate and affluent merchant class, led to Hiromichi's firm conviction that such a market could be found to support his new, reader-friendly edition of *Genji*.

Chapter Three

FROM MORAL CONTENTION TO LITERARY PERSUASION

Noguchi Takehiko (1937–) has argued that within Hiromichi's *Appraisal of Genji* we find the workings of what a modern scholar would call "literary interpretation" (*bungaku hihyō*):

> The "*shaku*" of the title stands for commentary while the "*hyō*" stands for what we would now call "literary interpretation." This work contains a deliberate attempt to use commentary and criticism as a means of "performing" *Genji* in a fascinating way as if it were a musical score. This is done by combining the text with an intelligent selection of commentary and criticism that encompasses the history of previous commentary from an astute interpretive perspective.[1]

Noguchi goes on to explain that he sees the *Hyōshaku* as a work of literary interpretation, because Hiromichi does not approach *Genji* from the outlook of a Confucianist, nor from the perspective of a nativist. Instead, he approaches the text as if it were nothing other than a work of literature.[2] Hiromichi's experience working with a variety of literary genres and critical traditions made it possible for him to approach criticism and commentary from this perspective. The eclectic taste in literature and criticism characteristic not only of Hiromichi but of the vibrant and diverse culture of Osaka provided him with the breadth of experience necessary to appreciate the significance of these interpretive methods. Understanding their significance made it possible for him to deliberately emphasize elements that define *Genji* as a work of narrative fiction rather than a work of didactic literature or lyric prose. His predecessors touched upon the crucial elements behind this approach, but Hiromichi was the first to successfully integrate them into an interpretive theory that could be consistently applied to the text. In doing so he directs the reader's eye to passages of fiction that create the appearance of reality and the reader's attention to compositional techniques that indicate artistic accomplishment on the part of the author. In his interpretive remarks on specific passages, he frequently concludes his notes on literary style and structure with "such is the author's remarkable use of the brush" (*sakusha no ito medetashi fudezukai nari*), or her "skillful use of language" (*bun no takumi nari*). In the commentaries that preceeded his the standard expression used to conclude a remark on literary style was "the previous passage is wonderous" or "extraordinary" (*myō nari*). The expression *myō nari* is simply meant to draw the reader's attention to a specific passage, but it also subtly builds on the tradition of "secret" commentaries by implying that the author's use of language somehow defies explication. In aggregate, this expression leaves the reader with the impression that the construction of the text is in some way beyond ordinary comprehension, as if it is miraculous or sacred. In contrast, the language Hiromichi employs is more descriptive. He draws the reader's attention to the specific elements of literary style and structure to be found in the text as something remarkable, yet also open to interpretation, analysis, and appreciation.

Hiromichi intended to cover all fifty-four chapters of *Genji*. Illness prevented him from seeing such an ambitious project to completion, but, fortunately, the first installment of his *Appraisal*, published in 1854, contains his treatise on the work as a whole. By 1861, he had managed to publish the second installment of the *Hyōshaku*, with detailed commentary covering the text up to the eighth chapter of the tale. At age forty-nine, only two years after the second installment's publication, Hiromichi succumbed to health problems that had plagued him for many years. He died in 1863, leaving his greatest efforts unrealized beyond the eighth chapter of the *Genji*, "Hana no En" ("Festival of the Cherry Blossoms").

The published volumes of Hiromichi's final work can be divided as follows:[3]

"General Remarks" [*sōron*]: volumes 1–2:

> Both volumes first published in 1854. Hiromichi surveys major issues related to the commentary and criticism of *Genji*. He reviews prominent theories developed prior to the *Hyōshaku*, evaluates their relative merits, and supplies his own analysis. The second volume also contains an exposition of his own interpretive strategy for reading *Genji*.[4]

"Main Text" [*honbun*]: volumes 3–10:

> Volumes 3–6, published in 1854, reproduce the text of chapters 1–4 in*Genji*. Volumes 7–10, published in 1861, reproduce chapters 5–8 in*Genji*. Hiromichi corrects numerous transcription errors and includes various marks and glosses to simplify reading the text in the original.[5] He also includes a preface and running commentary, in the form of headnotes, for each chapter.

"Philological Annotation" [*Genji monogatari goshaku*]: volumes 11–12:

> Grammatical, philological, and morphological analysis substantiating annotation to the main text of *Genji*. Hiromichi considered this

> material to be too important to omit, but felt that placing it in the introductory material or headnotes would distract from more immediate concerns when reading the tale.
>
> "Supplementary Annotation" [*amari no tokigoto*]: volume 13:
>
> The first half of the volume (fascicle 13) supplements the chapters published in 1854, the second half (fascicle 14) supplements the chapters published in 1861. Additional annotation, correction, and supplementary information relating to historical references, customs, and objects discussed in the text. Again, he considered the information contained in this volume to be important, but did not want its inclusion to interfere with the presentation of the main text.

Previous commentaries followed one of two formats. First, there were works in the style of the earliest commentary, Fujiwara Teika's *Okuiri* (ca. 1227), which quoted key lines from *Genji* followed by relevant annotation and interpretation. Commentaries subscribing to this format contained an introductory section. The emphasis of these commentaries was line-by-line annotation. These works were to be used as a reference or companion guide to a complete copy of *Genji*. Second, there were works defined more by interpretive argument than by annotation, such as Tameakira's *Shikashichiron* and Norinaga's "General Introduction" to *Tama no ogushi*. Hiromichi's *Appraisal* combines both approaches into a single work. The first two volumes cover general topics, including his evaluation of various theories on the author's intentions in composing *Genji*. He also presents his own interpretive approach to appreciating the overall structure of the work. The remaining volumes provide close philological analysis and interpretive commentary accompanying the development of the narrative, line by line, and in some cases word by word. The result is a surprisingly effective critical analysis that transcends many of the limitations of previous scholarship on *Genji*.

Hiromichi's unique approach to interpreting *Genji* can best be understood by examining the treatise he sets forth in his "General Remarks." The "General Remarks" section is organized under seventeen main topic headings. The topics addressed range from an analysis of the title *Genji monogatari* to the use of poetic allusion in the text. What follows is a selected translation and an analysis of the three topics that most clearly illustrate Hiromichi's approach to interpreting *Genji*: "The Design of the Monogatari and Norinaga's *Mono no Aware* Theory," "The Main Point of the Monogatari," and "Commentaries on *Genji*."

THE DESIGN OF THE MONOGATARI AND NORINAGA'S *MONO NO AWARE* THEORY

In this section Hiromichi introduces the reader to Norinaga's *mono no aware* theory. He praises Norinaga's development of this theory and points out that nearly all of *Tama no ogushi*'s second volume is devoted to it. However, his comments are not made without providing some critical balance. First, he calls into question Norinaga's philological explanation for the term *mono no aware*. His discussion begins with a quotation from the second volume of *Tama no ogushi* in which Norinaga explains the following:

> *Aware* is the sound of the sigh one makes upon being moved by the sight, sound, or sensation of something just as people now say "*aa*" and "*hare*." For example, when one looks at a flower or the moon and is moved one says, "*Aa*, what a beautiful flower," or "*Hare*, what a lovely moon." *Aware* is the combination of these two expressions. For the same reason we pronounce Chinese characters such as *wuhu* ["to sigh"] as "*aa*" when we read Chinese texts [*kanbun*].[6]

Hiromichi then adds the following comment of his own:

> Somehow this seems to be wrong. The expression "*aa*" can be found in old texts as well as contemporary speech, but the utterance "*hare*" is not something that one finds in any [old] texts nor is it something that one hears in contemporary speech. Perhaps it is something peculiar to Norinaga's Ise dialect. I really can't agree with Norinaga's point here. Rather, I believe that *aware* itself is an expression of the speaker's emotion. Other than this, the theory put forth in *Tama no ogushi* is extremely good.[7]

Hiromichi's criticism of Norinaga's explanation for the origin of the term *aware* does not alter the significance of Norinaga's theory, but it does show how Hiromichi held Norinaga's interpretive technique to the same standard of philological rigor as any other interpretive theory. His comment, that perhaps the explanation is based on a peculiarity in the dialect of Norinaga's native region, sounds somewhat dismissive. However, we should not overlook the fact that Hiromichi took such matters quite seriously. The note he provides concerning the appearance of the expression "*hare*" in various contexts is evidence of this interest and his scholarly approach to the subject. Hiromichi provides an additional headnote to this passage, which reads:

> In the Saibara collection of ancient songs there is a song in which the chorus chants "*hare*."[8] But people no longer chant in this way. Also, in the *saigoku* region [central Honshū] it is said that people in the *tōgoku* region [northern Honshū] chant "*haresate*" while most people chant "*hatesate*." But I don't think that these uses of the term help to explain the origins of the term "*aware*."[9]

Hiromichi's wide-ranging interests in philology and regional culture discussed in the previous chapter can be seen in this note. In disputing Norinaga's explanation he not only draws upon historical sources but also a knowledge of dialects and regional speech in contemporary Japan.

Hiromichi then refers the reader to Norinaga's explanation of the term *mono no aware* as it applies to *Genji*. In part, his quotation from *Tama no ogushi* reads as follows:

> We say that a person is sensitive to the poignancy of things [*mono no aware o shiru*; "knows *mono no aware*"] when he comes into contact with something moving and responds in a way that we understand. Similarly, we say that a person is insensitive to the poignancy of things [*mono no aware o shirazu*] or is "heartless" [*kokoro naki hito*] when he comes into contact with something that should certainly move him and yet he remains untouched by it. . . .
>
> *Genji* depicts all the particularly moving things that reveal such poignancy to the reader [*aware o misetaru mono*]. It portrays a wide range of events both at court and in private life that are interesting, wonderful, and magnificent. . . . The author leaves nothing out of her description. She describes everything in such an exceptional way that the reader might feel in his heart and mind that "this could be real" [*geni samo aran*]. Having been written in this way, when one reads *Genji* it is as if one were with Murasaki Shikibu, listening to her relate in vivid detail the feelings of a person who is before her very eyes [*ma no atari kano hito no omoeru kokorobae o kataru*]. By analyzing the behavior and disposition [*shiwaza kokoro no omomuki*] of both the good and bad characters who appear in the monogatari one is able to understand how each one responds to things in a certain way and how each one thinks in a certain way when faced with particular circumstances. As a result, one understands how good characters behave in this way and bad characters behave in that way. One thus becomes familiar with the general way in which people anywhere in the world might think and feel. This is what Chinese texts call "knowing the ways of the world" [*ninjō setai ni yoku tsūzen koto*]. I doubt there is anything that equals reading *Genji*.[10]

Hiromichi concludes: "Certainly, this theory is accurate. It is as if [Norinaga] were able to see into the deepest reaches of author's heart and mind. There is something I would like to add here." Rather than questioning the validity of Norinaga's *mono no aware* theory, he uses the points raised by Norinaga to introduce the fundamental issue of how scholars approach the interpretation of literature and scholarship in general:

> Scholars [*gakumon to iu koto suru hito*] both past and present only learn from what they find in books [*fumi*] and don't pay much attention to the realities [*utsutsu*] of the world before their own eyes. They are only able to see things in a well-reasoned manner familiar to them from books and try to apply this way of thinking to everything

with which they come into contact. In general, scholarship means learning the "ancient way" [*inishie no michi*]. This consists of becoming completely familiar with the way things were in the past. The world in which we live is then understood by comparing it to the state of things in the past. Scholars think this is the way things should be done. However, if one strictly follows their line of reasoning one discovers that there are very few cases in which knowledge from the past can be applied to present circumstances without modification. Nevertheless, they try to follow this reasoning closely and arrogantly carry it out in various ways. . . . This is an unfortunate and distressing circumstance because it means that there is absolutely no field of scholarship that encompasses what we call "knowing the ways of the world." However, if one were to read a monogatari such as *Genji*, come to thoroughly understand human feeling [*hito no kokoro*] and the ways of the world, and then go on to read the great variety of other books in the world then each book would come to have great meaning. There is no mistaking this. For this purpose there is certainly nothing that surpasses *Genji*. Long ago the master, Hosokawa Yūsai [1534–1610][11] was asked,

"What is the most important text to rely upon if one wishes to comprehend the world?"

He replied, "*Genji monogatari*."

Perhaps, Yūsai had a similar idea in mind when he answered this question.[12]

At first it would seem that Hiromichi's goal is simply to expand upon Norinaga's claim that there is no greater work than *Genji* in its realistic portrayal of humanity. However, there is a great deal of history behind the development of Norinaga's interpretive approach that Hiromichi leaves unsaid in his presentation of the *mono no aware* theory and his comments that follow. Hiromichi's selective quotation from *Tama no ogushi* focuses on the interpretive aspects of Norinaga's theory while avoiding much of the ideological debate that portrayed Confucian and Buddhist interpretation as a malevolent force to be exorcised from one's reading of the monogatari. Due to Norinaga's forceful rejection of didactic interpretation, Hiromichi was able to divorce his interpretation completely from moralistic concerns. This development allowed Hiromichi to focus on critical technique rather than ideology. In particular, Hiromichi rejected the notion that commentary should seek to transmute the moral or ideological values of antiquity so that they might serve as a guide to contemporary society. Essentially, he sought to displace the function nostalgia played for nativist scholars in appraising *Genji*. The resulting change in the focus of *Genji* criticism brought into view an entire range of literary insights that had long remained just beyond the scope of serious inquiry.

To uncover the path that Hiromichi followed in eliminating moralistic argument from his approach to literary criticism it is necessary to retrace several of the steps taken by Motoori Norinaga. In retrospect, one could say that Norinaga replaced the didacticism of Buddhism and Confucianism found in earlier commentaries with his *mono no aware* theory. Essentially, knowing *mono no aware* came to take the place of knowing good from bad as the standard by which Norinaga argued *Genji* should be judged. In adapting the critical term *mono no aware* from traditional Japanese poetics to an interpretation of *Genji*, Norinaga was able to emphasize aesthetic merit over didactic value in his evaluation of literature. However, he was unable to completely free literary criticism from its ideological perspective on fiction. His interpretation of *Genji* rests on two interdependent assumptions borrowed primarily from the Confucian critical tradition. The first assumption is that texts from antiquity contain immutable truths. The second is that evaluation of prose should be based on an assessment of the author's character and intentions. Confucianists believed that the mythological age of the sage kings produced authors of unparalleled virtue and works of eternal truth. For nativists, Japan's ancient past, before the influences of Buddhism and Confucianism had taken hold, came to be viewed as the age of a naturally harmonious Japanese spirit similar to China's idealized antiquity. Nativists argued that as Japanese authors increasingly imitated Chinese writings, the pure Japanese spirit came to be polluted by foreign ways. A corollary to this view was that because the past was a repository of such absolute values as truth and virtue, one should apply what one learned from studying the past to problems of the present. This approach was typified by the ancient learning (*kogaku*) school of Confucian studies and the belief in an idealized ancient way among nativist scholars.

For Norinaga, belief in an ancient way meant that the contemporary reader had to reject the bias imposed by Buddhist and Confucian teachings and return to the pure Japanese spirit of ages past to truly appreciate a text such as *Genji*. At his home in Matsuzaka, he reserved the second story for his study of ancient and Heian period literature, while the ground floor was devoted to his medical practice. It is said that Norinaga imagined he was transported to an earlier age in climbing the stairs to the second story, and that he left concerns of the contemporary world behind to better appreciate the sentiments being expressed in early literature. Similarly, he urges the reader in *Tama no ogushi* to immerse himself in the study of ancient texts to participate in the spirit in which Murasaki Shikibu composed *Genji*. Norinaga ultimately becomes quite dogmatic in his insistence that those who do not follow his approach to interpreting or appreciating the tale fail to see it for what it is meant to be. Hiromichi, on the other hand, views the knowledge gained through the careful study of early texts as a key ingredient of scholarship (*gakumon*) and serious inquiry rather than spiritual transformation. He argues against imposing the values of the past on one's actions in the present, including scholarly inquiry, because it is impossible to overcome the changes wrought by time. Hiromichi believed that the reader should strive to become knowledgeable about history and past customs to fully appreciate the nuances of earlier texts, but there was little to be gained from imposing ancient ideology on contemporary life.

A familiarity with Tominaga Nakamoto's critique of religious tradition (see chapter 2) may have provided Hiromichi with the inspiration to approach scholarship and literary interpretation from this perspective. While Hiromichi refers to Nakamoto and his ideas by name in an earlier work, he makes no direct reference to his writings in the *Hyōshaku*'s "General Remarks." Regardless of the path by which Hiromichi reached this new perspective, he did succeed in redefining an important aspect of literary interpretation as it applies to *Genji*. Specifically, he liberated his critical approach to literature from ideological argument. If we refine Hiromichi's argument as it appears earlier, we reach the conclusion that a belief in Buddhism or Confucianism is not what distorts one's reading of *Genji*. Rather, it is the imposition of morality and ideology from the past on our reading of a work that is much more than a one-dimensional moral lesson. Hiromichi advocates reading *Genji* as if the messages it contains about human nature and society are of paramount importance. In other words, *Genji* should be read on its own terms, as a realistic portrayal of human drama in prose fiction rather than as a work of didactic literature.

Hiromichi's argument in this section may at first seem an isolated statement of limited significance. However, its implications can be seen throughout his approach to literary interpretation. For example, separating his critical approach from ideological dispute allowed Hiromichi to integrate interpretive concepts and terminology derived from the tradition of Confucianism to his reading of *Genji*. The impact of these interpretive concepts and terminology can also be seen in Hiromichi's theory of the "principles of composition," which is discussed at length in a later section of the "General Remarks." This theory and its development will be examined in greater detail in chapter 4.

The impact of his argument can also be seen in the next two sections of the "General Remarks." In these sections Hiromichi advocates reading *Genji* on its own terms from two different perspectives. The next section describes his attempt to move beyond interpretation that imposes a single, absolute meaning on the entire monogatari. Instead, he emphasizes the role individual interpretive strategies play in conveying the complexity of *Genji* as a whole. The section after that concerns the general development of commentary on *Genji*. Hiromichi returns to the issue of scholarly methods to emphasize that it is careful analysis rather than ideological argument that establishes the foundation for effective commentary and criticism.

THE MAIN POINT OF THE MONOGATARI

In this section Hiromichi introduces Andō Tameakira's theory that the author's main point (*ichibu daiji*) is to present readers of *Genji* with a moral allegory. He then summarizes Norinaga's arguments against this position. Through this comparison Hiromichi is able to highlight the contradictions and limitations inherent in Tameakira's moral allegory theory as well as Norinaga's *mono no aware* theory. This sets the stage for Hiromichi to promote his own critical approach and to establish the points that distinguish his interpretation from the theories of his immediate predecessors.

The focal point of Tameakira's theory is the illicit affair between Genji and Fujitsubo. Since Fujitsubo is both a favorite consort of the emperor and Genji's stepmother, the child resulting from their union introduces a particularly disturbing moral dilemma to the story. This incident profoundly affects the actions and behavior of Genji, Fujitsubo, and their child, who will become Emperor Reizei, as the narrative progresses. All three interpreters struggle to preserve the ambiguity of this illicit act as it is described in the tale. Such phrases as "the matter concerning Emperor Reizei" (*Reizei in no onkoto*) and "the corruption" (*mono no magire*) are used throughout the discussion in the *Shikashichiron*, *Tama no ogushi*, and the *Hyōshaku* to denote a topic so taboo as to inspire circumlocution, even in the theoretical discussion of a fictional event. While all three interpreters do their best to avoid referring explicitly to this disruption of the imperial line, they find its significance in terms of *Genji*'s overall plot and structure important enough to warrant detailed discussion and analysis. Hiromichi begins this section by citing the opening lines of the sixth essay, "The Main Point [of the monogatari]" (*ichibu daiji*), from the *Shikashichiron*:

> Concerning the "matter" [*onkoto*] of the Emperor Reizei: Some say that because *Genji* is a fictional tale one mustn't take it too seriously. Others say that a delicate subject of this nature is best left undiscussed. There are still others who say that this matter is most unpleasant and it alone is reason enough to avoid reading the entire monogatari. I must point out that in expounding such theories these people demonstrate their failure to grasp the spirit in which Murasaki Shikibu composed *Genji*. I shall now attempt to put forth a hypothesis of my own and await the judgment of those who are more knowledgeable than I am on this subject.[13]

Because the affair between Genji and Fujitsubo is not openly described in the monogatari, Tameakira cites passages from the text that point to its occurrence. He quotes from a scene in the "Kiritsubo" chapter, where Genji expresses a preference for Fujitsubo over his own wife, Aoi, as evidence of the author's intention to foreshadow Genji's illicit affair. He then points to the scenes from the "Wakamurasaki" chapter, where Genji's meeting with Fujitsubo and the pregnancy that soon follows their meeting are described. This is followed by a scene from the "Usugumo" chapter, in which Emperor Reizei comes to realize that Genji is his true father. Finally, Tameakira refers to the illicit affair between Genji's last wife, the Third Princess (Onna San-no-miya or Nyōsan), and Kashiwagi as evidence of the author's interest in portraying the consequences of Genji's actions later in life.[14] After assembling the textual evidence that such an affair did indeed take place, Tameakira points to various figures from Japanese literature that he believes may have inspired Murasaki Shikibu to portray such infidelity:

> One cannot help but mention the Empress Nijō in the *Ise monogatari*,[15] Kyōgyoku Miyasundokoro in the *Gosenshū*,[16] and Lady Kazan in the *Eiga monogatari*.[17] These women all lacked a certain strength of character and were clearly overcome with passion, but fortunately they never succumbed to "the corruption" [*mono no magire*] which befell Fujitsubo.[18]

Hiromichi continues by observing that Tameakira also refers to certain "incidents" (*koto*) that compromised the imperial lineage in China's ancient past.[19] Tameakira then concludes:

> It is unsettling for us to think of such incidents when we read of them happening in other countries. Needless to say, in terms of our own country, which has an imperial lineage unbroken since Amaterasu bestowed this sacred land upon us, one can scarcely imagine a corruption of the imperial line ever coming to pass. Yet Murasaki Shikibu contemplated the possibility that someday there might be a woman in service to the court with such a feckless heart as to corrupt the imperial bloodline. When one reads this allegory [*fūyu*], which takes into account such a remote possibility, one must conclude that Murasaki Shikibu—despite her [handicap of] sex—possessed character and knowledge in such equal proportions that her natural ability to perceive things was comparable to that of a great Confucian scholar. Furthermore, the story of Kaoru [the illegitimate child of the Third Princess and Kashiwagi] is intended to illustrate heaven's punishment [of Genji] for evil acts. . . . This entire matter [*kono ikken*] is the main issue of the monogatari as a whole [*ichibu no daiji*]. Those who teach *Genji* must be familiar with it.[20]

Tameakira goes on to explain in greater detail how the depiction of such events can be understood as a moral allegory:

> If the imperial line were to be sullied only once by the blood of a Minamoto or Taira there would be considerable anxiety and men would turn their backs on the state just as the great orator Lu

> Zhonglian (J: Ro Chūren) became disillusioned with affairs of the imperial court of his time and left the capital for the eastern sea, never to return.[21] This being the case, Genji's visit to Lady Fujitsubo's quarters and the birth of [the future] Emperor Reizei constitute a grave transgression. It is fair to say that the sin of illicit intercourse [*kan'in*] weighed heavily upon Genji. However, the affair did not result in an unacceptable corruption of the imperial line. Emperor Reizei is a descendant of Emperor Kiritsubo—in the sense that he is Kiritsubo's grandson [through Genji]—and therefore represents the true imperial lineage descending from Emperor Jimmu [660–585 B.C.].... Furthermore, the author composed the monogatari in a way that ultimately allows the son of Emperor Reizei to be passed over and replaced by Emperor Suzaku, who is a more direct descendant in the imperial line. Is this not a superb [stroke of the author's] brush [*kibishiki fude ni arazu ya*]? ...The author must have intended the narrative to be this way. Murasaki, with her profound sense of discretion [*yōi fukaki*], most certainly realized that her monogatari would be introduced to the imperial court. Therefore she must have composed it with this in mind. It is unthinkable that she would have depicted such corruption without realizing what she was doing. The allegory found in this fictional tale is designed to prevent any corruption of the imperial line from ever taking place. Though I doubt that such an incident could ever come to pass.[22]

This passage contains one of the few instances where our interpreters resort to an explicit statement that illicit intercourse occurred in the monogatari. Tameakira was forced to draw attention to this detail in order to argue that Genji's actions were improper but technically did not lead to a corruption of the imperial line. As he observes, it is the subtlety of this distinction that allows the story to serve as a cautionary tale against future corruption of the imperial line without taking the offensive step of actually portraying such an event. Later in this section Hiromichi notes that Tameakira wisely chose the term allegory (*fūyu*) rather than the phrase "the encouragement of good and chastisement of evil" (*kanzen chōaku*), commonly associated with Confucian criticism, to characterize the depiction of this event in *Genji*. The term *fūyu* connotes the deliberate use of ambiguity to imply a certain conclusion, while *kanzen chōaku* assumes a direct correspondence between actions and their results.[23]

Hiromichi moves directly from Tameakira's theory to Norinaga's arguments against it. In the second volume of *Tama no ogushi*, Norinaga attempted to discredit Tameakira's allegory theory by attacking his exposition point by point.[24] In doing so, Norinaga set out to prove that the author's larger purpose (*ōmune*) could be explained by her motivation to depict the poignancy of things (*mono no aware*) rather than her desire to create an allegorical narrative. Hiromichi introduces Norinaga's argument with the following quotation from *Tama no ogushi*:

> To take "the corruption" relating to Emperor Reizei as an allegory and consider it to be the most important issue [of the entire work] is to adopt the attitude of a Confucianist and mistakenly read *Genji* as if it were nothing but a Chinese text. To do this constitutes a failure to truly appreciate the monogatari. . . . Tameakira encourages the reader to look for particular signs [of a moral lesson] and unreasonably pursues the argument of an allegory.[25]

Hiromichi then cites several of Norinaga's specific arguments against Tameakira's theory. He begins with Norinaga's attempt to undermine the didactic aspect of Tameakira's theory. For example, Norinaga argues that if Genji realized his affair with Fujitsubo was wrong then it does not make sense that he should go on to seduce Oborozukiyo once he discovers that she is betrothed to Emperor Suzaku:

> If we pursue Tameakira's line of reasoning, how does it follow that later Genji should have gone in secret to visit Oborozukiyo and had an affair with her? If indeed the author's intention were to describe this [affair with Fujitsubo] as Genji's terrible blunder, then why would she subsequently depict his relationship with Oborozukiyo? If indeed the author's intention had been to compose an allegory to discourage such acts, then would not she be encouraging the opposite in describing Genji's affair with Oborozukiyo?[26]

Hiromichi later comments on this criticism by referring back to Norinaga's own *mono no aware* theory. He points out that according to Norinaga's argument:

> The monogatari is composed so as to make human feeling its foundation [*nasake o moto to shite*] and *mono no aware* its main concern. This being the case, Genji feels compelled to pursue Oborozukiyo despite the fact that he knows it is something he should not do. Since this is a point to which Norinaga constantly returns it can hardly be used to argue against Tameakira.[27]

This response succinctly characterizes the way in which Hiromichi's critical approach differs from that taken by his predecessors. Tameakira and Norinaga both set out to establish a single, absolute principle that could explain the greater significance of *Genji*. By definition, these two theories must be at odds, because each claims to have penetrated to the true beliefs of the author and her main purpose in composing the monogatari. Hiromichi states that in general he finds Tameakira's argument the more persuasive of the two. Yet he finds it difficult to agree entirely with either theory. As can be seen in the passage just quoted, he finds that both theories contribute to our understanding of the monogatari. Tameakira's moral allegory theory provides readers with a rational explanation for the depiction of *Genji*'s illicit affair in terms of the work as a whole. On the other hand, Norinaga's *mono no aware* theory offers a persuasive explanation for *Genji*'s appeal as a fictional work while at the same time avoiding moral justifications. Hiromichi judges each theory in terms of its practical application to the text. Because he sees both theories in terms of interpretive function rather than ideological integrity, he has no interest in arguing that the validity of one theory naturally excludes the other as Norinaga did.

While avoiding ideological rancor, he also subtly returns to the most valuable aspects of each approach. In the case of Norinaga's comments, he emphasizes the point that the effectiveness of the *mono no aware* theory is based on the notion that fictional characters are placed in extraordinary circumstances to reveal a full range of "human feeling." This being the case, Hiromichi reminds readers that the depiction of immoral behavior and the fact that characters are aware that they are doing something wrong, but cannot prevent themselves from doing so, should be understood as heightening the intensity of emotion conveyed in the work. If one were to overlook or discount such scenes, then one would run the risk of eliminating or distorting some of the most emotionally powerful passages in *Genji*.

The distinction between Hiromichi and his predecessors on this point can best be illustrated by turning to his treatment of the intentions of the author. For both Tameakira and Norinaga, determining the author's intentions was an integral part of their interpretive approach, because it allowed them to refute Confucian and Buddhist condemnation of *Genji* based on ideological grounds. Tameakira argued that Murasaki Shikibu's intentions were virtuous. Therefore, immoral aspects of the text could be interpreted as ultimately serving virtuous ends. Norinaga argued that the author intended to portray the poignancy of things rather than compose a morally instructive text. Therefore, moral and didactic criticism failed to account for the true artistic merit of Murasaki Shikibu's work. Similarly, Norinaga argues that Tameakira ultimately fails to appreciate the meaning of *Genji* because he does not understand the author's convictions concerning the purpose of the monogatari. After quoting extensively from Tameakira's and Norinaga's conflicting theories on the main point of *Genji*, Hiromichi offers the following assessment:

> Of these two theories, which one is better? All of this involves understanding the innermost thoughts and feelings of the author [*mina tsukurinushi no shita ni omoeru koto nareba*]. Consequently, there is no way that people from a later age can add anything to the discussion. However, because these theories have already been advanced, it is impossible for me to simply ignore them. I must include something of my own opinions on the subject here. Between these two

> theories, I think that Tameakira's is the more reasonable of the two. Tameakira's *Shikashichiron* is completely based on Confucian teachings from Chinese books—just as Norinaga points out in *Tama no ogushi*. However, I believe that to a certain extent the author's intention was probably to create an allegory. As for why I think so. . . .Various things must be taken into consideration, but we know from what is written in the author's diary that several copies of *Genji* were in circulation among members of the court during Murasaki Shikibu's lifetime. . . .Therefore she must have considered how she might write about such unsettling matters in a discrete way so as to avoid bringing trouble upon herself. She must have had something similar to allegory in mind.[28]

In evaluating the two major interpretive theories to shape *Genji* criticism before him, Hiromichi concludes that neither one can be proved correct, because it is impossible to know the intentions of the author. While he acknowledges that it is potentially useful to hypothesize as to her motivations and literary influences, he also accepts the fact that any attempt to determine her intentions can result in nothing more than speculation. Therefore, Hiromichi is not interested in perpetuating the argument that one can appreciate the literary value of the entire work based on such subjective criteria as the author's intentions. However, he is interested in argument based on fact rather than speculation. He concludes that Tameakira's theory is more persuasive because it makes sense in terms of the details we encounter in reading *Genji* and the author's diary.

As Hiromichi's explanation continues, it becomes increasingly clear that he perceives these theories to be interpretive tools rather than expressions of ideology. Such things help make sense of puzzling details in the text but do not necessarily determine every aspect of it. In the paragraph that follows, he continues his evaluation of Tameakira's theory but explains that he agrees with it only as far as the details of the text bear it out:

> Does it seem that I agree with Tameakira's theory? Actually, I find it extremely difficult to agree entirely with him. In general, the matter of Emperor Reizei does seem to be an allegory. However, Kashiwagi's illicit relationship is more clearly an indication of the negative consequences [*mukui*] of a person's actions than it is an allegory. In the case of Kashiwagi, the law of karmic retribution [*inga*] plays out before our very eyes, just as was taught under the Buddhism of Murasaki Shikibu's day. However, the results of *Genji*'s actions are not described in such a transparent way. Rather than employing a style that clearly indicates the monogatari is an allegory she makes it ambiguous [*kakimagirawashitaru*] so that each person might read it in his own way [*hito no kokoro no yuku mama ni*]. She deliberately wrote

> it this way to conceal what was controversial—in the way women so often do.[29]

In evaluating Tameakira's theory, Hiromichi not only accepts the possibility that Murasaki employed the Confucian concept of allegory but also suggests that she drew upon Buddhist concepts of cause and effect to give shape to her narrative. However, his conclusion to all of this theoretical debate is that the author deliberately left the story open to interpretation. Rather than seeing this ambiguity as a flaw in the story or a limitation of interpretive theory, he sees it as a technique consciously employed by the author, to great effect. In a later section, he develops this idea to explain how the deliberate use of ambiguity contributes to the literary sophistication and sense of realism that are touchstones of Murasaki's compositional style.

Hiromichi goes on to observe that he also finds Tameakira's allegory theory persuasive because it confirms the validity of his own interpretation of *Genji*'s overall structure. His structural theory is fully explained later in the "General Remarks," but he alludes here to one point that he finds particularly relevant. In terms of the overall structure of the monogatari, Hiromichi considers Genji and Fujitsubo central characters and the dynamic of their relationship to be an important element of the monogatari. He believes that the author emphasized the importance of this relationship in a very subtle way by referring to them with epithets that are similar in meaning:

> Beginning in the "Kiritsubo" Chapter Genji is referred to as "the shining lord" [*hikaru kimi*] while Fujitsubo is known as "the lady of the radiant sun" [*kagayaku hi no miya*]. It is possible to see their relationship as being foreshadowed [*fukuan*] from this point onward. Accordingly, one might see their affair as being the central concern of the monogatari [*monogatari no naka no mune*] and everything else as being an attempt to elaborately cover up for it. Therefore, in terms of this specific incident I think that one can say the author had certain intentions in mind. Well then, what is it that the author was thinking? Now [such a long time after the author lived] it is very difficult to know what her intentions were. If we are to draw conclusions [based on this incident, we should limit ourselves to saying that] this incident had to do with a disturbing matter. I shall leave my analysis at that.[30]

It is interesting to note that Hiromichi has taken Norinaga's expression referring to the "larger purpose" of the monogatari—*ōmune*—and modified it to more closely reflect a structural approach to *Genji*. Hiromichi refers to the affair between Genji and Fujitsubo as being "the central concern" of the monogatari—*monogatari no naka no mune*. This change can be seen as Hiromichi's way of distinguishing his interpretive approach from Norinaga's. The emphasis of Norinaga's interpretation was ultimately ideology. He argued that readers needed to understand, and accept, the lofty and essential convictions that Murasaki Shikibu held to be true in order to appreciate *Genji*. To this end, the second volume of *Tama no ogushi* is devoted to explaining what he saw as the "larger purpose" that should determine the way *Genji* should be read. Rather than attempting to define the entire monogatari in terms of a single, comprehensive concept or ideology, Hiromichi points to an event that occupies a position of central importance within the complex structure of the entire work. By indicating a structural center to *Genji*, Hiromichi helps the reader appreciate where many of the smaller details fit in relation to the overall framework of the story. This structural approach allows the reader to interpret *Genji* in a systematic way based on details in the text rather than on assumptions concerning ideology or the motivations of the author.

Hiromichi never dismisses Norinaga's *mono no aware* theory as being unimportant to an appreciation of *Genji*. However, in this section, he does criticize Norinaga's efforts to selectively interpret *Genji* to refute Tameakira's theory. Norinaga argues that the affair between Genji and Fujitsubo was included by Murasaki Shikibu not as an allegory for real-life concerns over the preservation of the imperial line but rather as a plot device that would later allow Genji to rise to the pinnacle of importance in the narrative. Norinaga's interpretation makes sense insofar as the affair between Genji and Fujitsubo ultimately leads Emperor Reizei to confer the title of honorary emperor (*dajō tennō*) upon Genji in recognition of the fact that he is his true father. However, Norinaga further argues that this event is necessary because the author intended to portray Genji as the most moving character in the monogatari. To achieve this goal she composed the story to allow Genji to rise to a position of ultimate importance. Norinaga uses this argument to explain why Genji is depicted as having an affair with Fujitsubo and ultimately to explain why he is elevated to a rank equivalent to emperor. For Norinaga, this theory precludes any moral or allegorical intention on the part of the author.

Hiromichi criticizes this interpretation on several counts. He points out that Genji's successes as well as his misfortunes are recorded in the monogatari. If Murasaki Shikibu had wished to move the reader merely by portraying *Genji*'s good fortune, then she would have omitted the details of such unfortunate events as Murasaki's death. He then faults Norinaga for disregarding other events of great significance in the monogatari because they do not fit with his *mono no aware* theory. By omitting these events from his discussion, Norinaga strengthens his argument against Tameakira but ends up presenting a distorted view of *Genji*. Norinaga's interpretation fails to take into account the events that occur after the nineteenth chapter, "Usugumo," in which Emperor Reizei decides to grant Genji the title of honorary emperor. Specifically, Hiromichi points to Tameakira's discussion of the illicit affair between Kashiwagi and the Third Princess, which takes place sixteen chapters after "Usugumo," in the "Wakana ge" chapter.

In summarizing Tameakira's allegory theory Hiromichi shows how a connection exists between two events that take place at chronologically distant points in the narrative. From the earliest chapters of the monogatari, details foreshadow the illicit affair between Genji and Fujitsubo. This affair, once it takes place, influences the course of events leading up to the abdication of Emperor Reizei in the thirty-fifth chapter, "Wakana ge." In the thirty-sixth chapter, "Kashiwagi," we see the results of Genji and Fujitsubo's affair echoed in the birth of Kaoru, who is the product of an illicit affair between Kashiwagi and Genji's wife. Kaoru then becomes the main romantic figure of the final chapters in *Genji*. Hiromichi's preference for Tameakira's theory over Norinaga's is based on an appraisal that places a higher value on internal textual evidence than ideology. Tameakira's theory makes it possible for Hiromichi to argue that the illicit affair between Genji and Fujitsubo is the central concern of the tale's overall structure.

In summing up his argument against Tameakira, Norinaga offers the following conclusion:

> There are many places in Tameakira's theory regarding the illicit affair [*mono no magire*] that miss the mark, but the subject matter is disturbing [*kashikokisuji*] so I'll not discuss it further. Suffice it to say that this incident should not be taken as an allegory. While such an occurrence is something that was exceedingly unacceptable in times past as well as today, monogatari are unique unto themselves [*monogatari wa monogatari nareba*]. What is important in this world does not necessarily become the most important issue of a monogatari. Furthermore, the affair is no more than a single incident in terms of the entire monogatari.[31]

Hiromichi returns to this statement later in his discussion of Norinaga's argument against Tameakira. In refuting Norinaga on this point, Hiromichi provides an unusually direct contradiction:

> Norinaga writes, "monogatari are unique unto themselves. What is important in this world does not necessarily become the most important issue of a monogatari. . . ." But what are we to make of this statement? I, on the other hand, think that the great issues of a monogatari are written on account of important things in this world [*saru yo no naka no daiji no tame ni ichibu no monogatari wa kakitaru mono no yō ni oboyuru nari*].[32]

In a final effort to discount the allegory theory, Norinaga argued that the fictional world of the monogatari bears no relationship to the concerns of the real world. If we wish simply to reject all aspects of moral concern from our examination of literature, then such an argument might seem appealing. However, upon further consideration, it becomes clear that Norinaga painted himself into a corner on this point. If there is no connection between the issues that define the monogatari and real-life issues that concern its readers, then there is no reason to expect that anyone would want to read a monogatari or find it interesting. To pursue Norinaga's argument in a logical manner, as he formulates it here, would undermine the validity of his own *mono no aware* theory as a tool in interpreting *Genji*. Hiromichi wisely avoids further analysis of Norinaga's argument on this point and simply asserts his own views on the subject. While Hiromichi does not accept Tameakira's notion that moral didacticism defines every aspect of *Genji*, he does accept the notion that there appears to be a conscious moral purpose behind an important aspect of its composition. According to Hiromichi, this moral purpose is derived not only from elements of Confucianism but also from elements of Buddhist thought. This makes it possible to see that the fictional world of *Genji* depicts concerns that would resonate with the experience and imagination of its readers.

Throughout this section the *Shikashichiron* and *Tama no ogushi* are cited extensively. Hiromichi avoids directly criticizing Norinaga's interpretive approach but provides extensive quotation to expose the contradictions in Norinaga's theory, using his own words. At the beginning of this section, Hiromichi quoted Norinaga's declaration that Tameakira fails to grasp the true meaning of *Genji* and unreasonably urges readers to interpret the work according to his own ideological bias. Ironically, Hiromichi's insightful comparison of the two theories leads us to the conclusion that Norinaga's reading suffers most from ideological bias, while Tameakira's theory—which is admittedly moralistic in perspective—produces a more effective strategy for reading *Genji*. In his treatment of Tameakira and Norinaga, he demonstrates an appreciation for the complex nature of literary criticism. He is willing to concede that moral issues play a legitimate role in interpreting how a work of fiction is evaluated, but in qualifying his praise for both Tameakira and Norinaga, he makes it clear that neither didacticism nor nostalgia should overshadow an appreciation for the tale in all its beauty and complexity.

COMMENTARIES ON *GENJI*

In this section Hiromichi provides an overview of *Genji* commentary prior to the *Hyōshaku*. His comments include brief evaluations of the relative merits and failings of the most influential premodern commentaries with an emphasis on five major works: the *Kakaishō*, the *Kogetsushō*, the *Genchū shūi*, the *Shikashichiron*, and *Tama no ogushi*. The *Hyōshaku* is not unique in this regard. In fact, Hiromichi's review covers many of the same works Norinaga mentions in the first volume of *Tama no ogushi*. However, Hiromichi's comments lack the argumentative tone that defines Norinaga's treatment of commentary outside the nativist tradition. Rather than finding fault or elevating the status of certain scholars, Hiromichi reviews previous commentaries to establish why one work tells us more about *Genji* than its predecessors. At times he speaks harshly of commentaries from the past, but his anger is usually directed at interpretive failure rather than ideological difference. In essence, he attempts to provide the reader with an outline of the historical development of *Genji* commentary and criticism.

Hiromichi begins his discussion with the *Kakaishō* because it is the first work to provide comprehensive annotation on *Genji* rather than simply a collection of marginal comments on certain aspects of the text. However, even with this early commentary, he notes that numerous errors make it an unreliable source of annotation. He adds that most of the early commentaries following the *Kakaishō* simply repeat the errors of their predecessors.

The next major work to draw Hiromichi's attention is the *Kogetsushō*. He notes that the *Kogetsushō* contains the entire text of *Genji* and is widely available in a printed edition (*surimaki*). In addition to being widely available and presenting the complete text in a more readable format, Hiromichi remarks that the annotation in the *Kogetsushō* should be of interest to the reader because it contains a selection of the best annotation from prior commentaries. However, he also notes that it fails to cover the same passages that are omitted from earlier commentaries, so one cannot say that it presents much in the way of new annotation.

Hiromichi then echoes the assessment expressed in *Tama no ogushi*, that the *Kogetsushō* reproduces many of the errors found in older works and often proves to be unreliable. However, Hiromichi's observations go beyond Norinaga's critique of individual commentary. After referring the reader to *Tama no ogushi* for a detailed discussion of the errors contained in the *Kogetsushō*, Hiromichi goes on to establish a historical and ideological framework that encompasses virtually all commentary and criticism of *Genji*. He begins by observing that it seems odd to argue that these older commentaries, highly valued by Kigin in his compilation of the *Kogetsushō*, should prove to be so unreliable. One would expect that their proximity in time to the composition of *Genji* would make them more reliable, not less. In addition, he notes that they were generally written by men in service to the imperial court, to whom he refers as the "revered ones who lived above the clouds" (*kumo no ue harukanaru onkatagata*). One would expect members of the nobility to be a reliable source of information on the details of their own culture. To explain the often puzzling errors found in these earlier commentaries, Hiromichi refers back to the secretive and unscholarly methods to which the medieval aristocracy felt strongly attached:

> The *Kakaishō*, *Kachō yōjō*, and other commentaries that appear in the *Kogetsushō* date from an age closer to antiquity than our own and were produced by revered men of noble rank, so you might ask how it is that they contain so many passages that seem to be wrong. Let us consider the reasons. In general, learned men since the Heian period [*nakamukashi yori konata no monoshiribitotachi*] have relied upon

> a loathsome practice, which some call "esoteric transmission" [*hisetsu*], to explain all manner of things. According to this tradition even the most insignificant details had to be concealed from outsiders. These commentaries were only to be secretly transmitted [*himetsutaete*] among a few people rather than to be seen and studied by many. Therefore no scholarly attempts were made to confirm their annotation by examining a variety of texts from the past or thinking about how the information might be proved true or false. Most annotation was simply recorded verbatim, as if being learned by rote memorization [*soraoboe no mama ni*], without any attempt to analyze or question its accuracy. One would expect that because these learned men belonged to such noble families they would be familiar with old ceremonies, events, manner of dress, and common objects associated with life at court. Yet, if we compare their commentaries to old texts we discover that there are many places where the commentaries provide explanations that seem to be wrong. I believe this is due to the fact that much time had passed between the composition of *Genji*, in the reign of Emperor Ichijō [986–1011], and the age in which these commentaries were written. Laws and regulations governing affairs changed considerably during this span of time. In particular, life at the imperial court changed drastically following the Jyōkyū disturbance [1221] and the Kemmu restoration [1334].[33] Furthermore, the world familiar to the commentators was also one of frequent turmoil. There are things which were entirely familiar to the early commentators so they never thought to provide annotation. There are also places where annotation exists, but in terms of small details we can clearly see that the compiler did not understand what he was writing about. It is therefore very difficult to rely on the explanations from these commentaries.[34]

Hiromichi identifies the tradition of esoteric transmission as the primary factor behind the inaccuracy of older commentaries. He also recognizes that the enormity of cultural and social change since the time of *Genji*'s composition only compounds the difficulty of providing accurate annotation for many passages. Hiromichi was certainly not the first scholar of the Edo period to note the unreliability of medieval commentary. Nativist scholars often lamented the pernicious influence Confucianism had on the study of Japanese texts and attributed the failure of earlier commentaries to the ideological corruption of their compilers. His predecessors, Keichū, Tameakira, Mabuchi, and Norinaga, had all remarked on these failings in their own commentaries on *Genji*.[35] However, Hiromichi stands out for developing his observations on the systematic failure of medieval commentary into a practical periodization of *Genji* scholarship. He argued that the esoteric tradition followed by the compilers of these older commentaries was broken by Keichū in his *Genchū shūi*. The implications of Keichū's scholarly technique were so profound that Hiromichi described the *Genchū shūi* as marking a division between two major eras in the history of *Genji* commentary. He continues from the passage just quoted:

> Consequently, I now refer to commentaries from before the *Kogetsushō* as "old commentaries" [*kyūchū*; lit. antiquated commentaries] and generally avoid citing them. However, in cases where the substance of the annotation does not vary much [from one work to the next] I follow the practice of citing the old commentary first and then citing only a few [examples from later works].[36] The *Genchū shūi* by the priest Keichū discusses the inaccuracies found in these "old commentaries." He took the passages with contradictory information and corrected them based on an examination of various ancient texts. It is a fascinating and remarkable work. The author was extremely well informed about many things. He did not simply follow the interpretations found in other poetic anthologies. Instead, he compared ancient texts to provide accurate interpretation. As a result, he made not a single unfounded assertion. In our age he was the first to practice what is called "evidential scholarship" [*kōshōgaku*]. His *Genchū shūi* greatly changed the nature of commentary on *Genji*. Therefore I distinguish the commentaries that follow it by calling them "new commentaries" [*shinchū*]. Having said this, the *Genchū shūi* itself is primarily devoted to correcting errors found in old commentaries and generally is not useful in reading the text of *Genji*. Therefore I do not cite it frequently [in my annotation of the main text].[37]

Hiromichi is most impressed by Keichū's scholarly methods and the accuracy of his conclusions. This point attracted the attention of Norinaga as well. In *Shibun yōryō* (1763), he observed:

> The *Genchū shūi* contains many remarkable observations due to the exceptional ability of its author, Keichū. Everything he writes is based on proof derived from the comparison of ancient texts without any reference to the baseless theories of his day. There are many new and remarkable opinions to be found in this work. In the study of poetry [*kagaku*] there is truly no one to equal Keichū.[38]

In terms of content and language, Norinaga's comments clearly seem to have inspired Hiromichi in his assessment of Keichū's work. However, as we have seen in earlier sections, Hiromichi refuses to limit the scope of his analysis to certain scholarly traditions or genres as Norinaga did. Here he goes far beyond the boundaries of Japanese literature to suggest that Keichū's analytical methods are similar to those belonging to the branch of learning called "evidential scholarship." The school of evidential scholarship (*kaozhengxuepai*; J: *kōshōgakuha*) developed as a reaction to neo-Confucianism in late Ming-period China. By the Qing dynasty, it had come to dominate Confucian scholarship in China by providing an objective and empirical foundation for the study of history and literature. In late-eighteenth-century Japan, a school noted for its eclectic use of scholarship from various branches of Confucianism (*setchū gakuha*) was the first to adopt the methods of evidential scholarship from China. Evidential scholarship went on to become an influential force in Japanese historiography through the Meiji period.[39] Based on the document-oriented philological analysis evident in the *Genchū shūi*, Hiromichi argues that Keichū should be considered the first Japanese scholar to employ such methods. However, a recent study of Keichū's work concluded that his annotative approach was primarily influenced by Buddhist methods of philological analysis, most likely derived from comparative textual practices introduced to Japan by the monk Kūkai (774–835).[40] While Hiromichi's argument has not stood the test of time, it is interesting to note that he chose to draw upon this element of contemporary Confucian scholarship—either from his reading of Ming- and Qing-period literary criticism or from his contact with Confucian scholars in Osaka—to broaden the scope of his own assessment of literary criticism and commentary.

Hiromichi considered the analytical methods adopted by Keichū as so profoundly altering the course of *Genji* commentary that he instituted the practice of specifically referring to works produced by Keichū and his successors as "new commentaries" (*shinchū*).[41] In *Genji shinshaku* Mabuchi had already begun to refer to certain commentaries as being "old" (*kochū*). He also proffered the opinion that the works of Keichū and Tameakira presented "new ideas" (*shin'i*) on *Genji*.[42]

Tsutsumi Yasuo's study of the history of *Genji* commentary (*Genji monogatari kenkyūshi no kisoteki kenkyū*) validates Hiromichi's periodization of *Genji* commentary while providing some additional interpretation from the perspective of a contemporary scholar. Tsutsumi observes that nativist scholars from Keichū through Norinaga tended to emphasize the originality of their own work and that of their immediate predecessors to establish the notion that they had revolutionized the process of *Genji* commentary by liberating it from the tradition of esoteric transmission. He remarks that nearly all modern scholars accept this distinction and tend to classify commentary before the *Genchū shūi* as "old commentary" (*kochū*) and commentary following it as "new commentary" (*shinchū*). However, he cautions that it is more accurate to characterize this distinction as rhetorical rather than substantive in nature. In most cases, premodern commentary following Keichū represents a reform of annotative practice rather than a revolution.[43]

Tsutsumi goes on to remark that this adversarial approach no longer dominates the discussion once we reach the *Hyōshaku*. Instead, we see rationally consistent and original interpretation occupying a position of central importance. He concludes that the work of Hiromichi's predecessors, from Keichū to Norinaga, contributed to the gradual development of *Genji* commentary, but it is in the *Hyōshaku* that we see signs of a clean break from the attitude of medieval commentaries.[44]

The next major work Hiromichi covers is Tameakira's *Shikashichiron*. Hiromichi cites two reasons the student of *Genji* will want to take note of this work: First, Tameakira provides an interpretation that takes into account the overall meaning of *Genji* (*monogatari no ōmune o ronji*).[45] Second, he utilizes his knowledge of Murasaki Shikibu's diary to refute numerous errors perpetuated by old commentaries. He agrees with Norinaga's assessment that "In general, Tameakira thinks of *Genji* as if it were written to illustrate the ideas found in Chinese books. He therefore fails to take into account *Genji*'s [unique] qualities as a work of narrative [fiction]."[46] He concedes that Tameakira's Confucian bias detracts from his theories but reminds readers that even Norinaga sometimes advances theories in *Tama no ogushi* that one might find difficult to accept (*ikanizo ya oboyuru kotodomo arite*). This remark simply adds to Hiromichi's argument that Tameakira's interpretation should not be entirely dismissed simply because its basis is in Confucian methods of interpretation. Hiromichi concludes that the *Shikashichiron* should be understood as no less important than Keichū's *Genchū shūi* because it was one of the first works to break free from the influence of "old commentaries."

Hiromichi remarks that there are numerous commentaries he has failed to mention. However, he makes it clear that the interpretive standard set by Norinaga's *Tama no ogushi* is the one against which he compares all other scholarship. He praises *Tama no ogushi* not only for its attention to detail but also for its attempt to define a theory penetrating to the main point of *Genji*.

What stands out in Hiromichi's treatment of previous commentary here and throughout the "General Remarks" is that he is willing to concede that even the best interpretive strategy is only an imperfect tool for extending one's grasp of the vast reserve of aesthetic accomplishment to be found in *Genji*. To impose a single, comprehensive interpretive principle on a work of such length and complexity inevitably forces readers to overlook certain aspects of the text.

In *Tama no ogushi*, Norinaga cites numerous passages where characters in the tale respond emotionally to their surroundings. Genji, being the main character of the story, is the principle character to whom Norinaga refers in developing his *mono no aware* theory. Norinaga argues that unsympathetic characters are depicted as being insensitive or unresponsive to their surroundings. His prime example is Kokiden, Genji's main adversary, who fails to respond appropriately to even the most moving of scenes before her very eyes. To Norinaga this correlation proves that Murasaki Shikibu's main concern was to show readers that sympathetic characters are sensitive to the poignancy of things (*mono no aware o shiru*), while unsympathetic characters are insensitive.[47]

Hiromichi does not dispute Norinaga's conclusions concerning the author's intentions in this section. In fact, he suggests that the reader refer to Norinaga's examples as they appear in *Tama no ogushi*. However, in a section titled "The Description of the Setting and Seasons in the Work" near the end of his general remarks he skillfully recasts Norinaga's argument to suit his own interpretive approach. To do this he shifts our attention from the author's intentions to her skillful use of detail in composing *Genji*. Specifically, he builds on Norinaga's praise for the moving description of seasons and natural surroundings to argue that such details enhance the aesthetic quality of the work by making it seem more real to the reader. Hiromichi includes the following illustrative example in his discussion:

> In the theater, the stage is set in accordance with the season depicted in the story and the appearance of the characters accord with the story's content as much as is possible. This realistic portrayal of things [*kotogara no makotomekite*] is what makes an impression on the audience. Think of a scene in which the seasons and setting do not correspond. For example, imagine a stage set with flowers coming into full bloom that depicts the appearance of a fiercely jealous avenging spirit. Or, suppose there is a scene in which a cheerfully dressed young noblewoman peacefully stands in a raging storm set in the shadows of an embankment. Is there anyone who would immediately say, "Yes, that scene seems real?" It is the same with the description of a scene in a monogatari.[48]

While descriptions of the seasons and natural surroundings are important, Hiromichi cautions readers against concentrating on the beauty of such passages to the exclusion of other elements of the text. In this case, he complains that it is the mark of an inexperienced reader to praise the beauty of these passages while overlooking other qualities to be found in the text:

> When a passage is composed so that the surroundings and season correspond [to the passage's mood] the passage is made even more joyful or gloomy. However, it is quite foolish to simply praise a monogatari for its description of surroundings and seasons. It would be like praising a play based solely on its various scenery and props.[49]

To guide the inexperienced reader in fully appreciating the tale, he suggests that they apply his theory of the principles of composition. He warns that readers who fail to see principles of composition at work in *Genji* often assume that it is enough to glean passages that contain moving descriptions of natural beauty from the text. However, such efforts only result in "a collection of elegant expressions" that fails to reflect the true beauty and complexity of *Genji*.

This points to a deeper concern Hiromichi had regarding the application of Norinaga's *mono no aware* theory. He clearly does not wish to deny the contribution Norinaga's theory has made in appreciating *Genji*. If, however, it is seen as the only tool available for evaluating *Genji*, then there are many remarkable aspects of the text that will remain beyond the reader's grasp. Hiromichi presents his own theory of the principles of composition as a complementary interpretive tool to those provided by Tameakira and Norinaga. Tameakira's theory allows readers to view the overall structure of the text in terms of a single, unifying theme. On the other end of the spectrum, Norinaga's *mono no aware* theory emphasizes the poetic and lyric quality underlying the author's composition of isolated scenes. Hiromichi's own theory bridges the gap that exists between these two ideologically driven strategies for reading. By focusing on interpretive technique, he makes it possible to approach the text in terms of the integrity of its composition and subtle control of nuance and detail. These are the qualities that define it as a masterpiece of literature rather than a persuasive ideological tool.

TRANSCENDING THE LIMITATIONS OF TRADITIONAL STRUCTURE AND FORMAT

Following his "General Remarks" on commentary and criticism, Hiromichi includes a brief section of explanatory notes to the main text (*tōsho Hyōshaku hanrei*; "explanatory notes for the commentary and criticism that appear in the Headnotes [to the main text]"). This section includes miscellaneous notes concerning the integration of previous commentary and his own interpretation with the main text of *Genji*. Hiromichi also provides a list of other commentaries referred to in his annotation to the main text. The list includes twenty-three commentaries that precede Keichū's *Genchū shūi* and six commentaries following it. A translation of this section, with Hiromichi's explanatory notes and brief annotation on the commentaries he mentions, can be found in the notes at the end of this book. This section also includes definitions for the major terms Hiromichi uses in applying his principles of composition theory to the main text. He provides definitions for such terms as *foreshadowing* (*fukuan*) and *principal* and *auxiliary characters* (*shukaku*). (See the following chapter for a detailed discussion of these terms and a translation of Hiromichi's definitions for them.)

Hiromichi does not discuss critical theory or present new analysis in this section. In keeping with his preference for interpretive function over ideological argument, he points out in his explanatory remarks that he has limited his annotation in the main text to comments that further the reader's understanding of *Genji*. His selection thus provides us with a comprehensive compilation and an implicit evaluation of prior commentary and annotation as it was understood by a leading Edo-period *Genji* scholar. In addition, his selection of annotation based purely on its practical value in interpreting the text represents the culmination of efforts begun by Keichū and Tameakira to correct much of the misinformation found in medieval commentaries. However, in the *Hyōshaku*, Hiromichi simply omits misleading information rather than arguing against it. As a result, the *Hyōshaku* is arguably the first major work of commentary and criticism to integrate the complete text for chapters of *Genji* with annotation devoted more to clarifying the meaning of the text than to ideological argument.[50]

GUIDING THE READER

A final section following the "General Remarks" consists of a catalogue of miscellaneous entries concerning the format of the text (*honbun yaku chū hanrei*; "explanatory notes on the translation and notation that accompany the main text"). The innovations in format that these notes describe may at first seem trivial. In fact, previous scholarship on the *Hyōshaku* has nearly always overlooked this section of Hiromichi's "General Remarks." However, in practical terms, Hiromichi's innovations in formatting play a crucial role in guiding the reader through the text. The last major work before the *Hyōshaku* to integrate the complete main text and annotation was Kitamura Kigin's *Kogetsushō*. The *Kogetsushō* followed the practice of previous centuries in presenting each chapter of *Genji* as one seamless flow of text. Other than the division between chapters, breaks in the text were reserved almost exclusively for marking the beginning and end of poems.

In his presentation of the main text, Hiromichi introduced a series of marks—several of which he assumed readers would be familiar with from reading Chinese texts—to identify breaks in the narrative flow where he felt such changes might not be readily apparent to the inexperienced reader. On the broadest level, he used an L-shaped block (⧠)to mark the end of major divisions and a small bar (-) to mark smaller breaks in the story line. These divisions are similar to the small headings in bold text accompanied by paragraph breaks indicating important shifts or events in the tale that are found in modern editions of *Genji*. A brief comparison of the *Hyōshaku*'s division marks with the modern Shōgakukan edition of *Genji* suggests that while section breaks in the modern edition appear much more frequently than division marks in the *Hyōshaku*, there is a surprisingly high correlation between divisions indicated by Hiromichi and those found in the modern edition. In other words, Hiromichi's division marks appear with less frequency, but when they do appear, they consistently correspond to major divisions of the narrative that modern scholars and editors have incorporated into the formatting of the modern edition of *Genji*.

Running inside the line of text Hiromichi includes a double circle mark (circle within a circle) to indicate more subtle but equally important shifts in the text. He refers to this double circle mark as something that alerts the reader to a change from "this to that" (*kare to kore to koto wakatsu hyō*). He goes on to explain:

> I have included this mark to alert readers to places in the text where there is a shift [in subject] from one thing to another, a shift [in voice] from the personal to the third person [narration], places where it is difficult to distinguish between a question and its response, as well as places where an aside has been inserted into the main description.[51]

These marks largely correspond to paragraph breaks one finds in modern editions of the text. For example, the first appearance of the double circle mark in Hiromichi's text indicates a shift from the description of Genji's birth and the emperor's affection for Genji and his mother to an explanation as to why Genji's mother was so vulnerable in her position at court. In the English translations by Seidensticker and Tyler, this break is clearly indicated by the shift from the paragraph that begins "His majesty must have had a deep bond with her . . ." to the following paragraph that begins "Her rank had never permitted her to enter His Majesty's common service."[52] Hiromichi draws the reader's attention to the fact that an important shift in narrative perspective has taken place here. In the original, this mark allows the careful reader to register that the information following the double circle mark should be understood as providing information not about the feelings of the emperor but concerning Lady Kiritsubo's position at court. This is the type of guidance that can make all the difference in following the flow of the narrative.

Hiromichi uses a double circle mark alongside the text as well. In his explanatory remarks, he notes that he includes a short series of double circles alongside the text to indicate the presence of a "key word" (*ganmoku no go*) in the text. He explains:

> These marks are placed to the right of words frequently used to evoke a particular atmosphere or to indicate the mood of a scene or to indicate a phrase that foreshadows something in the narrative. A similar mark is used in Classical Chinese texts to draw the reader's attention to a crucial term. Readers should pay particular attention to the passages indicated by these marks.[53]

Hiromichi's identification of such "key words" embedded in the text to evoke a particular atmosphere for a scene or passage became an influential avenue of academic analysis of the text in modern scholarship on *Genji*.[54]

Hiromichi also remarks here that in many places he has included a translation (*utsushikotoba*) alongside the main text. It would be fair to characterize the material Hiromichi provides as a literal gloss into contemporary language rather than anything approaching a complete translation. He acknowledges that the experienced reader may find it disturbing to see such common language associated with Murasaki's elegant prose. However, his experience in teaching *Genji* has taught him that it is useful for the beginning student to have a simple translation to clarify the meaning of the original text. With this in mind, he has included these keys to translation in the printed edition of the text itself to assist the reader and provide some guidance at crucial or particularly complicated passages in the text. He suggests that the familiar reader can disregard such material if he finds it distracting.[55]

Hiromichi's preference for interpretive function distinguishes his work from that of his predecessors in this area as well. In his linguistic treatise *Tama arare* (1792), Norinaga promoted composition using ancient vocabulary and grammar (*inishie buri no fumi*) to improve one's understanding of the ancient way. He believed that one had to know ancient language well enough to properly compose poetry in it to appreciate the literature of Japan's past.[56] While he expressed resentment against medieval commentary and the elitist methods of the aristocracy, he continued to approach *Genji* and other texts from antiquity as if they were documents written in a sacred language. For Norinaga, a true appreciation of *Genji* was tied to the supremacy of native sentiment and ideology. In essence, he argued that the reader must abandon the polluted values of the present and embrace the idealized sentiments of the past to appreciate the meaning and poignancy (*mono no aware*) of *Genji*. As the previous chapter illustrated, Hiromichi dismissed this interpretive approach as the product of ideological conflict rather than true scholarship. He argued that the world had changed too much to impose what can be gleaned from texts of the past on beliefs and actions in the present.

The logical extension of Hiromichi's argument is that reading fiction for its value in promoting nostalgia ultimately fails, because such analysis is incompatible with both the nature of the text and the goal of scholarly pursuit. In part, he avoided making this point too clearly, because it represented a challenge not only to the way *Genji* was read but also to the way all literary works were interpreted by nativist scholars. Rather than highlight his rejection of ideological argument, he provides specific interpretive tools to help the average reader pull the text of *Genji* from the past into the present. These tools include innovations in formatting, and commentary and the inclusion of colloquial equivalents for archaic language, all designed to make the meaning of the prose more transparent to the average reader. Most important, he relies on scholarly analysis rather than on dogma to interpret *Genji*.

It has been observed that in medieval Europe the first translations of Cicero and Horace from classical language to the vernacular tended to be extremely literal in nature. As translation methods developed and philology became an accepted area of scholarship, there was a tendency to move from literal translation to sense-oriented translation.[57] A similar process was at work in Edo Japan. The seeds of philological analysis planted by Keichū in the first century of the Edo period had taken root by Hiromichi's day. As a result, he was able to include literal vernacular glosses alongside the original Heian language in his printed edition of *Genji*. The earliest works that fall under the category of vernacular translation of *Genji* date from 1704 with the *Fūryū Genji monogatari*. Ryūtei Tanehiko's *Genji* parody, *Phony Murasaki and Rural*

Genji, built upon this conceit in the following century. However, these works were written as adaptations of *Genji* rather than as true translations. It is not until after Hiromichi's innovations that we see the publication of sense-oriented vernacular translations of *Genji* worthy of scholarly consideration.[58] Hiromichi's inclusion of vernacular glosses represents an important intermediary step in the production of accurate translations of *Genji* in the Meiji period. Hiromichi's innovation demonstrated the value of scholarly analysis over ideological persuasion in interpreting *Genji*. This refocusing of philological argument made it possible for later scholars to undertake the complete and accurate translation of *Genji* into modern Japanese.

CONCLUSION

In 1884, three decades after Hiromichi first published his "General Remarks" in the *Hyōshaku*, Henry James published an essay titled "The Art of Fiction." In his essay James wrote that when fiction depicts life or attempts to portray real-life concerns in a serious manner rather than resorting to comedy or drama, one often encounters the suspicion that the author has somehow been deceitful or immoral. However, it is this suspicion that denies the novel its true right as a work of art:

> [The novel] must take itself seriously for the public to take it so. The old superstition about fiction being "wicked" has doubtless died out in England; but the spirit of it lingers in a certain oblique regard directed toward any story which does not more or less admit that it is only a joke. Even the most jocular novel feels in some degree the weight of the prescription that was formerly directed against literary levity: the jocularity does not always succeed in passing for orthodoxy. It is still expected, though perhaps people are ashamed to say it, that a production which is after all only a "make-believe" (for what else is a "story"?) shall be in some degree apologetic—shall renounce the pretension of attempting really to represent life. This, of course, any sensible, wide-awake story declines to do, for it quickly perceives that the tolerance granted to it on such a condition is only an attempt to stifle it disguised in the form of generosity. The old evangelical hostility to the novel, which was as explicit as it was narrow and which regarded it as little less favourable to our immortal part than a stage-play, was in reality far less insulting. The only reason for the existence of a novel is that it does attempt to represent life.[59]

For James it was the depiction of sensuality and sexuality that particularly brought this issue to mind. He believed that the "English novel" often failed to realistically portray the sexual aspect of a character's life and consciousness in fiction. Authors omitted such description to avoid offending public sensibility and social convention. James saw such emotions and actions as an integral part of human life. To avoid their portrayal out of concern for propriety was to deny fiction its true self. In fact, he argued that it was important for the author to have a conscious moral purpose in composing fiction because morality was a real human concern. However, James believed that it was even more important for the author to possess the "purpose of making a perfect work" than it was for him to be concerned with moral purpose.[60] By this he meant investing the fictional world with events and concerns that fully resonate with the experience and imagination of the author and reader.

James's argument holds a particular relevance to our examination of *Genji* commentary and criticism. The "old evangelical hostility" toward fiction of which he speaks can be seen in the condemnations and distortions of medieval commentaries on *Genji* and against fictional literature in general. The flourishing of *gesaku* literature in the Edo period with the widespread publication of such comic and dramatic genres as *sharebon, kokkeibon*, and *ninjōbon* indicates a desire to escape the weight of this moralistic prejudice against fiction. It is precisely for this reason that *gesaku* literature has been described as "a diverting amusement for an otherwise serious man."[61] In this same context it would seem that Tameakira and Norinaga offered apologies for the realistic depiction of humanity they encountered in *Genji*. Tameakira's allegory theory was a way of apologizing for the immorality depicted in *Genji*. Norinaga rejects the apology offered by Tameakira. Instead, he argues that there is no conscious moral purpose to be found in the work. According to Norinaga, the fictional world of the monogatari operates beyond the concerns of real life because it is based on the lyric, aesthetic principle of *mono no aware*.

James would surely have agreed with Hiromichi's view that such an approach is no truer to the nature of *Genji* than is Tameakira's moralistic apology. To reject all conscious moral purpose in *Genji* is to deny its power to portray the concerns of real life. Hiromichi's argument throughout the "General Remarks" demonstrates that he had moved beyond the need to apologize or explain away the moral transgressions depicted in *Genji*. As his own theory of the principles of composition attempts to demonstrate, the defining characteristic of *Genji* is not its moral purpose but rather its deliberate and artful way of creating a work of prose fiction that allows the reader to experience and engage with a fictional world in a meaningful and satisfying way. Hiromichi rejected the notion that *Genji* was a sacred or an ennobling text that was the exclusive property of the aristocracy. Instead, he sought to make the tale in all of its complexity available to a popular audience. In his *Appraisal of Genji* he was not satisfied with simply reducing the essence of Genji's greatness to a single theme that lent itself to ideological argument. It is for this reason that he acknowledges the interpretive power of Norinaga's *mono no aware* theory but also urges the reader to look beyond it to appreciate how the text conveys a sense of the tale's characters and the world they inhabit that is so sophisticated in its construction that in reading *Genji* one experiences a very immediate, inescapable sense of satisfaction. Hiromichi's suggestion that the tale's greatness derives from the kind of completeness that allows readers to "scratch in all the places that itch" is as defiant as James's bold move to write in frank terms of the sexuality and sensuality of his characters. Both Hiromichi and James challenged the interpretive conventions of their time by urging readers not to turn a blind eye to the aspects of fiction that contribute to its ability to convey experience with a sense of complexity and nuance that approaches real life.

Chapter Four

EXPOSING THE SECRETS OF THE AUTHOR'S BRUSH

> Fiction [*fabula*] is a form of discourse, which, under guise of invention, illustrates or proves an idea; and as its superficial aspect is removed, the meaning of the author is clear. If, then, sense is revealed from under the veil of fiction, the composition of fiction is not idle nonsense.
>
> Giovanni Boccaccio, *Genealogy of the Gentile Gods*

Chapter 3 examined Hiromichi's treatment of previous scholarship on *Genji*, focusing on his efforts to overcome the limitations inherent in dominant critical theories of the Edo period to emphasize the importance of interpretive function over ideology in *Genji* criticism. To accomplish this goal he crossed boundaries that had previously divided two opposing ideologies, Confucianism and national learning, or nativist scholarship. Having established the scope and content of Hiromichi's criticism of previous *Genji* scholarship, our discussion moves on to examine the interpretive techniques and insights that he brought to the field from other scholarly traditions.

Specifically this chapter will examine Hiromichi's attempt to move beyond the limitations he pointed to in Tameakira's reading of *Genji* as a Confucian allegory and Norinaga's reading of the work in terms of his *mono no aware* theory. In introducing his own interpretive theory, Hiromichi hoped to bring the literary qualities of *Genji* to life in a way that could be understood and appreciated by any reader—from the Confucian scholar or nativist to the common reader wishing to discover "why *Genji* has received so much praise."[1] The method he introduces in the *Hyōshaku* for achieving this goal provides a key to reading the text. This key, called the "principles of composition," functions as a system of interpretive concepts designed to unlock the complexities of *Genji*'s long, elaborate narrative and to provide access to the compositional elements that define its greatness as a work of literature. In his application of these interpretive principles to *Genji* Hiromichi often sums up his analysis by reminding the reader that it is meant to draw attention to yet another example of "the author's remarkable use of the brush" (*sakusha no imijiki fudezukai nari*).[2] This expression clearly distinguishes Hiromichi from his predecessors who ultimately sought to legitimize their analysis in terms of larger moral, didactic, or political concerns.

HISTORICAL SOURCES FOR THE "PRINCIPLES OF COMPOSITION"

Hiromichi acquaints readers with the general scope of his interpretive theory in a section of the "General Remarks" to the *Hyōshaku* titled, "The Presence of Principles of Composition in This Monogatari." This section presents the historical and theoretical information necessary to appreciate Hiromichi's innovative approach to the interpretation of *Genji*. He begins the discussion by drawing a close connection between the "principles of composition," which he believes give shape to the narrative, and the literary sophistication that has come to be associated with the text:

> Praise for this monogatari requires no exaggeration on my part. The more one reads [*Genji*] the more difficult it becomes to express how exceptional it is. Therefore, I believe this monogatari is not written in any ordinary style, but rather it has been thought out and composed with various "principles of composition" [*nori*] in mind from the very beginning.[3]

These opening lines are noteworthy because they address the composition of *Genji* without direct reference to the personality or intentions of the author. As we saw in chapter 3, Hiromichi was critical of commentaries that attempted to interpret *Genji* based on the intentions of the author. He believed that such an analysis could only result in "idle speculation" because the author lived such a long time ago that it was impossible to know her mind with any certainty.[4] Hiromichi introduces his own interpretive theory by drawing our attention away from areas of speculation to the realm of observable phenomena. Specifically he begins by discussing *Genji*'s merits in terms of what was written, how it differs from other written works, and how his analysis of these facts has led him to conclude that certain techniques were used to construct the text. This establishes the empirical tone of his interpretive approach by focusing on the evidence available to both reader and commentator as it appears in the text. Because the focus of inquiry remains on the text, the commentator becomes an active guide in directing the reader's attention to those places in the text that reveal the literary accomplishments of the author. By sharing in the commentator's vision of the text, the amateur reader can join the scholar in reading and appreciating *Genji* as a great work of literature.

While his interpretive approach to the text is based on empirical analysis, the principles of composition, which serve as the focal point of his interpretation, belong to the realm of concept and theory. He never states that the number of principles at work in the text is finite, or that one passage of *Genji* exactly corresponds to a single principle of composition. In fact, he even resists rigidly associating the concept of the "principles of composition" with a single Chinese character or character compound. His first reference to what I have translated as the "principles of composition" corresponds in the aforementioned passage to the combination of two Chinese characters. In modern Japanese, these characters in combination are read *hōsoku*. The compound consists of a character meaning law, technique, or model—*hō*—and a second character with a similar meaning, but also with the implication of being in accordance with laws—*soku*. Historically, these characters may both be assigned the native Japanese reading *nori* in isolation. Hiromichi takes pains to assign the native Japanese reading *nori* to the characters as they appear in compound form. A few lines later, he uses only the first character of the compound—*hō*—and assigns it the reading of *nori*, to represent the same concept. This instability continues throughout the text, with the concept I translate as the "principles of composition" being alternately represented by a single character, the two-character compound, or the phonetic reading *nori* independent of any Chinese characters. Hiromichi may have resorted to this native reading because readers of his time were likely to associate the character *hō* with its use as an expression of Buddhist or Confucian doctrine. By obliging such readers to apply the native pronunciation for this term, Hiromichi subtly discourages them from equating his literary concept with "principle" in a moral or religious sense associated with Chinese philosophy or religion.[5] Conceptually, Hiromichi's literary principles are similar to moral or religious ones in that they express fundamental laws that can be known or understood and used as a guide to action. However, they play no role in governing action in a moral or religious sense and are entirely defined by their aesthetic utility in the composition, interpretation, and appreciation of literature. Hiromichi's interest in preserving this distinction between literary and moral or philosophical principles will become apparent as he discusses the historical and theoretical basis for his interpretive approach.

The presence of various principles of composition in *Genji* leads Hiromichi to conclude that the author must have become familiar with these principles through contact with other works of literature. He thus views her literary experience, rather than divine inspiration or pure genius, as the legitimate explanation for the high level of artistic achievement evident in *Genji*. He bases this conclusion on his familiarity with principles of composition found in other works of literature:

> I have yet to find anything in Japanese literature [*wagakuni no fumi*] that I could say exactly corresponds to these "principles of composition." However, the principles of composition one finds in Chinese works are generally not so different from those in *Genji*. So, initially,

> we might say that these principles came from Chinese literature. Having said that, the principles of composition found in Chinese literature come from a later period than *Genji*, thereby making it impossible to argue that Chinese principles are the source of those found in *Genji*. The first people to write things down did not discuss such principles. Rather, later generations saw the remarkable qualities of those early works and in trying to learn from them provisionally attached names to the passages worthy of comment. This is where the principles of composition came from. They were all only temporary names. Texts of ancient times were not consciously written with these principles in mind but rather passages were labeled as such at a later date, thereby making it possible to criticize and interpret them. It is due to the presence of such principles that these texts are understood to be so remarkable.[6]

As discussed in chapter 2, Hiromichi was familiar with a wide range of literary genres, including the prose fiction of Takizawa Bakin. It is likely that his idea for the principles of composition was originally inspired by the summary of critical terms Bakin included in his postscript to the ninth volume of *Hakkenden* (1835).[7] There is no single source for the list of critical terms Bakin presents in *Hakkenden*, but one work that appears to have had great influence on his development of these terms is an edition of the Chinese novel *Shuihu zhuan* (J: *Suikōden*, The Water Margin, ca. 1644), which includes extensive editorial comments by Jin Shengtan (J: Kin Seitan, 1608–1661).[8] Jin Shengtan is noted for bringing a style of commentary known as *pingdian* (J: *hyōten*, "critical punctuation marks") to a new level of sophistication in the interpretation of narrative fiction in China. In the process of carefully reading Bakin and works of Chinese vernacular fiction Bakin often emulated, Hiromichi became well versed in the methods of *pingdian* criticism associated with commentary editions of fictional works published during the Ming (1368–1644) and Qing (1644–1912) dynasties. He demonstrates an extensive knowledge of *pingdian* criticism in later sections of his "General Remarks." This expertise will become increasingly apparent as specific terms related to his theory of the principles of composition are examined in greater detail in this chapter and in chapter 5. However, at this point, he merely wishes to provide the reader with a general historical and theoretical grounding for his critical approach to the text and refrains from going into a detailed explanation of technical terms.

Hiromichi points out that the style of commentary he considers the basis of his principles of composition theory did not appear in China until after *Genji* was composed. This assessment of the development of *pingdian* commentary as it was applied to works of narrative fiction appears surprisingly accurate. Contemporary scholarship dates the earliest application of *pingdian* commentary on a work of narrative fiction to the thirteenth century.[9] However, as Hiromichi also indicated, the basic techniques of *pingdian* criticism can be found in the commentary editions of works of poetry and classical prose dating back to at least the Tang dynasty (618–907). From the mid-Ming dynasty (1368–1644), *pingdian*-style criticism was used with increasing frequency in the publication of commentary editions of major historical texts such as Sima Qian's *Shiji* (J: *Shiki*, Records of the Historian) and Ban Gu's (32–92) *Hanshu* (J: *Kansho*, History of the Han Dynasty) to direct readers' attention to noteworthy places in the composition of these works.[10]

Earlier in the "General Remarks" to the *Hyōshaku*, Hiromichi devotes considerable space to a discussion of the author's sobriquet "Her Ladyship of *The Chronicles of Japan*." He concludes that the author of *Genji* was known by this name in recognition of her knowledge of historical works. Hiromichi theorizes that it was not only the *Nihongi* (*The Chronicles of Japan*, 720) that Murasaki Shikibu was familiar with but "all the great national histories as well."[11] Hiromichi thus concludes that she was probably familiar with major works of Chinese history such as the *Shiji*. However, he also believed that she would not have been conscious of having learned anything called the "principles of composition" from the *Shiji* or of intentionally having applied such a technique to her composition of *Genji*:

> In the case of *Genji*, the author did not knowingly apply these principles of composition in her writing. She had been exposed to a wide variety of Chinese texts and was therefore very familiar with Chinese classics. These principles were undoubtedly transmitted to her without any conscious effort on her part [*onozukara*]. I hardly need to mention that there are principles of composition in Sima Qian's *Shiji* and that this work has long been the object of interpretation. However, *Genji* and the *Shiji* vary greatly in both language and content, so I shall not insist on claiming that the author of this monogatari modeled [*naraitaru*] her work on the *Shiji*.
>
> While I say that we cannot assume Murasaki Shikibu learned from Sima Qian, zealous scholars of our country [*hitaburu naru mikuni no gakusha domo*] are apt to find displeasure in my (mere) suggestion that *Genji* is in any way similar to Chinese writing. There are people who would accuse me of a crime for saying as much, but I must emphasize that this is simply a theory.[12]

As a student of literature who associated himself with the lineage of nativist scholarship, Hagiwara Hiromichi was well aware of the important role national identity had come to play in the study of Japan's classical literature. During the Edo period, nativist ideology evolved from the concern that the teachings of Confucianism, Buddhism, and the analytical ways of the Chinese intellect (*karagokoro*) were impediments to the expression of genuine feeling and instinct. According to this ideology, Confucian thought had the potential to diminish one's ability to appreciate the sentiments that characterized works of classical Japanese literature. Kamo no Mabuchi came to view the analysis of ancient Japanese texts as being crucial to the proper understanding of native literature and viewed Chinese learning with suspicion.[13] Similarly disposed, Motoori Norinaga came to perceive all Chinese texts as a potential source of contamination of the true Japanese spirit (*mikunigokoro*). He believed that one had to maintain constant vigilance against such contamination.[14]

It is with these rebukes in mind that we must read Hiromichi's cautious introduction to his own interpretive theory of *Genji*. As we saw in chapter 3, Hiromichi embraced the interpretive advances in *Genji* criticism made possible by nativist scholarship. Yet he was unable to share in their unqualified rejection of all things foreign or Chinese. His eclectic reading habits had led him to the conclusion that many of the compositional techniques at work in *Genji* bore a striking resemblance to techniques discussed in the critical editions of Chinese popular fiction.[15] These techniques helped the reader understand and appreciate the aesthetic merit evident in the text and, as Hiromichi perceived them, had little to do with Confucian morality or Buddhist philosophy. However, Hiromichi realized that the association between things Chinese and Confucian didacticism remained so strong that any reference to works in Chinese, such as the *Shiji*, in the context of interpreting *Genji* was likely to be perceived as an implicit endorsement of a Confucian reading of the text.

To affirm his allegiance to things Japanese, Hiromichi introduces the relevance of Japan's sacred religious tradition, Shinto, to his interpretive theory. Much of the language used in his explanation is borrowed from nativist scholarship, thus signaling to the reader that he intends to judge *Genji* within the framework of the Japanese literary tradition rather than a Chinese or Confucian perspective. Specifically, he reassures his readers that the sacred speech used in Shinto ceremony, *norito*, and the style used to record Imperial decrees, *senmyōgaki*, are in no way inferior to the style found in the great works of Chinese literature from which the principles of composition evolved.

> In the past, a writing system borrowed from China [*kanbunshō*] was used to record things, as everyone knows, and the only documents written in Japanese were sacred Shinto prayers [*norito*] and Imperial decrees [*senmyō*.][16] With this monogatari [*Genji*], a work characterized by "literary style" [*bunshō*] somehow appeared for the first time in the Japanese language. Monogatari prior to *Genji* merely told stories by stringing together words. More precisely, they lacked what one would call a literary style. *Genji* marks the first appearance of this wonderful literary style [in Japanese]. Originally, literary style corresponded to what was called elegant expression [*aya kotoba*], indicating a technique by which the material being recorded was embellished in such a way as to cause the reader to experience an exceptional

> sense of enjoyment [*yomu hito ni medetaku omoshiroku kikishimuru*]. This is different from writing in which things are expressed just as they would be in conversation. The first character [*bun*] in the expression "literary style" [*bunshō*] means to possess a sense of beauty or to beautify, while the second character [*shō*] means to possess a distinct sense of beauty. I mention this simply because one should keep it in mind.[17]

Great works of narrative fiction, whether in Chinese or Japanese, must have what Hiromichi called "literary style"—*bunshō*.[18] According to his view, reading prose that has literary style moves the reader, because the text conveys a sense of vitality and beauty. Prose without literary style might convey the same information, but because its construction lacks literary sophistication, it fails to move the reader in the same way. Hiromichi emphasizes that the goal of his interpretation is to help the reader understand and appreciate the literary sophistication of *Genji*. Specifically the principles of composition allow him to give names to the qualities of literary style that make prose aesthetically pleasing. He goes on to point out that it is not that Japanese literature lacks literary style, but simply that the Japanese have never resorted to the "exaggerated" (*kotogotoshiki*) process of giving names to the impressive passages in narrative fiction the way the Chinese have.

> Our country has never followed the Chinese practice of attaching such overstated [*kotogotoshiki*] names [as literary style] to written documents [*koto*, "things"]. However, the sacred prayers and such [*norito nado*] I mentioned earlier contain expressions that are elegantly arranged with a unique vitality so that if one looks at them one realizes they are unlike the words we usually utter. It is said that it is best to avoid excessive adornment of language, but a sentence only constructed with care to detail [*omou koto o tsubutsubu to kaku*] that lacks charm [*okashiki fushi mo naku*] cannot be said to possess literary style. The term "literary style" comes from the Chinese, but a similar concept to that of literary style has always existed in Japan. One should think of sacred [Shinto] prayers and Imperial decrees as having these qualities. Therefore, while it is probably inaccurate to say that this monogatari's style is a direct imitation of the *Shiji*, we can say that it is written in the hand of someone who had read the *Shiji* and in trying to write an interesting story was naturally influenced by this work.[19]

Hiromichi seems to be drawing upon his sense as a poet to define what constitutes literary style in prose. Ki no Tsurayuki's (868?–945?) preface to the first Imperial anthology of poetry, the *Kokinshū* (c. 905) defined the essence of Japanese poetry as the transmission in words—*kotoba*—of what was found to move the heart—*kokoro*—of the poet. As traditional Japanese poetics evolved, the balance of *kotoba* and *kokoro* was often used to assess a poem's quality based on its style—*sama*—and integral form—*sugata*. Hiromichi applies the poetic notion that literary style is derived from this balance to suggest that a similar balance must be struck in the composition of prose. He asserts that the story and the language in which the story is told must strike the proper balance of vitality, beauty, and charm before a text can be said to have literary style.

Hiromichi then suggests that it would have been easy for him to invent entirely new Japanese terms to classify and explain the elements of literary sophistication in *Genji*, but it made more sense to adapt those aspects of narrative fiction criticism developed in China—which I have characterized above as *pingdian* criticism.

> When one compares the *Shiji* and *Genji*, one discovers great differences in content and style, so that it is clearly a mistake to say *Genji* is written in imitation of the *Shiji*. However, no one can deny that *Genji* is the first work written in Japanese worthy of being characterized as having literary style [*bunshō*]. In any case, when one comments upon [*hyō*] the literary style of this monogatari to bring the wonderful techniques in it to the surface [*sono medetaki yoshi o arawashi izutsu*] one naturally points out the names of the principles of composition that exist in the work. One cannot help but point to these principles in trying to explain why such passages are worthy of comment to those who wish to learn to write well. This is how they come to understand [*satosu*] such things. That being the case, it is just as simple [for me] to point out the [existing, Chinese] names for these principles of composition as it is for me to make up different [i.e., Japanese] names for all of them. However, these principles have already been transmitted to Japan from China, so that even if I were to give the terms different names someone would probably say that I had modeled my terms on those from China. Rather than concern myself with such a pointless exercise that would probably just lead to confusion, I have studied the so-called "principles of composition" [*nori*] that can be found in later generations of various compositional rules [*bunpō*] in China. What is more, I have appropriated some of the terminology in order to interpret *Genji*. Dear reader, please keep these points in mind, and do not judge me too harshly.[20]

Rather than gloss over any indebtedness he feels to Chinese criticism, Hiromichi appears eager to fully disclose his familiarity with Chinese sources. It would seem that he is making a conscious effort to confront head on the anxiety of Chinese influence that so troubled earlier scholars of the nativist tradition. In setting the stage for his argument, he emphasizes that for a long time the Japanese wrote almost exclusively in a language borrowed wholesale from the Chinese. As he points out, this does not diminish the fact that Japanese has always had a beauty and vitality of its own. He goes on to suggest that his definition of literary style, while derived from the Chinese, could be applied with equal success to Japanese texts such as *Genji*. In fact, he asserts that it is counterproductive to reinvent interpretive theory specifically for Japanese literature when other suitable theories are to be found.

Hiromichi is also confident that any careful reader who has understood his interpretive theory will be able to recognize certain principles of composition as they exist in the text of *Genji*. He therefore assumes that the presence of principles of composition in the text is a matter of objective fact, not speculation. From this perspective he argues that introducing readers to such interpretive principles will improve their appreciation for the literary style and sophistication of *Genji*. He does not attempt to conceal the fact that his technique is in part derived from Chinese critical methods—what Motoori Norinaga had warned was the interpretive hazard of allowing the Chinese intellect (*karagokoro*) to dominate the Japanese spirit (*mikunigokoro*).

One particularly revealing passage is Hiromichi's reference to the role he believed his interpretive approach could play in helping readers understand the compositional techniques at work in the text so that they might go on to master these techniques in their own writing:

> One cannot help but point to these principles in trying to explain why such passages are worthy of comment to those who wish to learn to write well. This is how they come to understand [*satosu*] such things.

Genji had long served as a model for the composition of poetry, but Hiromichi is concerned that without appreciating the principles of composition at work in the text, students of literature will not be able to move beyond the process of "simply stringing together evocative passages taken from various places in *Genji*, and other works, and then making exaggerated claims to have composed prose of a particularly great literary style" [*kotogotoshiku bechi ni bunshō to zo iu naru*].[21] To compose prose in Japanese with true literary style he believes it necessary to have an appreciation for the principles of composition. He has applied his principles of composition theory to *Genji* precisely because it is the ideal model for studying the composition of prose. He goes on to express disappointment that older commentaries (*mukashi yori no chūshaku*) are particularly lacking in the type of interpretation necessary for understanding the principles of composition at work in *Genji*.[22] The logical conclusion of this is that Hiromichi's principles of composition theory presents the ideal approach to appreciating *Genji*, which he sees as the exemplar of literary style for Japanese prose. In addition, he suggests that mastery of these same principles will improve one's ability to compose prose worthy of admiration.

"PRINCIPLES OF COMPOSITION" AND LITERARY STYLE

Having exposed the historical sources for his principles of composition, Hiromichi goes on to point out that in fact he is not the first commentator to recognize the potential of this interpretive approach to *Genji*. Given the Chinese origins for his principles of composition, it is not surprising that his first example of their previous application to *Genji* comes from a commentator whom both Norinaga and Hiromichi characterized as approaching interpretation of *Genji* from the perspective of a Confucian, Andō Tameakira. Hiromichi quotes from a section titled, "Literary Style without Equal" (*Bunshō musō*) in Tameakira's *Shikashichiron*:

> The entire work [*Genji*] conveys a sense of nobility and comfort [*fūki onjun*] and is composed in the literary style [*bunshō*] of the Imperial Court. However, one also encounters scenes set in nature—where a character has left the secular world behind to lead a spiritual life [*sanrin shussei ari*]; scenes of city life and rural life; and scenes of poverty and distress. Human feelings and natural surroundings are depicted in every chapter with a vitality that makes it seem as if the characters were standing before one's eyes [*ma no atari sono hito ni mukae*] or one were inhabiting that very scene [*sono tokoro ni asobu ga gotoshi*]. The entire work serves as a chronicle of Genji's life, so naturally a variety of styles [*tai*] are employed. One finds introductory and closing passages [i.e., prologues and epilogues], passages of narrative and of dialogue, and correspondence from letters. The "rainy night discourse on women," in the "Hahakigi" Chapter, is especially extraordinary [*koto ni kimyō naru*]. Others before me have also commented upon the sentences and paragraphs of this scene. As I said in the preface, it consists of dialogue in which characters object and acquiesce as they discuss central issues as well as more tangential ones. The discussion ranges from broad topics to specific ones; from mundane subjects to refined ones; and from very complex issues to simple ones. Chinese compositional techniques [*morokoshi no bunpō*] such as "periodic fluctuation" [*polan*; J: *haran*], "sudden setback" [*duncuo*; J: *tonza*], "retroactive correspondence" [*zhaoying*; J: *shōō*], and "foreshadowing" [*fuan*; J: *fukuan*] are naturally [*onozukara*] included. The narrative pace [*kimyaku*] is serene and magnificent, the mode of expression [*bunsei*] is smooth and graceful.[23]

Tameakira inserts a note here to indicate that he originally wrote these comments as a preface to the section of the "Hahakigi" chapter in which Genji and his companions spend the night discussing the merits and failings of different types of women—a section often referred to as the "rainy night conversation" (*amayo monogatari*). However, his note points out that these comments should not be limited in scope to the "rainy night conversation." He writes, "This is not something that one sees only in the 'rainy night conversation,' similar care is taken by the author throughout the work."

In the passage just quoted, Tameakira uses the same word—*bunshō*—that Hiromichi defined earlier as "literary style." Tameakira sees the atmosphere of nobility depicted by the story as determining *Genji*'s aesthetic quality and sophistication as a work of literature. As the passage progresses, it begins to seem that Tameakira does have some of Hiromichi's same points in mind concerning the composition of *Genji*. Specifically he refers to "Chinese compositional techniques" that he associates with such positive stylistic qualities as magnificent narrative pace and graceful mode of expression. Unfortunately, Tameakira's development of the notion that there is a connection between compositional technique and the literary sophistication of *Genji* ends there. He fails to develop any deeper relationship between technique and literary style and instead focuses on the virtue of the author and her place in relation to other great authors. Hiromichi's quotation from Tameakira's *Shikashichiron* continues:

> *The Tale of Genji* is on the same level as the *Shiji*, the *Zhuan-zi*, and works by Han Yu (768–824), Liu Zong-yuan (773–819), Ou Yang-xiu (1007–1070), and Su Shi (1037–1101). The fact that it was written by a woman (makes it) both rare and admirable. Murasaki Shikibu is truly the only person in days past or present to possess such ability. While one speaks of "the two great authors, Murasaki Shikibu and Sei Shōnagon," Sei's ability was meager, and she was apt to try too hard to give the appearance of being clever. This makes her somewhat unpleasant. One can't really say that Sei Shōnagon is the equal of Murasaki Shikibu.[24]

Hiromichi's quotation ends there, but in the *Shikashichiron* Tameakira's discussion of literary style quickly turns to authorial intention rather than compositional technique. He assures readers that even though *Genji* portrays fictional events, it was written with the intention of inspiring moral behavior in others. The reader who understands Murasaki Shikibu's noble intention will appreciate that *Genji* is "indeed the essence of the way of poetry" [*ge nimo kadō no hon'i*].[25] Hiromichi's quotation serves to illustrate that Tameakira did recognize the presence of certain principles of composition in *Genji*. It demonstrates with equal efficiency that Tameakira chose to follow this interpretive insight in a completely different direction.

It is no mere coincidence that Tameakira and Hiromichi both refer to "principles" or "rules" of composition from China in their attempts to account for the literary style of *Genji*. Tameakira's interest in Confucianism necessarily brought him into contact with commentary editions of Confucian classics. Many of the commentary editions he encountered contained elements of what would evolve into the tradition of *pingdian* commentary that was to inspire

Bakin and Hiromichi more than a century later. The earliest sources for *pingdian* interpretation can be traced to editions of classical texts attributed to Confucius (551–479 B.C.) that contain critical commentary. Interpretive methods found to be useful in explaining the meaning of overtly didactic texts such as the *Chun qiu* (J: *Shunju* , Spring and Autumn Annals) were later applied to portions of the canon that were less openly didactic, such as the love poems of the *Shi jing* (Classic of Poetry), to bring out what was believed to be their underlying didactic meaning.[26] Beginning in the Song dynasty (960–1279), commentary editions of Confucian classics were produced to help students prepare for official civil service exams. Xie Fang-de (1226–1289) compiled one of the most influential editions of the classics used in exam preparation, the *Wenzhuang guifan* (J: *Bunshō kihan,* Model for Prose). The *Wenzhuang guifan* is an anthology of sixty-nine works from the Tang and Song dynasties with *juandian* (J: *kenten,* "circles and dots") interpretive punctuation to guide the reader in his understanding of each work.[27] The four terms that Tameakira lists to illustrate "Chinese rules of composition" can all be found in Xie Fang-de's *Wenzhuang guifan.*[28] He uses this information to assert that *Genji* should not be considered in any way inferior to the great classics of China. In Tameakira's view, the fact that Murasaki Shikibu used some of the same compositional techniques employed by the authors of Confucian classics is proof that she is their equal.[29]

As an integral part of China's literary tradition, elements of *pingdian* commentary had already begun to influence the work of scholars of Chinese classics (*kangakusha*) in seventeenth- and eighteenth-century Japan.[30] Numerous editions of Xie Fang-de's *Wenzhuang guifan* were printed in Japan under such titles as *Bunshō kihan hyōrin chūshaku* (Commentary on the Forest of Interpretation in *The Model of Prose,* preface dated 1791). An early reprint, or perhaps a copy from China, would be a likely source for Tameakira's application of "Chinese Rules of Composition" to *Genji.*[31] By the late eighteenth century, elements of *pingdian* commentary were employed as a method of instruction for students in Japan who wished to improve their compositional skills. The scholar of Chinese classical poetry, Emura Hokkai (1713–1788), wrote a manual for students in 1781 titled *Jugyōhen.* Hokkai's manual includes a section on composition in which he begins by cautioning the introductory student that the study of composition is a difficult endeavor, because "there are rules of composition for prose just as there are rules of composition for poetry" (*bunshō ni bunpō areba, shi ni mo shihō ari*), and one must be familiar with the rules to properly compose texts in both genres. He goes on to list four examples of principles of prose composition (*hōsoku*), all of which belong to the tradition of *pingdian* commentary: "the modulated rise and fall of narrative segments" [*qifu;* J: *kifuku*], "retroactive correspondence" [*zhaoying;* J: *shōō*], "dramatic modulation" [*yiyang;* J: *yokuyō*], and "reversal of argument" [*zhuanhuan;* J: *tenkan*].[32] Hokkai fails to define these principles or provide illustrative examples but implies that by carefully reading Chinese classics, the student will come to understand these principles and learn how to apply them to his own writing. Presumably, the editions of the classics to which Hokkai expected his students to turn contained *pingdian* commentary that would guide their reading and enhance their understanding of the principles of composition.

Hiromichi suggests that even scholars associated more closely with nativist scholarship than Confucianism made efforts to apply rules of composition to their interpretation of *Genji*. After quoting from Tameakira's *Shikashichiron*, he turns to Kamo no Mabuchi's *Genji monogatari shinshaku* (1758), saying, "One can find places where Mabuchi also tried to provide commentary for *Genji* based on rules of composition [*bunpō*]. I will now quote from the *Shinshaku* where he attempts to do this."[33]

> As far as the meaning of the text [*bungi*] is concerned, to bring up things before they have reached a conclusion is called "stretching out the main story" [*chōhon*, foreshadowing] or "consciously concealing things" [*fukuan*, foreshadowing]. There is a slight difference between the two terms, but in general they are the same. There are cases where the early event and the later event correspond to each other. This is called "retroactive correspondence"[*shōō*]. Also, there are certain cases where things are suddenly cut off in the story. These are called "sudden setbacks" [*tonza*]. There are places in the text [*bun*] where the author remarks on the events of the story by including comments that are addressed to someone outside the story rather than the people addressing each other in the story. These are called "words of the author" [*kisha no go*]. In common terminology, they are called "authorial intrusions" [*sōshiji*].[34] There are also places in passages of conversation where it isn't clear who is being addressed. My comments indicate the speaker, for example, "Genji" or "Murasaki no Ue." I also indicate where to end sentences with a mark to the side of the text ["period"] and where to break sentences in the middle ["comma"] with a small character read *tō* ["reading mark"]. To indicate small sections of the story [*shōdan*] I add a small box as follows [-]. To the larger sections of the story [*ōdan*] I add an ["L"-shaped] box, such as this [L]. By "larger section" I mean the conclusion of an important event of the story. There is no precedent for such things in [the texts of] our language, but I do this only to make it easier to understand the text. In addition to what I have already explained, there are other commentary methods [*chūhō*], but you should be able to understand them when you encounter them in the text. Therefore I am only providing representative examples here. For the most part, many of these are things that are not seen in earlier commentaries. Please pay attention to these things.[35]

Mabuchi's comments come from a section titled "General Remarks" (*sōkō*), which he originally wrote as a preface to a copy of the *Kogetsushō* in which he had inserted his own annotation on *Genji*.[36] It seems clear that he was familiar with the same tradition of textual commentary that inspired Tameakira's remarks on the rules of composition in *Genji*. Three of the terms he introduces—*fukuan* ("foreshadowing"), *shōō* ("retroactive correspondence"), and *tonza* ("sudden setback")—were also used by Tameakira. A fourth term, *chōhon* ("foreshadowing"), also belongs to the tradition of *pingdian* commentary.[37] The technique he applies to *Genji* of adding punctuation marks and certain symbols to indicate divisions between sections of the story is also closely related to techniques used in the *pingdian* commentary tradition. In an earlier section of his "General Remarks," titled "Literary Form" (*bun no sama*), Mabuchi's comments closely follow the points made by Tameakira in his "Literary Style without Equal."[38] However, Mabuchi fails to develop the connection between compositional technique and aesthetic merit beyond Tameakira's limited interpretation.

In Hiromichi's third and final citation concerning the origins of his interpretive approach, he takes a rather different tactic. Throughout the *Hyōshaku* he reserves some of his highest words of praise for Motoori Norinaga and his interpretation of *Genji* as it appears in *Tama no ogushi*. However, there is little in *Tama no ogushi* to suggest that Norinaga's interpretation of *Genji* was in any way inspired by Chinese principles of composition or a desire to analyze compositional technique.[39] Nevertheless, Hiromichi attempts to align his new interpretive approach with Norinaga's scholarship by focusing on those aspects of their interpretive approaches that they have in common. For this purpose, he focuses on Norinaga's admonition that one should read *Genji* with great care:

> One must penetrate deeply into the detailed places of the text and painstakingly appreciate [*komayakani ajiwau*] the author's care in their construction.[40]

Hiromichi adds:

> I have taken this often stated principle of Norinaga's as my own. Having read *Genji* many times with this in mind, I have discovered things that I did not expect to find. I have been surprised to discover how impressively these principles of composition have been applied to the text. I have added to the methods set forward by Mabuchi and put together this commentary, which I call the *Hyōshaku*.[41]

Hiromichi touches on the aspect of all three *Genji* commentators' work that resonates most strongly with his own interpretive approach. Paying close attention to the details of the text and noting the care with which these details are arranged are at the heart of his analysis of *Genji*. Tameakira, believing in the persuasive power of Confucianism and Chinese scholarship, made a special effort to point to the Chinese origins of the critical techniques he recognized in the composition of *Genji*. One might go so far as to say that he introduced Chinese interpretive terminology to his discussion of *Genji* because he hoped it would contribute to the prestige of the work. Mabuchi added the terms introduced by Tameakira to his commentary on *Genji* because they allowed him to expand his critical vocabulary. On the other hand, Motoori Norinaga expresses no interest in drawing our attention to specific interpretive terminology or techniques. Such methods probably struck him as contrary to the spirit in which the work was written. However, in quoting Norinaga, Hiromichi emphasizes that careful analysis and appreciation of the text are the goals he hopes to achieve. The principles of composition merely provide a language through which he can more effectively communicate his interpretation of the text to the amateur reader. Hiromichi further emphasizes this point by reminding readers that this approach is the basis of his title for the commentary. His approach consists of close reading of the text facilitated by commentary—*chūshaku* or *shaku*—and interpretation—*hyō*—of the way in which the details of the text are arranged. The combination of these two techniques constitues his unique method of appraising *Genji* in terms of its literary style and structure.

CONCLUSION

Hiromichi's citations from the *Shikashichiron* and *Genji monogatari shinshaku* indicate that earlier commentators saw certain principles of composition at work in *Genji*, just as he did. However, earlier commentaries fail to articulate a meaningful relationship between literary style and the principles of composition to the same level of sophistication that we see in the *Hyōshaku*. This difference can be better accounted for when we examine an important development in popular literature that took place in Japan during the late eighteenth century. This period saw the appearance of a new genre of literature, vernacular fiction (*baihua xiaoshuo*; J: *hakuwa shōsetsu*), imported from China. Chinese vernacular fiction contributed to developments in sophistication of language, style, character development, narrative structure, and use of historical detail found in the genre of popular fiction known as *yomihon*. The works of authors familiar with Chinese vernacular fiction typify developments detectable in popular fiction during this period. The popular fiction of Takizawa Bakin provides one example of this phenomenon.[42] Editions of Chinese vernacular fiction instrumental in effecting these changes included a style of *pingdian* commentary that was in widespread use in China throughout the Ming and Qing dynasties. However, this style of *pingdian* commentary was quite different from the form available to Tameakira in seventeenth-century Japan. *Pingdian* commentary found in anthologies of the Confucian classics, for example, Xie Fang-de's *Wenzhuang guifan*, was representative of textual commentary from the Song dynasty. In effect, *yomihon* authors—including Bakin and Hiromichi—had the advantage of being exposed to *pingdian* commentary as it had evolved over several centuries. To understand the dramatic difference in sophistication between *pingdian* commentary as it was applied to vernacular fiction in the Ming and Qing dynasties and commentary on Confucian classics from the Song dynasty, we need to return to our earlier discussion of the role that commentary on such works as the *Wenzhuang guifan* played in the preparation for civil service exams in China.

Civil service exams required students to demonstrate their mastery of large quantities of information found in classical texts and placed a premium on precise written expression. A student's comprehension was improved by following the interpretive comments supplied by the editor so that he could better understand the fine points and rhetorical techniques at work in the text. As a result, interpretive commentary influenced essay composition as well as comprehension and appreciation of classical texts. The competitive character of the exam system naturally brought about corresponding developments in the sophistication and originality of interpretive commentary supplied by editors of classical texts. As these interpretive techniques evolved, so did the role of classical texts. By the Ming dynasty, classical texts were not only considered repositories of historical and moral knowledge but also literary style. As a result, competence in the civil service examination came to be closely associated with mastery of composition and literary technique. Prestige associated with success in the exam system extended to other aspects of literary culture, creating an atmosphere in which interpretive techniques from the exam system were applied to other literary arts, such as the criticism of fiction and drama.[43] The work of Li Yu (Li Li-weng; J: Ri Ryūō; 1611–1680) provides one example of the way in which interpretive techniques from drama theory and classics commentary intersected to enrich the vocabulary of *pingdian*.

While noted for his success as a commentator of examination essays, Li Yu is most famous for his work on drama theory.[44] Of particular importance is his *Xianqing ouji* (J: *Kanjō gūki*, Random Repository of Idle Thoughts; 1671). Li Yu divides his discourse on drama in his *Xianqing ouji* into three major parts: the construction of the play, problems of staging, and bad theatrical practices.[45] In the section that covers construction of the play (*huqubu jieguo*; J: *gikyoku kekkō*) he advises the playwright to establish a central concept (*zhunao*; J: *shunō*, "controlling brain") for the play and to never lose sight of this concept in the placement of smaller details so that they eventually relate back to the central concept. He goes on to advise:

> Writing plays is something like the tailoring of clothing. In the beginning one cuts up whole cloth into pieces, and then one proceeds to piece together the cut fragments. Cutting something up into fragments is easy; it is piecing these back together that is difficult. The artistry of piecing together lies completely in the fineness of the stitching: if a given section happens to be too loosely connected, then

> holes in the composition [lit. "split seams"] will appear throughout the piece.[46]

Li Yu's advice to the playwright evidently found its way from drama criticism into the language of literary scholarship. Literary scholars after Li Yu took to evaluating works of narrative fiction by pointing out how the various chapters, sections, and episodes of a work of narrative fiction were sewn together by the author and how they were made to relate back to the central concept of the work.[47] Concepts used to critique the placement and composition of elements in portrait and landscape paintings such as spatial composition (*zhang-fa*; J: *shōhō*, "composition law") and subordination of elements (*binzhu*; J: *hinshu*, "guest and master") found their way into the critical language of *pingdian* through similar intersections in the criticism of painting and fiction.[48]

While this evolution of critical terminology led to increasingly sophisticated interpretation of the structure that held together works of narrative fiction, by the Ming and Qing dynasties it also contributed to what some literati criticized as an overly structured, mechanical approach to composition. Zhang Xue-cheng (1738–1801), in a section titled *Guwenshibi* (Ten Faults in Classical Prose) of his *Wenshitongyi* (General Principles of Historiography), criticizes teachers who employ *pingdian* commentary and terminology in instructing their students. His criticism serves as a concise summary of *pingdian* techniques and their widespread use at the time.

> When instructors teach [their pupils] the style and meaning of the Four Books and how to write examination essays, the essay must have technique [*fadu*; J: *hatto*] so as to comply with the formal requirements [*chengshi*; J: *teishiki*]. But technique is difficult to speak of abstractly, so they often use metaphors to teach their students. Comparing [the essays] to building, they speak of the framework [*jianjia*; J: *kankaku*] and structure [*jiegou*; J: *kekkō*] comparing [the essays] to the human body, they speak of the eyebrows and eyes [*meimu*; J: *bimoku*], tendons and joints [*jinjie*; J: *kinsetsu*]; comparing [the essays] to painting, they talk of "filling the pupils of the dragon" [*dianjing*; J: *tensei*] and "adding the whiskers" [*tianhao*; J: *tengō*]; and comparing [the essays] to geomancy, they speak of "lines of force" [*lailong*; J: *rairyū*] and "convergence points" [*jiexue*; J: *kekketsu*]. They make these up as they go, but it's all just for teaching elementary students [*chuxue shifa*; J: *shogaku shihō*] there is no help for it, so there is no need to upbraid them for it.[49]

As we can see from Zhang Xue-cheng's synopsis and somewhat reproachful evaluation, the vocabulary of *pingdian* criticism assimilated a wide variety of interpretive terms from other forms of art. The interpretive language of nontextual arts appears to have contributed a sophisticated appreciation for visual perception and spatial dimension to the tradition of literary interpretation. These terms, derived from the way in which visual elements and physical objects fit together to form an aesthetically pleasing whole, were introduced into the language of literary interpretation and then applied by editors of narrative fiction to literary works to explain literary structure and style. This expansion of the interpretive vocabulary available to explain the structure of the text resulted in a paradigm shift in literary interpretation. Commentators could facilitate a reader's appreciation of complex narrative structure and literary technique by relying on increasingly sophisticated *pingdian* terminology. Encouraged by the results, authors and editors strove to produce increasingly sophisticated works of fiction to challenge their readers and demonstrate their technical mastery. Hiromichi's perceptive reading of *pingdian* commentary, as he encountered it in Bakin's works and vernacular fiction imported from China, led him to apply this paradigm shift to his own interpretation of *Genji*.

Chapter Five

AMBIGUITY AND THE RESPONSIVE READER

Having dismissed the interpretive tools of his predecessors as failing to fully account for *Genji*'s value as literature, Hiromichi must now provide his own strategy for reading the text. For this reason, he introduces the most innovative aspect of his *Appraisal of Genji* with deliberate caution. In his "General Remarks," Hiromichi devotes the longest section to his exposition of what he refers to as *Genji*'s "principles of composition":

> I shall try to explain how these principles function. First of all, there are principles [*nori*] that hold true for the entire monogatari, principles that extend the length of individual chapters [*maki*], principles that cover particular sections [*kiri*], principles that exist within a particular passage [*kudari*], and principles that characterize a particular phrase [*kotoba*]. These principles are found even in the finest details and are extraordinary in their perfection.[1]

This statement immediately sets Hiromichi's critical approach apart from previous interpretations, because it implies that *Genji* is the product of literary craftsmanship from elements of greatest scale to smallest detail. In earlier sections of the "General Remarks," Hiromichi affirms Norinaga's argument that *Genji* is a superior work of literature that deserves careful reading and analysis. However, as we have also seen from Hiromichi's application of the *mono no aware* theory to the text, Norinaga's argument emphasizes the lyric temperament of the author at the expense of addressing the complexity of her compositional technique. As a result, Norinaga's *mono no aware* theory is most successful at providing a critique of *Genji* when it is applied to the work as an organic whole in terms of its artistic conception. Where this theory encounters rough edges associated with *Genji*'s complex narrative structure, it begins to fray and wear thin. Conversely, Hiromichi's interpretive theory provides a reading strategy that embraces and accounts for these same structural complexities.

In laying the foundation for his interpretive theory, Hiromichi explains that the complexity of *Genji* can be more easily appreciated when it is viewed as the product of compositional techniques governed by a consistent set of rules or principles. However, it should be pointed out that this assertion does not diminish his interest in appreciating *Genji* as an organic whole. He never suggests that his interpretive approach is meant to supplant Norinaga's *mono no aware* theory, nor does his assessment imply that *Genji* is simply the product of a formulaic application of certain rules. In fact, he points to the skillful application of these principles throughout the monogatari as further evidence of the author's extraordinary compositional talent. His discussion of specific compositional principles as they appear in the "Main Text" often concludes with a brief remark emphasizing that this principle is simply another example of the author's remarkable "use of the brush" (*imijiki fudezukai*).[2]

While Hiromichi believed that the presence of certain compositional principles was objective fact, he also realized that such literary sophistication would remain largely unappreciated without some guidance on the part of a commentator and diligence on the part of the reader. As a result, he places as much emphasis on reminding the reader to pay close attention to the text as he does to identifying specific principles of composition. His analysis concerning the principles of composition both in the "General Remarks" and the "Main Text" often concludes with a phrase such as, "One should take this into consideration and carefully read the monogatari so as to appreciate it," or "This is a remarkable example of a principle of composition; one should read the monogatari carefully to appreciate such things."[3] The frequent appearance of this rhetorical device suggests that the ultimate purpose of his principles of composition theory is to demonstrate how much is missed if one fails to pay close attention when reading *Genji*. In this sense, he is following the broad interpretive goal set by Norinaga of carefully reading the text to discover its literary qualities, yet he pursues this goal in a much more practical and systematic way.

Hiromichi's application of his theory of the principles of composition to *Genji* takes place in three distinct sections of the *Hyōshaku*. First, he continues from the passage translated earlier with an explanation of the way in which the principles of composition apply to the overall structure of *Genji*. Here he argues that seemingly unrelated incidents and gaps in the structure of *Genji* can be explained by reading the text in terms of its principles of composition. Second, he provides a list of specific terms related to the principles of composition and defines each term. This material is presented in a section titled, "Explanatory Notes for the Commentary and Criticism That Appear in the Headnotes [to the main text]," which directly follows his "General Remarks" on commentary and criticism.[4] Third, he applies the theory of the principles of composition to his annotation and interpretive commentary throughout the "Main Text" of the *Hyōshaku*. This chapter will attempt to integrate Hiromichi's theory as it is presented in all three areas of the *Hyōshaku*. The goal of this approach is to provide a synoptic analysis of Hiromichi's interpretive theory.[5]

"PRINCIPLES OF COMPOSITION" AND THE STRUCTURE OF *GENJI* AS A WHOLE

Despite the fact that Hiromichi's detailed commentary on the "Main Text" is only available to us for the first eight of *Genji*'s fifty-four chapters, his comments regarding the principles of composition demonstrate that his conclusions are based on a thorough analysis of the work as a whole. He begins his discussion of the overall structure of *Genji* as follows:

> In speaking of principles that apply to *Genji* as a whole, there are the lengthwise threads [*tate*, "warp"] of the passage of generations, years, and months and the crosswise threads [*nuki*, "weft"] of events in the lives of the characters that form the grand design [*omomuki*] of the monogatari. In terms of the passage of generations and time, as I have mentioned briefly before, one can speak as follows: As a stable base, we have the passage of time, primarily marked in the form of imperial reigns from the Kiritsubo Emperor to the Suzaku Emperor to the Reizei Emperor, to the present Emperor, Kinjō. . . . The corresponding divisions between the depiction of the rise and fall of Genji's fortunes and the passage from one imperial reign to the next, as mentioned above, constitute a principle of composition [in the tale]. The lives of various characters can also generally be compared and their ages calculated relative to each other. This is also a principle of composition.[6]

In commentaries as early as Fujiwara Teika's *Okuiri*, from the early thirteenth century, we find traces of an attempt to define the structure of *Genji* in terms of certain "series" or "groupings" of chapters—*narabi*.[7] Yotsutsuji Yoshinari's compilation of commentary on *Genji*, the *Kakaishō* (1363), includes brief notes indicating that the "Hahakigi" and "Utsusemi" chapters form a single unit, while the "Yūgao" chapter marks the beginning of another series. These chapters are considered "vertical series" (*tate no narabi*) because they depict events in chronological sequence. The "Suetsumuhana," "Yomogiu," and "Sekiya" chapters are considered "units that run on the perpendicular" (*ikkō ni yoko no narabi*) to these chapters because they depict events chronologically disjointed from surrounding chapters. The *Kakaishō* refers to the "Tamakazura" chapter as being a hybrid horizontal-vertical chapter because it contains elements that are chronologically related to surrounding chapters as well as elements depicted in retrospect from other parts of the story.[8] Later commentaries, such as the *Kachōyosei* (1472) and the *Sairyūshō* (1528), repeat this information with little variation or development.[9] Kamo no Mabuchi criticized these attempts at providing a structural interpretation in terms of horizontal and vertical units in his *Genji monogatari shinshaku*. He found that there were too many contradictions created by the theory for it to be of use as an interpretive strategy. In quoting from Mabuchi's *Shinshaku*, Hiromichi concludes that in many cases Mabuchi's criticism is justified, but he adds that the strategy should not be abandoned altogether.[10]

Hiromichi appears to have taken the concern for narrative continuity found in *pingdian* criticism and combined it with the traditional concept of horizontal and vertical chapter series to create a new metaphor for describing the overall structure of *Genji*. The fundamental connection between chronology and events in the narrative described by Hiromichi in the previous quotation may seem simplistic, but it serves his purpose well. In fact, contemporary critical theory in the West tends to define the basic elements of narrative along similar lines.

> Narrative is a verbal presentation of a sequence of events or facts (as in *narratio* in rhet. and law) whose disposition in time implies causal connection and point.[11]

As we saw in chapter 3, Hiromichi resisted the efforts of previous commentators to limit the meaning of *Genji* by allowing ideological concerns to dominate literary interpretation. Employing the metaphor of vertical and horizontal threads, he is able to account for the overall structure of *Genji* in a practical and systematic way without imposing an interpretation that is somehow contradictory or overly restrictive.

A cursory examination of the chronological structure and major events in the monogatari reveals that a meaningful pattern does emerge from their comparison. The overall chronology, viewed in terms of the passage of Imperial reigns, can be divided as follows:

> I. Chapters 1–8 ("Kiritsubo" to "Hana no En") are set in the reign of the Kiritsubo emperor.
>
> II. Chapters 9–14 ("Aoi" to "Miotsukushi") are set in the reign of the Suzaku emperor.
>
> III. Chapters 15–35 ("Yomogiu" to "Wakana-Ge") are set in the reign of the Reizei emperor.
>
> IV. Chapter 36 ("Kashiwagi") and on are set in the reign of the Kinjō emperor.

If we consider the four emperors in terms of their relations with Genji, it becomes clear that the Kiritsubo emperor (Genji's father) and the Reizei emperor (Genji's son) have familiar, sympathetic relationships with Genji, while the Suzaku emperor (Genji's half-brother and rival), the Kinjō emperor (son of Suzaku), and those closest to them are less likely to relate to Genji sympathetically. This dynamic of alternating sympathetic and unsympathetic reigns can then be factored into the overall chronology of the narrative. Based on Hiromichi's interpretation, we can summarize the vicissitudes of Genji's adult life in terms of the following four chapters and the key events that occur within them:

A. Events of the "Momiji no Ga" (7) chapter in which Fujitsubo, the emperor's consort, gives birth to Genji's son. The child eventually becomes the Reizei emperor, foreshadowing Genji's ultimate rise in stature to a position appropriate to the "father" of the emperor.[12]

B. Events of the "Suma" (12) chapter, in which Genji is forced to leave the capital and Murasaki to live in exile.[13]

C. Events of the "Fuji no Uraba" (33) chapter in which Genji is accorded the honorary title "Retired Emperor."[14]

D. Events of the "Minori" (40) chapter, in which Murasaki dies.[15]

The rise and fall of Genji's fortunes roughly correspond to the alternating sympathetic and unsympathetic Imperial reigns: the events of A fall within period I, the events of B fall within period II, and so on. However, this pattern only holds true for the structure of *Genji* on its largest scale. In terms of minor events, the two patterns do not overlap precisely. According to Hiromichi's metaphor, this is because they constitute two different types of threads in terms of the overall structure of the monogatari.

The complex dynamic between the narrative's chronological structure and the vicissitudes of Genji's fortunes provides the foundation for plausibility and verisimilitude in this fictional narrative. It is this dynamic that gives the rise and fall of Genji's fortunes an air of reality and unpredictability rather than the appearance of being a lesson in moral consequence. Genji's successes are augmented by favorable conditions set in motion by a sympathetic Imperial reign during some periods. The state of affairs, social standing, and psychological state of the story's main character thus work in concert to produce positive results for Genji at these points in the narrative. Similarly, selfish and irresponsible actions during unsympathetic reigns yield negative and inhospitable developments in the narrative fabric of the tale.

The consequences of each action, viewed individually, cannot be as easily explained. Even during sympathetic reigns, Genji's actions sometimes fail to meet with success. There is no fixed principle governing his actions or their consequences, just as we at times benefit and at other times suffer from the lack of certainty in the real world. However, the complex dynamic between the chronological flow of the monogatari and the experiences and actions of Genji's life prevents this lack of certainty from decaying into an arbitrary series of events. In terms of the overall structure of the monogatari, it makes sense that things go well for Genji at some points in the story, and that the tide turns against him at other points, because we must consider not only Genji's intentions and his actions but also the changes in his situation and environment as symbolized by the succession of Imperial reigns. Points at which Genji's irresponsible actions occur under a sympathetic reign or, conversely, he acts more responsibly during an unsympathetic reign represent less intense patterns in the fabric of monogatari. One could say that the forces working for and against Genji tend to cancel each other out in such places. These less dramatic points in the monogatari provide contrast and context for the more intense points where the forces of time and circumstance converge, elevating Genji to the height of success and later lowering him to the depths of failure.

This view of the overall structure allows us to understand why Hiromichi was able to reject earlier interpretations that imposed a single meaning on the entire work. *Genji* is more than simply a moral allegory or the portrayal of a fictional world designed to engage the sympathies of the reader—as Tameakira and Norinaga would have us believe. The characters and story depicted in *Genji* are too complex and, in some respects, too realistic to fit completely within such abstract notions. Hiromichi provides his theory of the principles of composition as a map to guide readers in exploring and comprehending the complexities of the narrative rather than reducing the entire work to a single meaning.

GAPS IN THE NARRATIVE AND HIROMICHI'S THEORY OF AMBIGUITY

The sophistication of Hiromichi's insight into the overall structure of *Genji* becomes even more apparent as he turns his attention to gaps in the chronological progression of the narrative. He points out that gaps in the narrative description constitute principles of composition at work. To arrive at the events depicted in the final chapter of *Genji*, some seventy-five years after Genji's birth, while at the same time maintaining internal consistency between the ages of Genji and other characters, it is inevitable that the description of some events be left out of the text. To elaborate upon Hiromichi's metaphor of fabric and threads, it is as if the narrative fabric has been folded in certain places. Readers can see where certain narrative threads begin and end and can guess at the pattern in between but are unable to see the material that the author has folded over and thus put out of sight in order to allow the story to move at a reasonable pace. Hiromichi's comment that follows stresses the fact that the author's aesthetic accomplishment lies not only in knowing how to weave the fabric of narrative but also which parts to display and which to hide from view:

> Within this [system of lengthwise and crosswise threads] there are always years that are a blank [for which we don't know what happens because nothing is described]. This is a principle [*nori*] of the monogatari. The approximately fifty years of Genji's life from the time of his birth are described in the fifty-four chapters of the monogatari. . . . In the case of the Uji chapters, the appropriate age of Niou no Miya can be determined based on Kaoru's age. This is also a principle of composition. Having established this structure, there are various prin-

> ciples of composition by which design is added to the telling of narrative threads that cross over the base threads of the passage of time [*nuki ni ayadorite katariyuku*].[16]

As mentioned earlier, Motoori Norinaga showed little interest in searching for compositional techniques at work in *Genji*. However, the one aspect of Hiromichi's principles of composition theory that closely follows Norinaga's work concerns time, age, and chronological continuity. Norinaga was very concerned with correcting errors made by previous commentaries in the calculation of Genji's age throughout the various chapters of the monogatari. Hiromichi shares this concern and often includes quotations from Norinaga's detailed computation of Genji's age in the introductory remarks for individual chapters in the *Hyōshaku*.[17] Because there are no specific references made to Genji's age between his coming-of-age ceremony in the first chapter and the passing reference to his becoming forty years old in the thirty-third chapter ("Fuji no Uraba"), close attention must be paid to the internal consistency and chronological continuity of the narrative if one wishes to properly calculate Genji's age.[18] Hiromichi's interest in the chronological gaps revealed by such an examination probably arose from performing these painstaking calculations and evaluating the detailed calculations made by Norinaga and previous commentators.

The chronological gap in the monogatari that has drawn the most attention is the absence of a scene depicting Genji's death. In the "Maboroshi" chapter, Genji reflects on the life of Lady Murasaki, mourns her death, and begins preparations for his own departure from the world. The following chapter, "Niou no Miya," begins with a reference to the fact that Genji has already died. To explain the absence of a death scene, commentators before Hiromichi often theorized that a chapter between the "Maboroshi" and "Niou no Miya" chapters (the forty-first and forty-second chapters in modern editions) once existed and was subsequently lost. This chapter came to be known by a euphemistic title referring to the death of an exalted person, "Kumogakure" ("hidden among the clouds").

Speculation regarding the existence of such a chapter seems to have begun very early in the history of *Genji* commentary. One of the first extant commentaries, the *Shimeishō* (ca. 1289), addresses this issue with the inclusion of a remark indicating that a "Kumogakure" chapter was not originally part of *Genji*.[19] Hiromichi follows the conclusion suggested by the *Shimeishō* and further argues that the author consciously avoided including a "Kumogakure" chapter in the monogatari. For Hiromichi, the decision not to include such details epitomizes the author's skillful application of a principle of composition that he calls "ellipsis" (*shōhitsu*).

> Among the finest examples [of principles of composition in terms of the larger structure of the monogatari] is the "Kumogakure" Chapter. We have a title for this chapter, but the author omitted the entire text of the chapter itself. This fact alone is most remarkable.

> Among all the works of Japanese and Chinese literature, from times past and present, there is no other work that employs such an extraordinary compositional technique [*fudezukai no imijiki sho wa hoka ni mata aru koto nashi*]. This is a remarkable example of the compositional principle of "ellipsis" [*shōhitsu*].
>
> In spite of this, there have been various commentaries that absurdly apply Buddhist theories [concerning missing works of scripture] to lament the loss of a "Kumogakure" Chapter. There were even people who felt such an unendurable loss at not having access to the contents of a "Kumogakure" Chapter that they cobbled together a worthless text of their own and gave it the name "Kumogakure" to stand in for a missing chapter. Such efforts betray a total lack of appreciation for the mind of the author and are thoroughly disagreeable.[20]

Hiromichi points to five different aspects of the text to substantiate his claim that the omission of a "Kumogakure" chapter epitomizes the complete artistic vision of the author.

First he argues that the author deliberately created a structural symmetry between the "Kiritsubo" chapter and the "Maboroshi" chapter to mark the beginning and end of Genji's role as the central character in the monogatari. Specifically he notes that in the first chapter Genji's mother, Lady Kiritsubo, dies, and Genji's father, the "Kiritsubo" emperor, utters a poem alluding to the loss of Emperor Xuanzang's beloved concubine Yang Guifei and the "wizard" who the emperor calls upon to find her in the netherworld from Bai Juyi's (772–846) narrative poem "The Song of Everlasting Sorrow" (*Ch'ang Hen Ge*; J: *Chōgonka*) as an expression of his grief. Following these events we encounter the scene in which the Korean physiognomist predicts the young *Genji*'s rise to a position of power. In the forty-first chapter, Genji's wife and greatest love, Lady Murasaki, has recently died, and Genji, having ascended to a position virtually equal to that of emperor, utters a poem alluding to the same poem and the same wizard that his father referred to in the first chapter. Genji thus marks the conclusion of his life, and presence in the monogatari, by uttering a poem in response to the one uttered by his father at the beginning of his life.[21] This theory is persuasive, because it makes the point that even without a chapter describing Genji's death, the story of his life maintains a structural balance in terms of its opening and concluding chapters.

Second, Hiromichi points out that the last poem associated with Genji in the "Maboroshi" chapter seems to be a final poem of the type one utters before dying (*Genji no kimi no jisei mekitaru uta*). By including this poem, the author allows Genji to indicate that he is emotionally prepared to leave this world.[22]

Third, Hiromichi praises the author for presenting the story of Genji's life in a way that is believable and aesthetically pleasing at the same time. He points out that the beginning of the "Niou no Miya" chapter clearly indicates that Genji has died and the story is about to move on to the activities of his heirs. He continues by arguing that in other fictional works, both Japanese and Chinese, the story usually comes to an end with a lengthy description of the central character's great prosperity. Hiromichi comments that this technique leaves the reader with the feeling of a contrived and an artless conclusion. On the other hand, Murasaki Shikibu allows her fictional tale to move toward a more credible ending. Genji's prosperity reaches its zenith in the "Fuji no Uraba" chapter (the thirty-third chapter). After this the monogatari turns to a description of some of the consequences of his earlier actions (*hōō*) and a decline in his circumstances. Hiromichi writes that by not including a lavish description of Genji's death, but rather omitting the scene altogether, the author avoids creating the slightest impression that this is an exaggerated or a fictional tale, leaving the reader to think that this is a story that actually could have taken place (*isasakamo tsukuri koto mekitaru koto naku, jitsu ni arishi koto goto oboete*).[23]

Fourth, Hiromichi considers the absence of a "Kumogakure" chapter from the opposite perspective. He notes that previous commentaries have tried to explain the omission of a scene depicting Genji's death by arguing that Murasaki Shikibu wished to avoid having to describe the boundless grief that all the other characters would doubtless experience at such an event. Rather than depict such an immense outpouring of grief, the author chose to conclude the story by portraying Genji as he mourns the loss of his greatest love.[24] Hiromichi thus credits the omission of a "Kumogakure" chapter with helping to maintain the deliberately refined tone of *Genji*. He expands on the conclusion offered by earlier commentaries to argue that the inclusion of a "Kumogakure" chapter would have forced the author to resort to an excessive description of grief and sorrow that would have detracted from the overall grace and restrained emotional tenor of the work.

Fifth, Hiromichi argues that the ambiguity of Genji's death is echoed in the ambiguity of the final chapter of the entire monogatari, *Yume no Ukihashi* ("The Floating Bridge of Dreams"). By interpreting the work structurally, it becomes possible to see that the main romantic heroes of the final ten chapters, Kaoru and Niou (referred to in the quotation that follows as "Niou no Miya"), represent the lingering presence of Genji in the story. He concludes his argument on this point as follows:

> In general, Genji's character is described as being somewhat self-centered, but he is also very sensitive to the feelings of others. He is deeply moving as both a colorful, expressive character and as an [introspective,] serious character. This is one of the things that makes him the central character of the monogatari. In terms of the principles of composition, Genji's presence lingers on [*nagori*; lit. is an aftereffect] in the story in the form of two characters: Kaoru and Niou no Miya. Kaoru, even more than Genji, is a subdued and

> moving figure. Niou no Miya is depicted as representing the more flamboyant and flirtatious side of Genji. . . . In order to distinguish between the motivations [*kokorobae*] of these characters it was as if she had entered into each character's heart and mind [*kokoro*] and was writing from that perspective. This is a most unusual and indescribably wonderful [technique].[25]

Hiromichi bases this argument on the notion that Genji is so strongly missed that the series of chapters following his death is shaped by a reluctance to see him vanish from the story. Therefore, Kaoru and Niou can be understood collectively as a "lingering presence" (*nagori*) or memento of Genji himself. Because Genji is the true main character of the monogatari, it is fitting that neither Kaoru or Niou should match him in emotional range or complexity. Instead, each represents a complementary dimension of his character. However, Hiromichi also points out that Murasaki Shikibu took pains to develop Kaoru and Niou as vivid, complex personalities in their own right, not merely as shallow reflections of Genji's character in the earlier chapters.

Because Kaoru and Niou stand in for Genji in the final section of the monogatari, it is only fitting that the conclusion of their story match the ambiguity surrounding Genji's final appearance in earlier chapters. This explanation points to an important structural link between the early chapters depicting Genji's life and the final chapters, centering on the lives of Kaoru and Niou. It also provides Hiromichi with an opportunity to expand upon his argument concerning the deliberate use of ambiguity in the construction of the monogatari.

Hiromichi points out that just as some readers composed a "Kumogakure" chapter to fill in for what was thought to be a missing description of Genji's death, others have imagined that a concluding chapter to the monogatari had also been lost. In its place they forged a final chapter, *Yamaji no Tsuyu* ("Dew of the Mountain Trail"), and then suggested that it was written by Murasaki Shikibu to bring closure to the tale.[26] He argues that it is understandable for readers to feel a sense of regret over the monogatari's coming to an end, but that to fabricate an additional chapter betrays a failure to appreciate the compositional artistry of the author.[27]

For Hiromichi, the structure of the monogatari in fifty-four chapters represents Murasaki Shikibu's complete artistic vision.[28] The principles of composition allow readers to appreciate this complexity in abstract terms. He also believes that they provide compelling reason to dismiss the notion that *Genji* is somehow marred by missing or incomplete chapters. In discussing the final chapter and the perfection of the overall structure of the tale, he writes:

> One can read *Genji* over and over again and never tire of it. There is no limit to the fascination to be found in this monogatari. Some people appended a chapter called "Yamaji no Tsuyu" because they felt dissatisfied with the monogatari's coming to an end. It is under-

> standable that they should feel this way, but adding a chapter betrays a lack of comprehension of the admirable intention of the author. The author has made use of the principle of composition known as "ellipsis" [*fude o habuku nori*] not because she has wearied of describing things, but because there are places that she feels are best omitted. The text of this monogatari is very detailed and complete [as it is]. In common speech we would say that with such perfection "one can scratch all the places that itch" [*kayuki tokoro e te no todoku yō naru sama nareba*]. When one starts out reading, it seems that *Genji* is quite long, but upon reaching this succinctly written ending, one realizes that the author consciously avoided writing any more than was necessary. This approach could not have been thought up by anyone other than Murasaki Shikibu.[29]

These remarks point to what is arguably the most significant unique aspect of Hiromichi's interpretive theory. A close analysis of *Genji*'s overall structure and literary style led him to the conclusion that it was not only what was written that determined the literary sophistication of the text but also what was omitted from the story. This principle applies to the description of major events as well as the composition of minor scenes. For Hiromichi, Murasaki Shikibu's mastery of the art of descriptive understatement was a sign of her creativity, reserve, and aesthetic sensibility. Her omission of certain details was an exercise in compositional virtuosity, because she had created a space in the narrative structure that allowed for the description of these details, but she chose not to reveal them directly to the reader.

The reader's imagination thus becomes engaged in filling in the gaps planted by the author in the perceptible pattern of the narrative. Hiromichi saw this technique as an important factor in the reader's response to the text. Readers who felt a sense of engagement with the text were likely to enjoy reading and re-reading it because it was sophisticated enough to repeatedly satisfy their curiosity and stimulate their imagination. In essence, Hiromichi formulated the basic points underpinning an aesthetics of ambiguity. He notes that through the skillful construction of narrative and careful omission of details, the author is able to construct a story with just enough left to the imagination that the reader is enticed to read more and to read again.

From a different perspective, one might conclude that Hiromichi's discussion of the principles of "ellipsis" and gaps in the narrative points to an appraisal of Murasaki Shikibu's economical use of description and language. Henry James had a similar technique in mind, which he referred to as "foreshortening," in his discussion of the modern novel. In stressing the close relationship between foreshortening and the artful composition of fiction, James concluded:

> The secret of "foreshortening"—the particular economic device for which one must have a name and which has in its single blessedness and its determined pitch, I think, a higher price than twenty other

> clustered loosenesses; and just because the full-fed statement, just because the picture of as many of the conditions as possible made and kept proportionate, just because the surface iridescent, even in the short piece, by what is beneath it and what throbs and gleams through, are things all conductive to the only compactness that has charm, to the only spareness that has a force, to the only simplicity that has a grace—those, in each order, that produce the *rich* effect.[30]

James refers to an author's failure to carefully and completely execute an idea or a theme in his composition of a novel as "looseness." For James, the technique of "foreshortening" was crucial to creating a sophisticated and compelling work of literature. Foreshortening was so important that its absence could not be compensated for by the correction of twenty "loosenesses" of execution or the brilliant turn of phrase. Similarly, Hiromichi points to Murasaki Shikibu's economical use of detail and language as a key element of her compositional technique. While he praises the author for her skillful execution of literary themes (allegory, for example) and incorporation of beautiful language, he finds that the principle of ellipsis plays an even more fundamental role in the creation of an engaging and artistically compelling work of fiction. Where James relies on lofty and exacting language in the previous quotation to express this idea, Hiromichi resorts to metaphors and familiar language to express the significance of this technique. Indeed, *Genji* can be said to produce what James called a certain *rich* effect, but it better served Hiromichi's purpose to suggest that this technique was instrumental in allowing the reader to discover an almost physical pleasure in carefully reading the text.

TECHNIQUES AND TERMINOLOGY

Having established the relationship between his principles of composition theory and interpretation of the overall structure of *Genji* in his "General Remarks," Hiromichi devotes an additional section to discussing the major terms that form the basis of his interpretive approach. While most of the terms featured in his interpretive theory would have been familiar to readers from other contexts, he includes definitions for each term, as if providing entries in a dictionary. The effect of this approach is to remove any sense of the esoteric from his interpretive strategy. Even in the case of terms that might seem self-evident to the careful reader, Hiromichi provides a definition so that anyone who reads the *Hyōshaku* can approach the text with the same understanding of these critical terms.

The section that follows his "General Remarks" to the *Hyōshaku* begins with an introduction to the terms that form the basis for his principles of composition theory:

> Among our writings in Japan there is almost no criticism of literary style [*bunshō*]. Most of the critical techniques on literary style are

> found here for the first time. Therefore I have followed the practice from China as I have explained earlier in this text. I have provisionally given names to the critical terms that follow. These terms are only for the beginning student of *Genji*. Some terms are taken from the Chinese. Some are taken from previous *Genji* commentaries. Some are developed by me and are being used for the first time here. All of them are designed to make it easy to understand the text. So it is not that I'm particularly set on using Chinese principles. Dear reader, please keep this in mind and be not suspicious of my methods.[31]

Hiromichi then provides an annotated list of the terms that figure prominently in his analysis of *Genji*. Occasionally he makes a distinction as to whether these terms apply to narrative segments (such as chapters, scenes, or phrases), the dynamic between two characters, or the function of inanimate objects. However, in practice, many of the terms refer to the relationship between not only characters but also narrative segments and inanimate objects. For example, the first term to be defined, relating to the dynamic between major and minor elements (*shukaku*), is applied at various points in the *Hyōshaku* to the relationship between major and minor characters in the story, major and minor chapters in terms of their relationship to the overall structure of the narrative, and the dynamic between two events or elements in the story.

The rest of this chapter is devoted to an examination of specific terms associated with Hiromichi's principles of composition. Each entry in this section begins with a translation of his definition of a term or a set of terms that are similar in function. This translation is followed by an analysis that incorporates Hiromichi's explanation and illustrative examples from the tale as a whole. Analysis is combined with information concerning the appearance of similar terms in works likely to have informed his critical approach to the tale. In translating these terms, I have occasionally relied on the nomenclature of structural criticism and narratology developed in relation to literary theory in the West.[32] In translation, the familiar nomenclature signals a precocious sense of modernity. However, the greater significance of Hiromichi's insights resides in his definition of these terms and their application to *Genji*. For this reason, I rely on Hiromichi's original terminology in Japanese rather than equivalents in translation where possible.

"PRINCIPLES OF COMPOSITION" UNIQUE TO THE *HYŌSHAKU* IN *GENJI* COMMENTARY

"Major and Minor" or "Principal and Auxiliary" Characters (*Shukaku*)

> In cases where there are two characters [who regularly appear together or in related circumstances during the course of the story], the more important character is referred to as the host and the one that serves

> the host is called the guest. The importance of this principle varies from one section of the text to the next. There are also [cases where the relationship between] chapters and paragraphs follow this principle. One should keep this principle in mind [when reading the text].[33]

The term *shukaku*—alternatively written with characters for master and guest *shuhin*—appears in the commentary edition of the *Sanguo yanyi* (J: *Sangoku engi*, Romance of the Three Kingdoms, preface, 1680), a work of narrative fiction in 120 chapters that was widely read in both China and Japan. The commentator of this edition, Mao Zonggang (J: Mō Shūkō, 1632–1709?), is considered one of the most influential editor-commentators of the *pingdian* tradition in China.[34] The term can also be found in the postscript to the ninth volume of Bakin's work of popular fiction, *Hakkenden*. Mao Zonggang, Bakin, and Hiromichi all use the term in their commentaries primarily to describe the relationship between a major character (*shu*) who is central to the development of the story and a minor character (*kaku* or *kyaku*) who in some way assists or supports the major character.

For the most part, Genji takes on the role of the major character in the narrative. However, Hiromichi points out that there is a certain pleasure for the reader in coming across the occasional scene in which Genji's role unexpectedly shifts from that of host character to guest character. For example, in the famous scene of the "rainy night conversation," found in the "Hahakigi" chapter, Sama no Kami (Captain of the Guards of the Left) has a long discourse on the different types of women men encounter in life. During this speech, Genji begins by asking Sama no Kami leading questions. This briefly continues, and then Genji falls asleep, allowing Sama no Kami to take on the role of the major character. In this scene the dynamic of Genji as the lead character and Tō no chūjō as his supportive companion is set aside, and in its place we have Sama no Kami taking the lead role, while Genji takes on a supporting role. Hiromichi comments on this scene in the following manner:

> The scene in which these two characters [Sama no Kami and Tō Shikibu no Jō] appear is extremely unusual. It would be tiresome simply to have Genji and Tō no Chūjō forever paired up so these two characters are added and the scene becomes a little more lively. However, it is amusing and unusual that Genji, who is usually the host character [*shu*], should play the part of the guest character [*kaku*] while Sama no Kami takes the part of host. It is only in the "rainy night conversation" that Sama no Kami takes the role of host character. Such an unexpected description is quite extraordinary.[35]

In terms of the reader's sense of the flow of the story, it is not so unusual that Sama no Kami should become the speaker and Genji the listener. However, when viewed in terms of the structure of the narrative, it is quite surprising to have a scene in which the character whom we have come to expect to play the lead should suddenly begin to play a supporting role to a minor character. However, if the characters in the story were never to act contrary to our expectation, then the story would lack a sense of excitement and variety. The implication of Hiromichi's remark here is that it is enjoyable to read the story, precisely because there are changes in narrative technique that the reader does not anticipate. Ordinarily readers would remain unaware of such a subtle shift in narrative structure, but through Hiromichi's adept application of the principles of composition, they are able to perceive this narrative device at work. Such comments provide concrete evidence that the text must be read with great care to fully appreciate the range of compositional techniques employed by the author.

"Lead and Secondary Characters" (*seifuku*)

> In the case of the military, one has a chief general and vice general. The main one is considered to be the Chief General or *sei*. And the one who follows the general is called the Vice General or *fuku*. There are places where this principle becomes more or less prominent.[36]

The term *seifuku* is used to define more exactingly the *shukaku* dynamic explained in the previous entry. The paradigmatic *seifuku* relationship is between Genji and Tō no Chūjō where Genji is the lead or host character—*sei*—and Tō no Chūjō is the secondary or guest character—*fuku*. This dynamic helps establish that one character in the pair can be expected to take the lead in terms of the story's development, while the secondary character facilitates the events set in motion by the lead character. In some places, Tō no Chūjō takes on the role of Genji's rival rather than his secondary character. The heightened tension that naturally arises between the two characters in this dynamic thus provides for interesting developments in plot and characterization.

Hiromichi also points out that the dynamic between Genji and Tō no Chūjō is echoed in the final chapters of the monogatari in the relationship between Kaoru and Niou. However, this example becomes quite complex in nature. Hiromichi argues that the lead/secondary-character dynamic of Genji and Tō no Chūjō is echoed in the relationship between Kaoru and Niou, while at the same time, the personalities of Kaoru and Niou together represent the "lingering presence" of Genji's character—one might even say the lingering fragrance of Genji—in the monogatari following his death.[37]

"Corresponding" or "Contrasting" Characters (*seitai*)

> Characters or objects that have the same importance without one being superior to the other are called *seitai*. They can be understood as contrasting characters who are of equivalent rank. [There is no distinction in quality or importance made between the two partners in *seitai*.] The character for equal is replaced by the character for opposition in the next term, *hantai*.[38]

This term appears in *pingdian* commentaries on Chinese vernacular fiction. Hiromichi's familiarity with the term from Chinese criticism probably inspired him to include it as an entry in the *Hyōshaku*. While he refers to the concept in his "General Remarks," he does not use it in any of his discussions of specific characters in the "Main Text."

"Opposing" Characters or "Character Foils" (*hantai*)

> This relationship is one of opposition. For example, when it rains versus when it is clear or daylight versus nighttime, and so forth. While they are not equals, the two characters are related to each other as opposites.[39]

The term *hantai* can also be used to define more exactingly the *shukaku* dynamic. This term appears in *pingdian* commentaries and in Bakin's interpretation of fiction. The paradigmatic *hantai* relationship is between Genji and the crown prince (Kokiden's son). Another example Hiromichi cites of character foils is the relationship between Lady Murasaki and the inelegant character of Suetsumuhana, who is featured prominently in the sixth chapter.[40]

In terms of opposing characters or elements Hiromichi notes that the tension between two forces can become a source of plot development—a term he later defines as the principle of "the seed of a narrative thread" (*kusawai*). The example he cites comes from the relationship between the opposing factions of the Minister of the Left (Sa-Daijin, associated with Genji's first wife, Lady Aoi, and Tō no Chūjō) and the Minister of the Right (U-Daijin, associated with the crown prince and Kokiden).[41] Poor relations between these two factions become the fertile soil from which we see the growth of such major events as Genji's exile from the capital in chapter 12.

Hiromichi points out that the presence of a character foil can be used not only to provide motivation for plot development but also to shed light on certain aspects of a character's personality.[42] Henry James referred to a similar principle as the "antithesis of characters." In James's estimation, the "ideal" antithesis in which two characters represent polar opposites is appealing as a concept but rarely successful in execution.[43] Perhaps Murasaki Shikibu found the deployment of "ideal" opposites in *Genji* similarly difficult. The two clear examples of character foils that Hiromichi identifies in the *Hyōshaku*, Genji/Crown Prince and Murasaki/Suetsumuhana appear only occasionally throughout the monogatari.

"Retroactive Parallel" and "Retroactive Correspondence" (*shōtai* and *shōō*)

> These two are largely the same, but retroactive parallel denotes the appearance of analogous events. These events are similar just as the light of the sun and the moon are similar, yet they are rivals just as

> the light of the sun comes from the east while the light of the moon still shines in the west in the morning. Retroactive correspondence, on the other hand, denotes the conclusion of a matter that appeared earlier but for some reason lingers on in the story or has yet to come to a resolution. The narrative thread of this matter reappears and can be understood as corresponding to the meaning or significance of a previous event. This is similar to the way in which the moon and stars reflect light that has come from the sun.[44]

The term *shōō* can be found in Mao Zonggang's commentary on the *Sanguo yanyi* and Bakin's *Hakkenden*. Bakin notes that *shōō* is sometimes referred to as being analogous to *shōtai*.[45] However, Hiromichi's definition attempts to establish a fine distinction between the two terms. These two terms can be considered complementary terms to *fukuan* and *fukusen* (two methods of foreshadowing), which appear later in Hiromichi's list. While foreshadowing performs the function of showing us a glimpse of something that is to happen later in the story, *shōō* designates a correspondence with something that happened earlier in the story. *Shōtai* refers to a correspondence between things that exist as parallel, but not intersecting, events in the story. For example, near the end of the "Hana no En" chapter, there is a scene describing Genji's participation in a wisteria festival. Hiromichi remarks:

> The scene of the wisteria festival at the Minister of the Right's estate corresponds to the festival of the cherry blossoms at the Emperor's residence earlier in the story.[46]

In terms of the flow of the story, the connection between the two festival scenes in the "Hana no En" chapter seems purely coincidental, but in terms of the structure of the narrative, one scene clearly represents a repetition of the other. For Hiromichi, this repetition of festival scenes provides the opportunity for the author to put her compositional talents to the test. She allows for a chance encounter between Genji and the younger sister of his nemesis, Oborozukiyo, following both festival scenes. Following the first festival scene, Genji seduces Oborozukiyo but fails to learn her identity. After the second festival scene, he again encounters her. This time he uses his wit and ingenuity to discover her identity while keeping their liaison secret. What is most telling for Hiromichi is that the repetition of festival scenes allows the author to skillfully repeat poetic allusions in new and different ways to add depth to the narrative.[47]

"Retroactive correspondence," or *shōō*, on the other hand, refers to events that are more directly linked in terms of the story. For example, in the "Yūgao" chapter, when Genji first hears from Koremitsu of the lowly circumstances of the Lady Yūgao, he immediately thinks back to the "rainy night conversation" of several chapters earlier. During this conversation, Genji's companions discussed the attraction they felt for a woman whose life has brought her a certain amount of hardship. Genji's recollection of this scene prompts him to express an interest in meeting Lady Yūgao. This recollection of a past scene is described as "retroactive correspondence" by Hiromichi.

The principle of "retroactive correspondence" contributes to an interpretation of the text, because it allows readers to appreciate the way in which Genji's actions are influenced by previous events. The use of this technique thus contributes to the psychological depth of Genji's character and the realistic way in which the narrative structure provides for his character development.

In his interpretation of dreams, Freud discussed a similar relationship between two events, which he termed *nachträglichkeit* ("afterwardsness" or "retroactive meaning"). Freud noted that in the course of recalling two events from one's past, one event naturally precedes the other chronologically. In *nachträglichkeit*, there is something about the second event that so fundamentally defines or alters our understanding of the first event that it brings new meaning to our understanding of the first event. In psychological terms, Freud's analysis points to the fact that temporality is distinct from consciousness. In literary theory, the term *nachträglichkeit* has been used to define the way in which repetition functions as an essential element of narrative.[48] Based on Freud's theory of "retroactive meaning," it is possible to argue that each event in a narrative acts upon those events that have come before. In particular, the repetition of an event allows readers to anticipate the way in which certain actions will play out in a story. Repetition thus allows a reader to either confirm or challenge his or her expectations of the way the event should play out. From the perspective of the critic, repetition provides the opportunity for the author to improvise in recycling the same images or story elements. Hiromichi's identification of the principles "retroactive parallel" and "retroactive correspondence" points to ways in which Murasaki Shikibu consistently relies on certain compositional techniques to refer back to, or recycle, images or details and to elaborate upon their original meaning as the narrative progresses.

"Narrative Interlude" (*kankaku*)

> There are cases in which the uninterrupted description of a single point would become too long and disturbing to the reader. To avoid offending the reader other details are inserted [into the narrative using the device of an "interlude" in the narration]. For example, in looking at a distant sea or mountain one sees intervening clouds and fog so that the view becomes more magnificent. This technique is often used in the middle of chapters.[49]

This term appears to have been developed by Hiromichi and does not have a direct precedent in *pingdian* commentary. The fact that Hiromichi applies the term to his interpretation of the "Main Text" only three times suggests that he had a specific incident in mind when he introduced this term in the *Hyōshaku*. All three cases in which Hiromichi uses the term *narrative interlude* relate indirectly to Genji's illicit affair with Lady Fujitsubo.

The primary example of his use of the term *narrative interlude* can be found in the "Momiji no Ga" chapter.[50] Hiromichi notes that fundamentally this chapter concerns the illicit affair between Genji and Lady Fujitsubo. The fact that Fujitsubo is about to give birth to a child as a consequence of her affair with Genji is the major force behind the development of events in the chapter. Hiromichi argues that the scenes with young Murasaki and Aoi no Ue do not significantly affect the course of events in the story, but their insertion does provide a distraction from the more serious, and potentially disturbing, matter of Fujitsubo's pregnancy.

Curiously, Hiromichi does not refer to the comical scene near the end of the chapter in which the old maid, Naishi, throws herself at Genji in relation to his principle of "narrative interlude." Instead, he focuses on the mock battle scene set up by Genji and Tō no Chūjō to restore Naishi's honor as further evidence that the dynamic between Genji and Tō no Chūjō is one of "principal and secondary character" (*seifuku*).[51] Perhaps Hiromichi was attempting to follow Murasaki Shikibu's lead in choosing not to overemphasize the stark contrast that existed between the gravity of Genji's immoral affair with Fujitsubo and the frivolity of his farcical affair with Naishi.

"Foreshadowing" (*fukuan* and *fukusen*)

> These two are largely the same. The technique of *fukuan* takes into consideration the outcome of something while quietly revealing parts of it, but hiding the [general] fact of the matter. *Fukusen* consists of the character with the radical for thread, and as such the thread is buried up to a distant point while occasionally revealing it from time to time. When you reach the outcome it is as if you could pull on the end of the thread to move all of the stitches. This technique is also called "shitamae" [alternatively read as *kekkō*]. *Shitamae* [more broadly] refers to the placement of details which the author has planned in advance.[52]

In *Hakkenden* Bakin provides examples of the terms *fukuan* and *shinsen*, then compares the two and explains the subtle differences between them.[53] Here Hiromichi seems to be applying the same distinction between the terms *fukuan* and *fukusen*. *Fukuan* is foreshadowing in which an element of the larger plot of the story is hidden within a small detail of the narrative in such a way that until the reader has a clear understanding of the larger plot, the significance of this detail cannot be appreciated. For example, in the "Kiritsubo" chapter of the *Hyōshaku*'s "Main Text," we find the following commentary by Hiromichi on the passage describing the Korean fortune-teller:

> This passage consists of an extremely skillful use of the technique of "foreshadowing" [*fukuan*] in which everything that will happen to Genji in his lifetime is thought of and made to be foretold by the Korean physiognomist. Pay close attention here. First [at his birth] Genji's superior appearance is noted, then his outstanding ability is noted, and by the time we reach this passage the technique of hearsay is used to foretell of the sum of Genji's life. The poems that follow all build upon the aftereffect of this passage and are simply in praise of Genji's superiority of appearance and ability.[54]

In other words, due to the inspired planning by the author, Genji's illustrious future and superior ability are foreshadowed in this simple detail. Meanwhile, with the foreshadowing technique of *fukusen*, the reader is occasionally shown small portions of the thread of the story and its importance but cannot guess as to its connection with the larger plot until he or she reads to the end. The paradigmatic example of *fukusen* can be seen in the trope of the apparition that appears throughout the "Yūgao" chapter.

In the "Yūgao" chapter there are fifteen different passages that Hiromichi singles out as examples of the "narrative thread of the apparition" (*henge no suji*).[55] The majority of these passages refer to "fox spirits" in one way or another, and they do not seem to bear any great significance in terms of the larger events of the chapter. However, once one reads past the scenes in which Genji avoids visiting his old lover, Lady Rokujō, and ends up seducing the young and vulnerable Yūgao, the collective importance of the apparition trope becomes clear. The apparition is a manifestation of Lady Rokujō's jealous spirit. In the scene where Yūgao suddenly dies, Genji sees the figure of a beautiful woman hovering over her. The presence of Rokujō's avenging spirit is closely associated with Yūgao's untimely death. Collectively, these "threads" foreshadow the major event of the chapter, Yūgao's death. Based on this, Hiromichi interprets them as examples of the compositional principle he refers to as *fukusen*.

"Comparative Description" (*yokuyō*)

> *Yoku* is the part that is suppressed, while *yō* is the part that is emphasized. From this comes the strength of the description. For example, with a rice husker, to make the mallet head go up, the pedal is pressed firmly, so that when something is to be emphasized an earlier part is specifically suppressed.[56]

The paradigmatic example of *yokuyō* is the relationship between Genji and his rival, the crown prince. From the beginning of the monogatari, Genji is portrayed as possessing a beauty that makes the emperor especially fond of him. In contrast, the emperor's first son is clearly destined to become crown prince and therefore is held in high regard by all, despite the fact that he shows no remarkable talents or traits. The passage immediately following Genji's birth reads as follows:

> The newborn [Genji] was particularly beautiful and the Emperor went in haste to see his new son. The Emperor's first son was born of the daughter of the [powerful] Minister of the Right and was therefore said to be treated as heir apparent without challengers, but this [new] son was beautiful beyond compare. While the first son was given his due, the Emperor's affection for the new child, whom he took as his own, knew no limits.[57]

In this passage, Genji, whose appearance is described as being magnificent, and the crown prince, about whom we are given not a single concrete detail of his appearance, are both introduced. Hiromichi provides the following commentary for this passage:

> Establishing the relationship of *shukaku*, "major" and "minor" characters, this passage provides the first description of the future Suzaku Emperor. Furthermore, Genji and Kokiden are posited as "opposing characters" [*hantai*]. [This passage provides] the first description of the strained relationship between them. The Emperor's first born son's stature is praised and then surpassed by the description of the intense nature of the Emperor's affection for the young Genji using the method of "comparative description" [*yokuyō*] extremely well here.[58]

Within this simple description Hiromichi points to three different techniques of composition at work. He points out that the relationship between Genji and the crown prince is that of "major and minor characters," the relationship between Genji and Kokiden is one of "opposing characters," and that the technique of "comparative description" (*yokuyō*) is skillfully used to emphasize Genji's vast superiority over his closest rival, the crown prince. The technique of "comparative description" allows the author to emphasize Genji's superiority without having to resort to exaggerated language. The crown prince is described as being "heir apparent, without challengers." At first this would seem to be the highest position any of the emperor's offspring might hold. However, Genji's importance is immediately elevated to a position even higher than that of the crown prince by referring to the boundless affection the emperor feels toward him. The absence of any description of the emperor's feelings toward the crown prince only serves to reinforce the gap that exists between the two characters.

"Control of Narrative Pace" (*kankyū*)

> As indicated by the characters this is a method of description. In calm passages it is done calmly. For example, on a warm spring day a maiden walking through a field [typifies a calm pace]. In quick

> descriptions, [the narrative pace] is like the gathering of a typhoon. [The pace of description for] this technique changes according to the passage.[59]

Hiromichi does not apply this term in his commentary on the "Main Text." This probably indicates that he envisioned a scene in a later chapter for which this term might aptly apply. Due to the lack of empirical evidence relating to the term, it is difficult to draw any specific conclusions in relation to his overall interpretive strategy. However, it should be noted that for this term, and several of the terms that follow, Hiromichi relies on metaphor to explain the significance of the principle at hand. Often the image on which he relies is reminiscent of stage directions for a dramatic work. The use of such terminology and imagery was probably meant to engender a sense of recognition for the average reader who frequented dramatic productions and was likely familiar with such language. This technique points to the fact that Hiromichi was interested in reaching a wider, and less scholarly, audience in his commentary on *Genji*.

"Reversal" (*hampuku/uchikae*)

> A reversal of expected outcome. Designed to surprise the reader, it comes suddenly like an evening shower in the middle of a calm evening. The scene suddenly reverses so that the circumstances change drastically. The author does this specifically to surprise the reader with something he wasn't expecting. For example, one can imagine a calm, clear evening where suddenly the light of the moon becomes obscured. It begins to thunder heavily and there is a sudden rain shower.[60]

This term is derived from *pingdian* commentary. Hiromichi relies on it only occasionally in his commentary on the "Main Text." As with the aforementioned term he relies on vocabulary and images familiar to the general reader to define the principle of composition at hand.

"Ellipsis" (*shōhitsu*)

> In cases where the description would be too long, making it short and only telling the beginning and end thereby making the reader guess what came between. A second type of ellipsis is to have a character tell of something that has already happened outside the narrative to inform the reader of an event. Another case is where the author wishes to avoid [the discussion of] something troubling. These are all three called *shōhitsu*.[61]

The term *shōhitsu* can be found both in Mao Zonggang's commentary on the *Sanguo yanyi* and Bakin's *Hakkenden*. Hiromichi's treatment of the first type of "ellipsis" has been described earlier in this chapter in relation to theories concerning missing chapters in *Genji*. In this discussion Hiromichi emphasized the importance that ellipsis plays in contributing to the overall sophistication and appeal that *Genji* holds for readers. He argues that the skillful application of ellipsis allows Murasaki Shikibu to express the complete artistic vision of her story without weighing the reader down with excessive detail. In addition, his interpretation points to an underlying connection between the principle of ellipsis and the type of textual ambiguity that he associates with aesthetic sophistication.

To see an example of ellipsis, we can turn to the "Wakamurasaki" chapter. Here there is a scene where Genji catches a glimpse of the young Murasaki through a gap in a hedge and manages to overhear the conversation between young Murasaki and her grandmother, Amagimi. Hiromichi provides the following commentary for this scene:

> From the grandmother's speech, the status of young Murasaki's mother and father is revealed using the technique of "ellipsis" [*shōhitsu*]. The technique is remarkably well applied here.[62]

In other words, the technique of *shōhitsu* is used to relate the story of Murasaki's circumstances (her mother dead, her father having abandoned her to the care of the grandmother) rather than using direct narrative description. This allows for an extremely efficient transmission of Murasaki's circumstances to the reader without encumbering the pace of the narrative.

"Lingering Presence" or "Resonance" (*yoha*)

> Secondary events following a major event in the story that represent a reluctance to let the residue of an event fade away. After writing the description of a great scene, the author regrets allowing the scene to disappear so she extends the description. After a great wave has come crashing in and receded, the small, shallow waves and bits of foam that linger on the shore are called *yoha*—also read as *nagori*. The principle of *yoha* is like this [in the monogatari].[63]

This term is also found in *pingdian* commentary. Hiromichi uses it to great effect in his discussion of the final chapters of the monogatari in which Kaoru and Niou serve as reminders of Genji's presence in earlier chapters. This principle was discussed in relation to the overall structure of *Genji* earlier in this chapter.

"Narrative Seed" (*shushi* or *kusawai*)

> When there is a gap between stories [in the narrative] that is difficult to bridge this technique is used. For example, Wakamurasaki's sparrow or Onna San no Miya's Chinese cat.[64]

This term appears to have been developed by Hiromichi to better define the way in which Murasaki Shikibu used certain compositional techniques to propel the development of the story in *Genji*. In his discussion of the monogatari's overall structure, referred to earlier in this chapter, he cites the rivalry between the factions associated with the Minister of the Right and Minister of the Left as an important source of plot development and an example of the element of the "narrative seed." In the previous definition he cites two examples related to the continuity of plot on a smaller scale. Rather than propelling the story forward, these examples are used to lend a sense of continuity to sudden jumps or shifts in the narrative as certain story lines in the monogatari evolve.

The example of Wakamurasaki's sparrow refers to a scene in the "Wakamurasaki" chapter in which Murasaki as a young child is secretly observed from a distance by Genji. From Genji's perspective, Murasaki is described as playing with other children. There is not much to be learned about Murasaki from this perspective other than the details of her physical appearance. It is not until Murasaki begins to cry about a sparrow she has lost that the focus of the narrative shifts from Genji's remote perspective to a more intimate view that provides Genji and readers of the monogatari with important details concerning Murasaki's personal life. Murasaki's tears attract the attention of the serving women around her, and this in turn leads them into a discussion of her unfortunate circumstances. The sparrow thus serves as a transitional device that allows the focus of the narrative to naturally shift from one perspective to another.

The example of Onna San no Miya's Chinese cat refers to two incidents in the "Wakana" chapters (New Herbs, part 1 and 2) in which a cat serves as a transitional device that allows Kashiwagi's relationship with Onna San no Miya to develop as a seemingly natural outcome of events in the monogatari. In the "Wakana-Jo" (New Herbs, part 1) chapter, a mischievous cat gets caught in a cord and ends up moving a screen so that Kashiwagi is able to catch a glimpse of Onna San no Miya. In the following chapter, which picks up the story of Kashiwagi some three years later, a kitten playing in the royal chambers serves as a reminder to Kashiwagi of the earlier incident in which he caught his first glimpse of Onna San no Miya. This recollection renews his interest in Onna San no Miya and later in the chapter serves to explain his efforts to arrange a secret meeting with her. After he forces himself on Onna San no Miya, Kashiwagi has a dream in which a cat approaches him. In his dream, he gives the cat to Onna San no Miya. This dream symbolizes the dynamics of their sexual relationship and Onna San no Miya's conception of a child. In this case the "narrative seed" not only provides a sense of continuity through various chronological transitions in the narrative but also embeds a symbolic image into the telling of the relationship between the two lovers. This example concisely illustrates the way in which a compositional principle contributes to the literary sophistication of the monogatari.

"Retribution" (*hōō*)

> [Also read as *mukui*.] This is the result that arises from certain actions. Something happens as a result of an action on the part of a character. The result is appropriate to the action.[65]

This term is closely related to the consequences of one's actions in terms of the Buddhist principle of cause and effect (*innen*). In general, it is associated with the consequences of a sinful or negative action. Hiromichi distinguishes between the sense in which the results of a character's actions are a matter of social force, which he associates with allegory and Confucian didacticism, and the sense in which the results of are a matter of self-imposed suffering, which he associates with the principle of "retribution." In his treatment of "retribution" and "allegory" he labels the emotional duress experienced by Kashiwagi as an example of "retribution" for his earlier transgression of having an affair with Onna San no Miya, Genji's wife at the time.

"Allegory" (*fūyu*)

> Actually occurred events, layered on an event of the story. By including this event in the story the author attempts to show readers the consequences of an action. Through these two principles [*hōō* and *fūyu*] we can guess at what was going on in the mind of the author.[66]

"Retribution" and "allegory" are both terms that can be found in previous *Genji* commentaries. As discussed in chapter 3, Andō Tameakira argued in the *Shikashichiron* that the illicit affair between Genji and Fujitsubo was a central event of the monogatari, which was meant to provide readers with a moral lesson through the interpretation of its allegorical meaning. This theory profoundly influenced Hiromichi's discussion of allegory in the *Hyōshaku*. Hiromichi's predecessor, Motoori Norinaga, rejected Tameakira's notion that allegory played an important role in shaping the overall structure of *Genji* by attempting to produce counterexamples from the text. Hiromichi sides with Tameakira in this debate by pointing out that a compositional technique can only be considered based in allegory if it contains the element of ambiguity. In rejecting Norinaga's point-by-point refutation of the allegory theory, he points out that if the details in the text were to correspond exactly to a moral lesson, then the story being told could not be considered an allegory. Instead, such a text would be considered a didactic work of literature following the technique of censuring evil and encouraging good (*kanzen chōaku*). By the same token, he refuses to completely accept Tameakira's assertion that allegory is the defining concept of *Genji*. This point leads him to conclude that *Genji* is too complex and sophisticated to be reduced to the illustration of a single moral principle.

"Context" (*bunmyaku* and *gomyaku*)

> *Bunmyaku* is the so-called [narrative] vein or fiber that joins one sentence [*bunshō*] together with the next. *Gomyaku* is the fiber that links one word to another. The way in which the meaning of events in the story pass through these ["narrative] fibers" [*suji*] by virtue of their being connected is similar to [the way in which blood circulates through] the blood vessels connected throughout the human body. There is also the term fiber or "*suji*" that is used in reference to foreshadowing [*fukusen*], but this is a different fiber or thread.[67]

These terms play an important role in integrating Hiromichi's interpretive theory from its broadest scale of overall structure to the smallest nuance of language. Because they are intended to address such a wide range of issues, it is difficult to define them any more precisely than Hiromichi has just done. In many cases, he uses the general concept of "context" and the specific term *narrative fiber* to identify places in the text worthy of the reader's attention, such as the reappearance of a character in the story from a previous chapter. The principle of "context" might be defined as a miscellaneous term applying to a broad range of compositional techniques and flourishes that Hiromichi identifies to ensure that they do not escape the reader's attention.

One aspect of this definition that prompts speculation is the unusual use of anatomical terminology. Hiromichi mentions in his preface to the "General Remarks" that it was at the insistence of his close acquaintances that he set his observations on *Genji* to print. In chapter 2 it was noted that Hiromichi lectured on *Genji* at Tekijuku, the school for Dutch learning and Western medicine founded by his friend, Ogata Kōan. It is possible that the anatomically oriented definition he provides for the aforementioned term resulted from his experience lecturing on *Genji* at a school for medical studies. He may have found such language effective in lecturing to an audience at least partially composed of students familiar with medicine and anatomy. On the other hand, it may have been his students' familiarity with Western principles of anatomy and circulation that inspired him to define the compositional principles "context" in this way. Such theories are not likely to lead to conclusive argument, but it is interesting to note that even during the Edo period, criticism of classical Japanese literature may have begun to assimilate principles derived from Western learning through the nexus of private academies such as Tekijuku.

TERMS FROM PREVIOUS *GENJI* COMMENTARIES

The remaining terms defined by Hiromichi are all taken from previous *Genji* commentaries. However, Hiromichi, did not simply duplicate the explanations of previous commentaries. There are many cases in which he improves upon the way these terms were used by prior commentators.[68] Specifically, he attempts to provide definitions that can be applied to the text consistently. In translating the terms that follow, I occasionally add observations relating to the way in which Hiromichi's definition or use of a term differs from previous commentaries.

"Close Correspondence" (*shubi*)

> This term indicates a place [in the text] where the beginning and end of something [such as an event alluded to in another text] match well [without contradiction] so that it should really be called "the matching of beginning and end [*shubi sōō*]." But it has always been referred to simply as *shubi* ["beginning and end" in *Genji* commentary] so that is how I refer to it.[69]

Hiromichi uses this term in identifying allusions to other works that resonate well with material in *Genji*. His first example in the "Main Text" is the close correspondence between the tragic story of Yang Guifei in "The Song of Everlasting Sorrow" and the story of Lady Kiritsubo. References to Yang Guifei in the opening lines of the Kiritsubo chapter are easily identified but Hiromichi urges readers to appreciate how developments in *Genji* consistently echo those in the Chinese tale as the chapter continues to unfold.[70] He points out that such "close correspondence" is evidence of the author's careful planning and deliberate construction (*yōi*) of the narrative.

"Textual Parallelism or Intertextuality" (*ruirei*)

> Events or words for which similar or parallel instances can also be found in another work or works. This can also refer to quotations from poems. All of these cases are called *ruirei*. This is a term used in commentary [as a form of annotation].[71]

This term is largely used to identify material alluded to in other works. It is primarily used to provide annotation rather than interpretation.

"Planning" or "Discretion" (*yōi*)

> This is where the author's thoughtful anticipation of events [or details] of the story makes the narrative work well. In general, that is what *yōi* refers to. An example of *yōi* is where Utsusemi's actions [in the "Utsusemi" chapter] can be described as betraying a great preparedness of thought.[72]

As Hiromichi's definition demonstrates, it is difficult to distinguish, in structural terms, where the careful planning and forethought apparent in a narrative character's actions should be attributed to the qualities of the character and where they should simply be attributed to the overall structure of the narrative under the direct control of the author or narrator. Ultimately, of course, all of the qualities and actions of narrative characters are the product of the author's imagination. However, it is important to distinguish between characters endowed by the author with the ability to plan and carry out sophisticated plots and those characters who are too simple, naïve, or ineffectual to accomplish such feats. Sophisticated, effectual characters serve different functions from unsophisticated, ineffectual characters in terms of the movement of plot and development of psychological aspects of the narrative. To this end, Hiromichi often distinguishes between instances where the unfolding of events should be directly attributed to the sophisticated structure set up by the author rather than the cleverness of the fictional characters involved. He does this by distinguishing between "planning on the part of the author"—*sakusha no yōi*—and simply "planning [on the part of the character]"—*yōi*.

Henry James refers to a similar concept as "literary arrangement." He specifies that careful "literary arrangement" allows the author to avoid "looseness" of conception and execution that will sap the novel of its artistry and grace.[73] In many cases Hiromichi makes the same association by pointing to passages in which the principle of "planning" or "discretion" serves as evidence of Murasaki Shikibu's remarkable compositional skill.

"Authorial Intrusion" (*sōshiji*)

> This term denotes words in the text that are not consciously uttered by a character in the narrative [*monogatari*]. They are comments that come from a place outside the narrative. As the words of the person who is telling the story they are understood to be those of the author. Among passages of authorial intrusion, there are places where the author temporarily assumes the thoughts or feelings of a character in the narrative. There are also places where the author speaks for a character in the narrative. Actually, these words represent an intrusion of the author into the narrative. Close attention should be paid to these passages.[74]

In his study of authorial intrusion in *Genji*, Enomoto Masazumi notes that Hiromichi's definition of *sōshiji* appears to be the earliest example available of the term used in the sense in which it is used by modern *Genji* scholars. He notes that Hiromichi's definition displays a sophisticated understanding of the fact that the voices of author, narrator, and character in the story all exist independently of each other. Enomoto believes that Hiromichi's sophisticated understanding of the term resulted from his comprehensive comparison of different instances where authorial intrusion was used in the text in order to provide a definition that could be applied consistently to all instances without contradiction.[75]

"Aesthetic After-effect" and "Aesthetic Satisfaction" (*yokō/nioi* and *yojō*)

> *Yokō* should be read according to the [native] Japanese pronunciation *nioi* ["fragrance"]. It is a term used to express praise for those feelings arising from a passage whose praise cannot be expressed in words. *Yojō* refers to the conclusion of an event in the story in which boundless *aware* [poignancy] is involved and is felt by the reader. The source of both of these cannot be exactly indicated in the story. I have only brought up this term to indicate where such an abundance of expression as cannot be explained in words exists in the story.
>
> There are other terms, but I have only discussed the major examples here. Other examples of principles of composition should be considered in a similar manner as they appear in the commentary.[76]

Hiromichi's final comments emphasize two important points. One is that he wants readers to understand that the terms defined do not completely account for the artistic and aesthetic accomplishment of *Genji*. As his definition of *yokō* and *yojō* implies, there is a certain aspect to appreciating the work that remains beyond expression in words. He is able to point out areas of particular compositional mastery or literary style, but ultimately these passages can only be described as indicative of sublime beauty, beyond the limits of technical interpretation.

This brings us to the second point in the passage just quoted, which Hiromichi uses to conclude his discussion of specific terms. Throughout the *Hyōshaku* he urges readers to use the principles of composition to enhance their own search for the meaning and appreciation of the text. As his remark indicates, we can only assume that Murasaki Shikibu relied on a wide range of compositional principles to execute the artistic vision she had for *Genji*. The specific terms and definitions that Hiromichi provides serve as a guide to the more prominent principles to appear in the text. However, he urges readers not to be misled into thinking that this is a finite list, or that the composition of *Genji* can be reduced to a simple formula. Each reader must carry out his or her own search for principles of composition in the text to appreciate the author's artistry at work.

CONCLUSION

According to Hiromichi's argument, the presence of compositional principles in *Genji* serves as concrete evidence of the author's genius in terms of both artistic conception and literary execution. The way in which he approaches this argument suggests that he is making a deliberate attempt to integrate the interpretive strategies he encountered in the works of Bakin and Chinese vernacular fiction with what he saw as the best aspects of previous *Genji* criticism.

As discussed in chapter 4, the dramatist Li Yu cautioned fellow authors and critics that the successful composition of a dramatic work required the author to carefully sew together various episodes so that they appeared to the audience as one seamless garment. In a similar vein, *pingdian* commentators of Chinese vernacular fiction were known to remark that the cohesiveness of long narrative texts was a sign of the technical mastery of the author. In his remarks on the *Sanguo yanyi*, Mao Zonggang praised this work of 120 chapters as being so skillfully constructed that "the entire work reads like a single sentence" (*yi-pian ru yi-ju*).[77] It is through *pingdian* commentary that he provided exacting analysis to substantiate this claim.

The sophistication evident in Hiromichi's interpretive strategy can best be understood in terms of his appropriation of critical terms and concepts from the tradition of *pingdian* commentary. While this point detracts from the claim that his interpretive technique is somehow unique, it should be noted that he was the first to approach the interpretation of *Genji* in such a systematic and practical manner by employing concepts and terminology from the tradition of Chinese vernacular fiction. Such strategies failed to make their way into the interpretation of *Genji* earlier because they belonged to what was considered an entirely different literary genre. Hiromichi's familiarity with a variety of interpretive strategies and his inclination to resist the ideological restrictions of established scholarship were established in chapter 2. It is these elements of his scholarship that made it possible for him to envision the potential benefits to be had by integrating *pingdian* methods of analysis with his interpretation of *Genji*.

Hiromichi challenged the notion that Norinaga's *mono no aware* theory was the best approach to interpreting *Genji*. The principles of composition were meant to provide an alternative to *mono no aware* in assessing the tale's merits as a work of prose fiction. In his discussion of the principles of composition he subordinates the term *aware* to a number of interpretive concepts, but never seeks to dismiss its importance. His theory of ambiguity is the capstone of this interpretive approach. Appreciating the literary style of the tale demands that the text be examined both for what it says and how it is written. Such analysis cannot be limited to the ideals of poetic criticism or the value of lyricism anymore than it can be circumscribed by the demands of didactic merit. Hiromichi's interpretive strategy requires that the narrative's ambiguities, ellipses, and chronological leaps be considered along with its descriptive elegance and poetic poignancy. In capitalizing on his skills as a poet and his stature as a critic of poetry, Hiromichi devised a system by which *Genji* could be appreciated for its literary style and the story it tells. In essence, this method follows the common practice of evaluating poetry based on an assessment of its form and content. From this perspective, his theory of ambiguity can be understood as a modification of Norinaga's *mono no aware* theory. This critical methodology also privileges internal, textual evidence over external concerns such as ideology, didactic merit, and nostalgia. While literary interpretation is never free of concerns beyond the text, such an approach is more consistent with the way in which contemporaries of an author evaluate a work of prose fiction than it is the promotion of a particular political or ideological agenda. In this sense, the *Hyōshaku* can be understood as enhancing Norinaga's contribution to the study of *Genji*. Norinaga idealized the values and language of antiquity in order to elevate the tale above what he perceived to be the cultural decay of his own time. This rescued *Genji* from moral and dogmatic condemnation, but limited its appreciation to an exercise in nostalgia. Hiromichi's innovations in format and commentary sought to realize Norinaga's interpretive achievement in a way that was meaningful for contemporary readers. Judged according to these terms, Hiromichi is the greatest scholar of *Genji* to take up Norinaga's legacy in the Edo period. His most important innovations have become a transparent part of the way the tale is read and reproduced in the modern era.

However, Hiromichi's accomplishments must also be measured in terms of their reception by successive generations. The *Hyōshaku* was well received and widely reprinted immediately following its initial publication. Curiously, it was not given a place of prominence in the study of *Genji* after the Edo period. Surveys of *Genji* criticism refer only briefly to the *Hyōshaku* as a minor footnote when they mention it al all. The most appreciative scholars simply refer to Hiromichi's work as the last major commentary to succeed Norinaga's *Tama no ogushi* in the premodern era.[78] Until recent decades, the impact of Hiromichi's interpretive theories beyond this conclusion remained largely unexplored. The next chapter takes up the argument that the low stature of Hiromichi's *Hyōshaku* is more than simply the result of accidental omission.

Chapter Six

TRANSLATING *GENJI* INTO THE MODERN IDIOM

TREE SPIRITS AND APPARITIONS

The Sarashina Diary stands out as one of the few extant accounts of how *Genji* was read in the Heian period. The author, known to us only as a daughter of Vice Governor Sugawara no Takasue, reflects back on her life, including her brief service at the Imperial court, in the form of a recreated diary. Early on in the diary, Takasue's daughter recounts her frustration at having seen only portions of *Genji* and wanting to know more. After receiving a copy of the entire tale as a gift, she indulges in a thorough reading of the text, chapter by chapter.

> Previously I had been forced to rush through [borrowed] portions of the text and had been frustrated by how little I understood of *The Tale of Genji*. Making myself comfortable behind a screen so as not to be disturbed, I started with the first chapter and made my way through the tale taking one chapter scroll then the next from its special case. This gave me such pleasure that I would not have wanted to trade places even with the Empress. Without stopping to rest during the day and into the night as long as I could stay awake with a lamp by my side I continued to read. In this way the text became second nature to me and I could easily imagine the story in my mind.[1]

This account of her mounting *Genji* obsession is punctuated by two ominous dreams. In the first dream she sees a Buddhist priest who urges her to learn the fifth volume of the *Lotus Sutra*. She recalls that this dream in no way distracted her from a compulsive reading of *Genji*.

> I told no one of this dream, since I couldn't bear the thought of studying such things. *Genji* consumed my waking thoughts. At the time I was still an unattractive young girl, but I imagined I would

> grow up to become a woman of unequaled beauty with long hair. I was so foolish as to imagine that when I grew up I would become just like Hikaru Genji's Yūgao or the Uji Captain's Ukifune.[2]

Shortly after this passage she mentions a second ominous dream in which a man advises her to offer prayers to the heavenly deity Amaterasu. Only after she has experienced many setbacks in life does she begin to wonder if there might not be a connection between her obsession with fictional literature and the misfortunes she has endured. These thoughts lead her to regret not having led a more pious life.[3] Her weaving together the account of fanatically reading *Genji* while awake and dreaming of religious pieties while asleep suggests that the earlier diary entries were deliberately constructed to convey the wisdom of an adult looking back on the errors of her youth.

The reference she makes to identifying herself with specific characters in *Genji* also reveals the hand of a self-conscious memoirist controlling the diary's composition. Yūgao and Ukifune do not seem like the most obvious characters to which a young woman might find herself drawn. Yūgao is the frail beauty pursued by Genji in the early chapters of the tale who dies a sudden and an unceremonious death. Ukifune is the troubled heroine of the end of the tale whose misfortune seems to grow with each passing chapter. It is tempting to conclude that Takasue's daughter chose these two characters spanning the length of the narrative simply to illustrate her command of the entire tale. However, being a close reader, she would certainly have been aware that both Yūgao and Ukifune suffer dearly at the hands of possessing spirits. If the text Takasue's daughter received as a gift at all resembles the text of *Genji* we read today, then the identity of the possessing spirit would have been most ambiguous and demanding to discern in the cases of both Yūgao and Ukifune. Unseen and unexplained malevolent forces are the most compelling elements the stories of Yūgao and Ukifune have in common. By bracketing her recollection of these two women with anxious dreams of religious devotion, Takasue's daughter expresses a subconscious fear for her own welfare. Might we not theorize that it is the ambiguity of the text in these places that forced Takasue's daughter to pause in her reading? To make sense of these scenes she was forced to review them in her mind and thus came to picture herself in the place of both women. This account provides valuable information as to how the author's contemporary responded to the text as a whole, and from that perspective which portions of the tale she found particularly engaging.

Ironically, the *Sarashina Diary*'s most enduring legacy is not of how *Genji* was read by Heian contemporaries of the author but rather why it should not be read with such abandon. After the Heian period, nostalgia for the lost world of *Genji* was often tempered by anecdotes reminding readers of the dangers inherent in fictional texts. These anecdotes echo the anxious dreams of Takasue's daughter, even when no direct reference is made to the *Sarashina Diary*. Many works of prose fiction from the twelfth and thirteenth centuries convey a continuing fascination with *Genji*, but this fascination is mixed with reports that Murasaki Shikibu was punished in the afterlife for the creation of such deviously interesting fabrications.[4] In subsequent centuries, textual commentaries framed their remarks on *Genji* within the context of these same didactic concerns. Edo period Confucian scholars Kumazawa Banzan and Andō Tameakira attempted to deflect this challenge to *Genji*'s stature by pointing to the morally redeeming aspects of the text.

Motoori Norinaga was effective in his efforts to overcome didactic criticism's position of dominance. His argument that to judge *Genji* as a guide to morality is to demonstrate that one has "failed to appreciate the intentions of the author" succeeded in banishing a highly compelling and long-standing ideology from the vocabulary of *Genji* commentary and criticism. To fill the resulting void, Norinaga promoted his *mono no aware* theory. This masterful command of rhetoric built upon centuries of reverence for *Genji* to lend credence to the notion that those who failed to acknowledge its stature were simply revealing their own shortcomings. He effectively cleared away one obstacle to a more appropriate appraisal of *Genji*, but introduced an equally compelling ideological impediment, the enduring link between nostalgia and cultural identity that had long played a role in the interpretation of *Genji*.

Hagiwara Hiromichi praises Norinaga's *Tama no ogushi* as essential reading for anyone seeking to develop an appreciation for *Genji*. However, he does not allow Norinaga's ideological position to dictate his own reading of the text. In discussing *Genji*'s overall structure, he boldly returns to the two characters who inspired dreams of religious piety in the author of *Sarashina nikki*. His concern for revealing the success of the text as fiction trumps Norinaga's wholesale condemnation of Buddhist and Confucian didacticism. He begins by highlighting similar details in the stories of Yūgao and Ukifune to illustrate their underlying structural affinity. These details allow him to establish that they are parallel characters when viewed from the perspective of the larger structure of the story. Structural similarities make the events leading up to Yūgao's demise resonate even more profoundly for the reader when they are witnessed again in the tragic unfolding of events in the Uji chapters. In the "General Remarks" to his *Appraisal of Genji*, Hiromichi writes the following:

> Yūgao had no one to rely on. Ukifune, too, was faced with the absence of anything to depend upon. Thus we can consider them to be a pair according to the structural principle of parallel characters [*shōtai*]. Furthermore, the "certain estate" [*nanigashi no in*, where Yūgao is taken by Genji] and the house at Uji [where Ukifune is hidden by Kaoru] are parallel settings.[5] On the one hand Yūgao is caught between two characters: Genji and Tō no Chūjō. On the other, Ukifune is caught between two characters: Kaoru and Niou. In terms of the timing, Yūgao is taken by Genji from Gojō on the fifteenth night of the eighth month [which is inauspicious according to the lunar calendar], while Ukifune is taken by Kaoru from the house in

> Sanjō on the evening of the thirteenth of the ninth month [also known to be an inauspicious day]. In both cases the women are taken by carriage. These similar details provide a clear indication that they are *structurally parallel*. One of them is fatally taken by a malevolent spirit [*henge ni torikurosare*], while the other is abducted by a tree spirit [*kotama ni kasume toraretaru*], making them *parallel characters* on this account as well. Employing the same technique [of the brush] with all these details the author indicates that in the case of women who are too retiring there awaits an unpleasant fate.[6]

In mentioning the fate of both women, Hiromichi builds upon the Edo notion that serious literature should ultimately serve to "extoll virtue and condem vice." This is the kind of interpretation Norinaga argued against with such conviction. However, Hiromichi makes the case that circumstance and psychological disposition, rather than immoral behavior, determine the unfortunate outcomes of both Yūgao and Ukifune. Hiromichi's ultimate goal is not to moralize but rather to persuade readers that the structural aspects of the story reveal the sophistication with which the text is composed. The details he uses in comparing the two characters underscore similarities in the descriptive texture of their stories rather than catalogue their virtues and vices. He does not allow moral didacticism to determine his interpretive strategy, but more importantly he does not exclude from his interpretation the possibility that reading *Genji* might help one better understand how a character's behavior and emotional disposition contribute to the development of plot. The stories of Yūgao and Ukifune, particularly in the way one echoes the other, bring to the foreground two critical issues that Norinaga would have preferred to avoid: textual ambiguity and the possibility that *Genji* can, and should, be valued for something other than its capacity to move the reader emotionally. In this case, he praises the tale because the thoughts and actions of specific characters contribute in such fundamental ways to major plot developments. Hiromichi emphasizes the parallel structure underlying the stories of Yūgao and Ukifune because this allows him to address precisely these issues. While there may be a moral lesson to be gleaned from the lives of these characters, it is the compelling way in which we can see their emotional flaws contributing to their downfall that he seeks to draw to the reader's attention. For him, such subtleties of composition establish *Genji*'s success as a work of prose fiction.

Hiromichi's reference to Yūgao and Ukifune returns to an issue that has provoked concern among readers and critics since the time of the tale's composition. However, he also pushes *Genji* commentary into new territory. Previous scholars primarily sought to advance philological and moral interpretation or to identify historical models and poetic allusions. Hiromichi integrates the most advanced theories of his day on all of these issues where they facilitate comprehension of the text. But in drawing upon his familiarity with the composition and interpretation of popular fiction, he also brings a keen awareness of literary style to his reading of *Genji*. This emphasis on the sophistication with which *Genji* was written ultimately leads him to consider aspects of the text often overlooked or dismissed by previous scholars. One sentence in the passage translated earlier is particularly noteworthy in this regard. Of the parallel construction of the characters Yūgao and Ukifune, he concludes:

> One of them is fatally taken by a malevolent spirit, while the other is abducted by a tree spirit, making them *parallel characters* on this account as well.

Hiromichi draws our attention to aspects of the story never directly described in the text. These are the same malevolent and violent forces that seem to have inspired Takasue's daughter's anxious dreams of religious piety. There are other examples of spirit possession and the supernatural in *Genji*, but the indistinct forces acting upon Yūgao and Ukifune make their cases of spirit possession stand apart from other depictions in the tale—where more clearly identifiable spirits are involved.[7] Precisely because Yūgao and Ukifune are subject to forces operating beyond what is visible or knowable to characters in the tale, readers must integrate disparate details from various chapters to gain a clearer understanding of these events. Hiromichi goes on to identify the possession of Yūgao as one of the five prominent examples of remarkable literary technique employed by the author that often escapes the notice of the unsophisticated or unfamiliar reader. He argues that it is a sign of the author's "skillful command of the brush" that her depiction of Yūgao's death by the possession of a spirit remains incomplete until the Rokujō Haven is introduced later in the text.[8]

Few premodern scholars of *Genji* chose to analyze instances of the supernatural at work in the tale in great detail. While the ambiguous identity of the malevolent spirit possessing Yūgao receives little treatment, the even more puzzling events surrounding Ukifune's possession are often overlooked, deliberately simplified, or distorted. Tsutsumi Yasuo notes in his survey of *Genji* commentary that Yūgao's death receives only a cursory and tentative treatment in most works before the Edo period.[9] This may be because depictions of the supernatural and spirit possession were fairly common in the literature of the tenth and eleventh centuries.[10] With more than enough thorny textual issues and poetic allusions to track down, scholars probably did not feel compelled to comment on the significance of a scene familiar from other fictional works of the period.

However, even as we approach modern *Genji* commentary, the analysis of these two scenes does not dramatically increase. This absence of commentary is revealing. Scholars writing on *Genji* for most of its thousand-year history chose to annotate aspects of the text that allowed them to show how issues outside of the text—ideological, moral, poetic, or historical—were relevant to what could be found in the text. The supernatural does not attract much annotation in most commentaries, because its greatest significance is to the fictional world created by the text and the psychological disposition of the characters inhabiting that world. Scholars compiling lessons for the real world naturally gloss over depictions of the supernatural, because they inherently contradict what they seek from the text.[11] However, because Hiromichi is ultimately concerned with literary technique and its ability to produce successful prose fiction, he finds depictions of the supernatural in *Genji* worthy of his attention. In this regard, Tsutsumi Yasuo argues that Hiromichi's annotation of Yūgao's spirit possession stands out as an important landmark in the transition away from the speculative and ideological concerns of medieval commentary and toward the more rational and analytical approach of modern textual analysis. Hiromichi's emphasis on internal consistency between small textual details and large plot elements makes this transition possible.[12]

To place Hiromichi's interpretive stance regarding the supernatural within a more meaningful context, we can turn to two annotated editions of *Genji*: the *Kogetsushō* and the *Nihon bungaku zensho Genji*. Kitamura Kigin's *Kogetsushō* was first published in 1673 and reprinted many times during the Edo and Meiji periods. It was the most widely circulated edition of *Genji* in early modern Japan. The first fully revised edition of *Genji* to appear in the Meiji period was published in 1890 by Hakubunkan as part of a compendium on classical literature titled *Nihon bungaku zensho*, edited by scholars closely associated with the establishment of academic programs devoted to the study of "the nation's literature" (*kokubungaku*).[13] The annotation associated with Ukifune's mysterious disappearance in these two editions provides a useful frame of reference from which to begin our examination of the Meiji and Taishō period reception of Hiromichi's interpretation of *Genji* in general and his treatment of the supernatural in particular.

THE DISAPPEARANCE OF UKIFUNE

The "Ukifune" chapter (chapter 51, "A Drifting Boat") closes with Ukifune in tears, the gentlewoman Ukon by her side pressing her to decide between two men. Incapable of imagining herself living with the decision to go to either Kaoru or Niou, Ukifune's thoughts return to the possibility of her own death and the resolution it will bring to so many troubles. Ukifune is unable to eat, unable to decide, and so overwhelmed by the possible consequences of her actions that she is no longer able to communicate with those around her. Earlier references in the chapter to people drowning in the nearby Uji River, tragic love triangles, and Ukifune's despondent demeanor suggest that her gentlewomen and her mother fear something terrible lies ahead. Familiar with her inner thoughts that everyone would be better off if she were dead, and that she might as well throw herself in the river, readers expect the worst. These suspicions are confirmed as the next chapter, "Kagerō" (chapter 52, "The Mayfly") opens with the panicked cries of gentlewomen discovering Ukifune is no longer with them. A literal translation of the opening lines reads as follows:

> There, attendants were wildly searching for the missing young woman, but they did not find her. Since it was like the morning-after scene from a tale in which a maiden has been abducted [under the cover of darkness] I shall dispense with further details.[14]

The *Kogetsushō* includes the following gloss for this opening line:

> "There (*kashiko niwa*) . . .":
>
> (1: *Sairyūshō*) Refers to the place where Ukifune threw herself [into the river to drown].
>
> (2: *Kachō yōjō*) At the end of the Ukifune chapter we saw the young woman contemplating suicide. Evidently a description of her throwing herself into the river was not thought necessary since no one [in the story] knows what happened.
>
> (3: *Kogetsushō shisetsu*) From this opening line to the words "dispense with further details" is narration by the author.[15]

At first the *Kogetsushō* style of commentary appears tedious and unnecessarily complicated. Three distinct notes from different commentaries spanning three different centuries fill the available white space at the top of the page to annotate the opening phrase of the chapter. However, a close reading of the original text reveals how vital each piece of information is to comprehending the peculiar nature of Ukifune's disappearance.

When confronted with the text alone, determining the context for the word "there" in the opening sentence is probably the first task that comes to the reader's mind. The first annotation supplies the necessary contextualization by citing a commentary compiled in 1528, the *Sairyūshō*: *There* refers to Uji, where we last saw Ukifune at the end of the previous chapter and, more specifically, the place where her gentlewomen suspect she must have thrown herself into the Uji River. Her attendants are desperately searching for some sign of her whereabouts, but the only thing they can point to is the last place they suspect she was: *There*! Sadly, their search is in vain. Literally, "it comes to nothing" (*kai nashi*).

The second notation, taken from an even earlier commentary, the *Kachō yōjō* (1472), explains that readers need not expect to learn the specifics of Ukifune's disappearance, since characters in the story itself do not know what happened. The poignancy of the opening phrase begins to reverberate more clearly with this comment. Ukifune's gentlewomen are not searching everywhere. The narrator's opening words suggest that they are drawn to a specific place because they have good reason to fear there is a location from which she must have thrown herself into the river. Readers are invited to imagine the frantic cries suggested by the opening line of the chapter: "*There*, she must have jumped from *there*." Tragically, the only people Ukifune can rely on do not even know what has happened to her because *they* were *not there* when

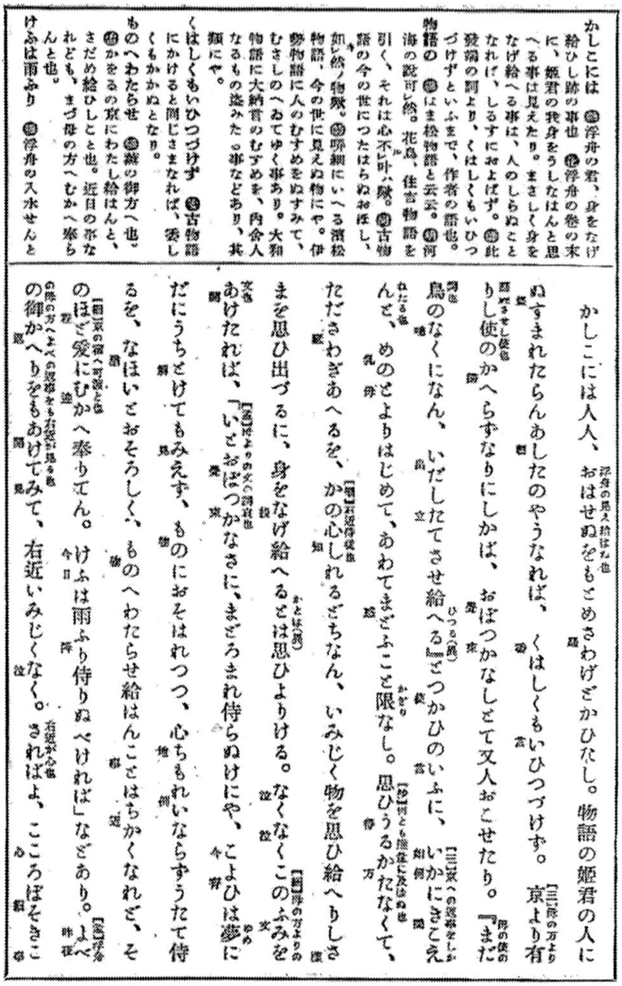
かしこには人人、おはせぬをもとめさわげどかひなし。物語の姫君の人にぬすまれたらんあしたのやうなれば、くはしくもいひつづけず。京より有りし使のかへらずなりにしかば、おぼつかなしとて又人おこせたり。「まだ鳥のなくになん、いだしたてさせ給へる」とつかひのいふに、いかにきこえんと、めのとよりはじめて、あわてまどふこと限なし。思ひうるかたなくて、たださわぎあへるを、かの心しれるどちなん、いみじく物を思ひ給へりしさまを思ひ出づるに、身をなげ給へるとは思ひよりける。なくなくこのふみをあけたれば、「いとおぼつかなさに、まどろまれ侍らぬけにや、こよひは夢にだにうちとけてもみえず、ものにおそはれつつ、心ちもれいならずうたて侍るを、なほいとおそろしく、ものへわたらせ給はんことはちかくなれど、そのほど愛にむかへ奉りてん。けふは雨ふり侍りぬべければ」などあり。よべの御かへりをもあけてみて、右近いみじくなく。さればよ、こころぼそきこ

FIGURE 2

Zōchū kogetsushō

(1927, based on original text from 1673, revised in 1890)
First page of the "Kagerō" chapter

she disappeared. The annotation reminds us of the fact that Ukifune is gone, and no one witnessed her disappearance. That is *all* we know.

A final comment indicates that this information is provided from the perspective of the author's narration of the story.[16] The annotation here literally refers to the words of the fictional narrator as "the author talking" (*sakusha no katari*). Enomoto Masazumi has observed that Hiromichi's definition of the term *authorial intrusion* (*sōshiji*) in his "General Remarks" to the *Hyōshaku* and his consistent application of the term to his line-by-line annotation of the first eight chapters of *Genji* provide the first case in which we see the term being applied in a way consistent with a modern understanding of the concept of authorial intrusion.[17] Since Hiromichi's line-by-line commentary for the "Kagerō" chapter is not available to us, we can only hypothesize that his sophisticated understanding of authorial intrusion afforded him a somewhat more nuanced appreciation of this scene than we find in annotation from the *Kogetsushō*. The author intrudes here to acknowledge that a melodramatic scene such as this is probably familiar to readers from previous tales they have heard. She tells us she knows better than to dwell on its description, because there is nothing new to be gained through such repetition.[18] It is equally possible that in drawing attention to the clichéd nature of this scene she is playing with her audience's expectations. In keeping with Hiromichi's theory of textual ambiguity (see chapter 5) we might also imagine that the author's description is deliberately vague here to produce an even greater effect when she later reveals that the events behind Ukifune's disappearance are far from ordinary.

The prior analysis of the opening lines of annotation may seem cumbersome when described in translation, but it is worth pointing out that this method of deciphering a text would have been transparent to a well-educated reader of the Edo period. It reflects the integration of textual exegesis, annotation, and interpretive attribution developed in China for the meticulous analysis of classical texts and modified over the course of centuries in both China and Japan to annotate documents ranging from sacred texts and historical chronicles to vernacular fiction. Within this tradition, exegesis was as highly valued as the original text.[19] A command of relevant commentary was often seen as indistinguishable from the process of appreciating the text itself.

While this style of commentary was highly revered in premodern Japan, it seems to have struck some scholars in the Meiji period as being unnecessarily mired in tradition. The *Nihon bungaku zensho* series promised to bring the classics of Japanese literature to a popular audience in a way never before possible. The editors included the following oblique condemnation of the traditional annotated textual format in their "introductory notes" to the first volume of the series:

> Books of old literature are scarce, difficult to obtain, and even the rare volume that comes to light is full of errors and not easy to understand. The reason we publish this series now is to make these books more easily obtainable, more easily readable, and to demonstrate the excellence of the national literature, which stands head and shoulders above Chinese and Western literature in a class by itself.[20]

The appearance of the *Nihon bungaku zensho* edition of *Genji* did signal an important change. Individual volumes in the series were affordably priced and widely available, meaning that *Genji* could now be read in the original, in its entirety, by a popular audience for the first time.[21] During the Edo period, parody and summary of the original story were widely available through such works as Tanehiko's *Phony Murasaki and Rural Genji*. Parodies of *Genji* were the province of the masses in the Edo period, but the original text largely remained the property of an elite group of readers despite the success of Kitamura Kigin's comprehensive collation of text and commentary in the *Kogetsushō*. The *Nihon bungaku zensho* edition of *Genji* is elegant and accessible, due in large part to its simplicity. Similar to Kigin's *Kogetsushō* and Hiromichi's *Hyōshaku*, the body of the original text is reproduced along with space at the top of each page for commentary. To facilitate ease of use, the text is clearly punctuated and broken down into paragraphs. Helpful pronunciation guides (*rubi*) for characters are provided alongside the text in small type. Unlike previous editions of *Genji*, nearly all nonessential information has been stripped from the textual commentary. Annotation is so pared down, in fact, that as one progresses beyond the introductory chapters in *Genji*, much of the space for headnotes is left blank, providing a visually pleasing white space along the top of the page. As a result, the headnotes, written in simple, direct language, are conveniently placed directly above the relevant passage in the original, where even the uninitiated reader can easily locate them. In the *Kogetsushō* and *Hyōshaku*, textual commentary for one page often runs into the headnote space for the following page until the commentary and text fall so far out of synchronization that full pages devoted to commentary alone often break up the flow of the main text.

The *Nihon bungaku zensho Genji* is, therefore, true to its editors promise, much more streamlined, rationally formatted, and simple to read. The reader is distracted only by what appears to be the most essential commentary. One by-product of this streamlined presentation is the tendency to simplify complexities of the original to avoid the involved annotation associated with traditional commentary. Nowhere is this tendency more striking than in annotation referring to Ukifune's disappearance. The "Kagerō" chapter annotation radically simplifies details pertinent to the structure of the opening lines. Notes running along the top of the text frequently refer to Ukifune's drowning in the Uji River as if it were fact, not rumor. For example, the same opening line of "Kagerō" annotated by the *Kogetsushō* is accompanied by the following gloss in the *Nihon bungaku zensho Genji*:

> Attendants were wildly searching for the missing young woman: Because Ukifune threw herself [into the river to drown] at this place her attendants are wildly searching for her.[22]

After working our way through the *Kogetsushō*, the *Nihon bungaku zensho* gloss seems refreshing in its concision. However, nearly all traces of the nuanced reading offered by the *Kogetsushō* are lost. Providing readers with an overly succinct and apparently omniscient interpretation destroys the sense that there is much we do not, and cannot, know based on this passage. The

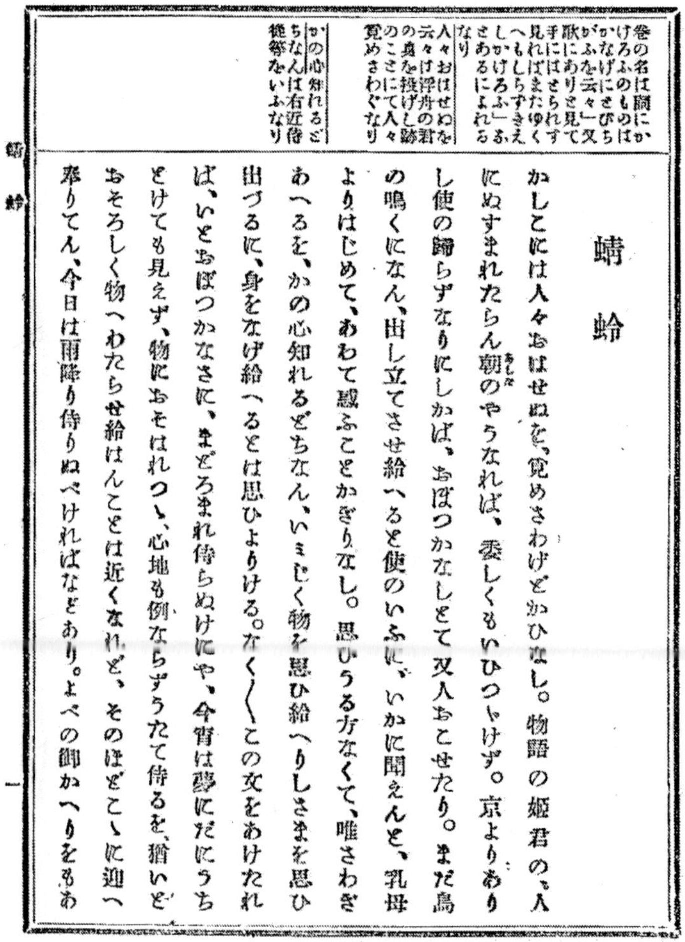

巻の名は蜻蛉にかげろふのものはかなげにさびちがふな云々」又歌にありさ見て手にはさられず見ればまたゆくへもしらずきえしかげろふ」ふさあるによれるなり

人々おはせぬを云々け浮舟の君の身を投げし跡のことにて人々覚めさわぐなり

かの心知れるごちなんは右近侍從者ないふなり

蜻蛉

かしこには人々おはせぬを、覚めさわげどかひなし。物語の姫君の、人にぬすまれたらん朝のやうなれば、委しくもいひつゞけず。京よりありし使の歸らずなりにしかば、おぼつかなしとて又人おこせたり。まだ鳥の鳴くになん、出し立てさせ給へると使のいふに、いかに聞えんと、乳母よりはじめて、あわて惑ふことかぎりなし。思ひうる方なくて、唯さわぎあへるを、かの心知れるどちなん、いみじく物を思ひ給へりしさまを思ひ出づるに、身をなげ給へるとは思ひよりける。なく／＼この文をあけたれば、いとおぼつかなさに、まどろまれ侍らぬけにや、今宵は夢にだにうちとけても見えず、物におそはれつゝ、心地も例ならずうたて侍るを、猶いどおそろしく物へわたらせ給はんことは近くなれど、そのほどこゝに迎へ奉りてん、今日は雨降り侍りぬべければなどあり。よべの御かへりをもあ

蜻蛉 一

FIGURE 3

Nihon bungaku zensho, Genji monogatari

(1890)

First page of the "Kagerō" chapter

authorial intrusion, indicating that the author is holding back in her description, is not even brought to the reader's attention.

The cumulative effect of this simplified style of commentary begins to emerge even more clearly as the Uji chapters unfold. In the following chapter, "Tenarai" (chapter 53, "Writing Practice"), the Prelate of Yokawa is led to the strange figure of a woman lying unconscious in the woods. We soon learn it is the body of Ukifune. As the Prelate and his entourage approach, someone asks, "Are you a demon? A god? Are you a fox spirit or a tree spirit?"[23] The imminent arrival of heavy rain forces him to take the woman to shelter before he can determine her identity. The *Nihon bungaku zensho* provides a helpful note here, reminding readers:

> "It looked like it was going to rain heavily. . . ." This phrase connects the downpour the night after Ukifune threw herself into the river to drown [*Ukifune no jusui*] with the weather conditions described in the *Kagerō* chapter the night following her disappearance.[24]

The phrase "Ukifune's having thrown herself into the river to drown" then becomes the set expression for referring to her disappearance throughout the rest of the chapter. A few pages later, we reach the passage where Ukifune begins to regain consciousness and recount the mysterious way in which she vanished from one place in Uji and then appeared in another. As her speech gains strength, she describes her confusion when she went outside to where she could hear the sound of the river at the Uji villa. She then describes an encounter with a "most beautiful man" who seemed to have taken her in his arms. She relates that he then left her in an unfamiliar place and vanished. Upon realizing that she did not accomplish what she intended to do (drown herself), she begins to cry. The headnotes for this passage provide the following commentary. (The first note on the page does not have a specific reference to a line of the text.):

> The description of Ukifune's intending to drown herself in the river does not extend beyond the scene at the end of the "Ukifune" chapter, so it is particularly interesting to see a detailed description of what she was thinking [*Ukifune no omou kokoro*] at this point in the story.[25]

This note is followed by annotation for the line "a most beautiful man approached me . . .":

> It seems the spirit appearing before her was that of Niou.

The last note on the page provides a specific annotation for the line "I did not accomplish what I intended to do . . .":

> This refers to her having thrown herself in the river to drown.[26]

The annotation and interpretation in the *Nihon bungaku zensho* edition focuses exclusively on Ukifune's mental state. The fact that this passage combines Ukifune's description of her mental state with an explanation of how she arrived at this new location is omitted altogether.[27] As we just observed, the editors glossed over the fact that little was known about Ukifune's disappearance at the beginning of the "Kagerō" chapter. As if to cover up for this oversimplification, readers are now told that this affords a fascinating insight into her mental state when she threw herself into the river. There is no effort made to explain that this passage provides an account of Ukifune's spirit possession and an explanation for how her body was mysteriously transported from the Uji River and into the woods.

The *Nihon bungaku zensho* annotation invites readers to conclude that Ukifune threw herself into the Uji River, and that the heavy rains carried her body downstream to where the Prelate and his entourage discovered her unconscious form. This conflation of rumor and textual ambiguity makes the story seem much less confusing and, ultimately, far more rational than the text suggests. In fact, it has become something of a convention in *Genji* scholarship to refer to "Ukifune's throwing herself into the river to drown" (*Ukifune no jusui*) when writing about the Uji chapters.[28] Scholarly editions of *Genji* published after World War II, such as Shōgakkan's *Nihon koten bungaku zenshū* (Complete Works of Classical Japanese Literature) and Iwanami's *Shin Nihon koten bungaku taikei* (New Compendium of Classical Japanese Literature), are careful to use precise terms when referring to Ukifune's "disappearance" or "abduction" (*shissō*). However, in recently published scholarly works focused on classical texts other than *Genji*, the vestiges of this interpretive shorthand remain. For example, the most recent scholarly edition of the *Sarashina nikki*, published in 1989 as part of the same Iwanami series *Shin Nihon koten bungaku taikei*, includes a footnote in the section from the *Diary* where Takasue's daughter imagines herself as "the Uji captain's Ukifune." This footnote reads:

> This refers to the young woman Ukifune loved by Kaoru. The unrecognized daughter of Prince Hachi no Miya, Ukifune is pursued by both Kaoru and Niou. In desperation, Ukifune throws herself into the Uji River [*Ujikawa ni tōshin suru*]. She is later rescued and takes Buddhist vows.[29]

More than a century after Hiromichi's publication of the *Hyōshaku*, when this scholarly edition of the *Sarashina Diary* was published, nuances of the text that Hiromichi explored and connected to a more comprehensive reading of *Genji* remained inaccessible or unappreciated by some of the leading scholars in the field of classical literature.

THE PROBLEM OF EDO

Hiromichi's interpretation of the disappearance of Ukifune provides just one example of the many ways in which the interpretive theories he sets forth in his *Appraisal of Genji* are consonant with modern *Genji* scholarship on a level that clearly sets him apart from his predecessors. At first it seems puzzling that scholars compiling the *Nihon bungaku zensho* edition of the text in the Meiji period would simply have overlooked his work. However, as the footnote just translated illustrates, the significance of Hiromichi's interpretive insights remained unappreciated even by some specialists in the field of classical literature in 1989. An examination of *Genji* reception and scholarship in light of Meiji-period political and cultural concerns helps to explain why Hiromichi's work has been consistently overlooked. In fact, it is possible to argue that in some cases it was deliberately ignored.

Texts on the history of *Genji* commentary and reception from the Meiji, Taishō, and early Shōwa periods devote little space to the *Hyōshaku*, when they cover it at all. Even scholars who have taken pains to recognize its interpretive merits are quick to point out that one cannot rely on the *Hyōshaku* alone, because it does not include a complete text of the *Genji*. A prime example of this sentiment can be found in *Kokubungaku no sekai* (The World of Japan's Classical Literature, 1939), in which Fujita Tokutarō (1901–1945) offers the following advice to students who wish to read *Genji* in the original language:

> In addition to the *Kogetsushō*, the text that should definitely be read by those who wish to study *Genji monogatari* is Hagiwara Hiromichi's *Hyōshaku*. . . . In contrast to the *Kogetsushō*, which is written in the old style, this work demonstrates the benefits of commentary from a new generation of scholarship based on more advanced techniques. The philological explanation is more helpful and detailed than what we find in the *Kogetsushō*. Various symbols are used to explain the style of composition [lit. the sense in which the sentences are connected]. Colloquially equivalent language is included next to the words of the main text. These and other techniques are employed so that anyone can easily appreciate the outstanding places in the story—as Hiromichi puts it, so that "one's hands can easily reach to scratch all the places that itch." In addition, there are places where we get a glimpse of literary interpretation and explanation from the author's perspective. By carefully reading this commentary one's appreciation for the understanding of literature of that time becomes appropriately rich. There is no question that a great deal of talent went into the making of this commentary. Unfortunately, the text is cut short at the "Hana no En" chapter so one cannot rely on this commentary alone. I believe that one can achieve an admirable understanding and deepen one's appreciation of the *Genji* by using this commentary to supplement a reading of the *Kogetsushō*.[30]

As established in chapters 4 and 5, despite the fact that Hiromichi was unable to publish a detailed commentary for all fifty-four chapters of the main text, the critical strategy as set forth in his "General Remarks" represents a complete and comprehensive interpretation of the tale. However, even if one finds merit in Fujita's claim and the *Hyōshaku* is evaluated only in terms of Hiromichi's interpretive argument as expressed in his "General Remarks," the failure of his work to be more widely received remains a question. In his survey of the history of *Genji* commentary (*Genji monogatari kenkyūshi*, 1937), Shigematsu Nobuhiro devotes an entire chapter to introducing readers to the *Hyōshaku*.

He begins by arguing that among the *Genji* commentaries produced during the late Edo period, Hiromichi's *Hyōshaku* merits the most attention.[31] He goes on to praise Hiromichi's treatment of Andō Tameakira and Motoori Norinaga's interpretive theories and paraphrases several points from the "General Remarks." His observations concerning Hiromichi's principles of composition theory are the least enthusiastic. Shigematsu praises Hiromichi for his development of this unique interpretive theory and acknowledges that in many cases its application to *Genji* seems reasonable, but, he cautions:

> If one follows this method of searching for "principles of composition" in the details of the text the complexity of Hiromichi's method becomes rather difficult to endure. One feels hard pressed to accept the validity of his over-emphasizing so many passages which otherwise might be considered as nothing more than one part of the work's rhetorical effectiveness [*shūjiteki kōka no ichibubun*].[32]

Shigematsu concludes that other than his tendency to overemphasize certain passages, Hiromichi lives up to and in some cases surpasses Norinaga in terms of his elaborate analysis and appreciation of the text.[33] While not denying the legitimacy of Hiromichi's interpretive approach, he suggests that readers are better off relying on a selective analysis of the tale. Ultimately, this argument dismisses Hiromichi's attempt to replace Nortinaga's *mono no aware* theory as the dominant mode of interpreting *Genji*. His conclusion implies that an emphasis on the analysis of literary style, internal textual consistency, and the principles of composition will result in tedium and unnecessary frustration in reading *Genji*.

In 1939 another prominent scholar of classical studies rejected Hiromichi's effort to challenge the preeminence of Norinaga's *mono no aware* theory. Sasaki Nobutsuna (1872–1963), best known for his work on the *Man'yōshū*, published an article in which he sought to resolve what he identified as a divergence of opinion (*isetsu*) between "Hiromichi's theory of *mono no aware*" and the theory espoused by Norinaga. Sasaki opens the essay by stating that in the interpretation of *Genji* "the original view clearly articulated by Motoori Norinaga concerning *mono no aware* remains uncontested." Explaining why Hiromichi's efforts to "faithfully transmit Norinaga's theory" had not yet come to wider attention, he claims that the particulars of Hiromichi's theory are clearly addressed in an unpublished treatise titled *Hongaku taigai* ("Presentation of the Main Teachings," preface dated 1846), but that the manuscript has never been widely circulated.[34] Hiromichi discusses Norinaga's *mono no aware* theory throughout the *Hyōshaku* but Sasaki directs readers to his earlier work, *Hongaku taigai*, for a more revealing exposition. In this treatise, Hiromichi promotes Tominaga Nakamoto's theory that religious and philosophical teachings develop and change in response to ideological difference (see chapter 2). Sasaki examines several passages in which Hiromichi applies this theory in arguing that *mono no aware* should not be understood as a static value, but rather it should be seen as evolving over time. He then argues that Hiromichi sought to "reconcile the contradictions that arose from the intersection of *mono no aware* and the spirit of samurai culture."[35] He explains that unlike Norinaga, who rigidly adhered to the ways of the past (*inishie no michi*), Hiromichi's understanding of the term tells us more about cultural values than it does the reading of ancient literature.[36] In the course of building his argument, he claims that in *Hongaku taigai* Hiromichi sought to address "morality as it related to the ancient way rather than constructing an argument related to theories of literature."[37]

Sasaki's analysis deflects Hiromichi's challenge to the *mono no aware* theory by reading his treatises on morality and literature in reverse chronological order. Hiromichi's argument is consistent from *Hongaku taigai* to the *Hyōshaku* in that it undermined the rigid connection Norinaga established between the meaning of *mono no aware* and Japan's past. However, the tenor of the times in which Sasaki wrote led him to reach conclusions that tell us more about a nation bent on promoting the values of the warrior than what Hiromichi contributed to the study of *Genji*. With these comments as the most extensive evaluation of the *Hyōshaku* available before World War II, it is not surprising that Hiromichi's work failed to receive wider attention. Despite a wealth of interpretive insights, the *Hyōshaku* failed to become an acknowledged landmark in the study of *Genji* commentary and reception until the generation of post World War II scholars came of age.

Noguchi Takehiko is one such student of *Genji*. Noguchi has remarked that it was not until his fourth full reading of *Genji*, when a specialist in Edo period fiction (Mizuno Minoru) brought Hiromichi's work to his attention, that he first became familiar with the *Hyōshaku*.[38] This is not surprising when one considers that an accurate typeset edition of Hiromichi's "General Remarks" on *Genji* did not appear in print until 1999. All of this might still lead to the impression that the relative obscurity of Hiromichi's scholarship is due simply to his failure to complete the detailed commentary on all fifty-four chapters of the main text before his death. However, Hiromichi's intellectual legacy reveals a more complicated reason behind the relative obscurity of his work when considered in light of the cultural and ideological atmosphere of the Meiji restoration. From the perspective of the Meiji scholar interested in promoting a national literature (*kokubungaku*), one might argue that Hiromichi erred most grievously on three accounts.

First, he acknowledged the Chinese, and thus the non-native origin of the interpretive theories he applied to *Genji*. This approach was unappealing to scholars looking to promote native literary genius. It defied the myth they were seeking to create of the unique nature of Japanese spirit and sentiment.

Second, he applied interpretive theory widely associated with Takizawa Bakin to *Genji*. His reference to the supernatural also evoked Bakin's literary style. Bakin's most successful novel of the Edo period, *Hakkenden*, provides a persuasive example of the supernatural's prominent place in popular fiction from the late Edo period. In *Hakkenden*, Bakin recounts the tale of eight fictional heroes, each embodying a different virtue associated with Confucianism or moral conduct. These heroes are born from the spiritual and symbolic marriage of an innocent young woman, Fusehime, to a courageous dog, Yatsufusa. Supernatural events, such as the transformation of gender and inanimate objects into living beings, are fundamental to plot development in *Hakkenden*. The novel assumes a willing belief in the magical powers of religious symbols and cultural ideas of premodern Japan to move forward with the adventures of its eight heroes. Bakin's overwhelming popularity made his works and his literary style synonymous with Edo period literature.

Finally, Hiromichi refused to perpetuate Motoori Norinaga's central tenet that *Genji* commentary must be purged of foreign and didactic methods of interpretation. This aspect of Norinaga's approach to *Genji* was particularly appealing to Meiji period thinkers, because it provided a convenient bridge from the nativist intellectual tradition of the Edo period (*kokugaku*) to the *kokubungaku* school's promotion of national literature in the early modern period. In rejecting moral didacticism from the interpretation of *Genji*, Norinaga distinguished his work from views that were characteristic of Edo ideology. As a result, Norinaga's reading of *Genji* struck early modern scholars as an enlightened, particularly modern reading of fiction by a native thinker. Ironically, Hiromichi's rejection of this dogmatic interpretive approach made his work appear as a challenge to Norinaga's precocious rejection of Edo ideology.

Paradoxically, those hoping to assert a sense of pride in the Japanese nation-state and national literature began flirting with notions of Western civilization and enlightenment (*bunmei kaika*) at this time. Politicians encouraged the citizens of Japan to abandon the culture associated with the Edo period and to embrace what were perceived to be the overwhelmingly superior aspects of Western civilization. In the early years of the Meiji period, things associated with premodern Japan were deemed feudalistic, unenlightened, and unappealing. This zeal to disassociate themselves with an inferior past often led to a radical and an irrational rejection of things evocative of the material culture and intellectual life in Japan before Meiji. The shotgun marriage of *kokugaku* to *bunmeikaika* that resulted from this flirtation provides us with additional insight into the failure of Hiromichi's scholarship to reach a wider audience. His reference to the supernatural elements to be found in *Genji* was highly evocative of Edo period popular literature. Such qualities would have been viewed as particularly primitive and irrational in comparison to Western standards of empiricism and rationalism. It was much more appealing to simplify *Genji* commentary and eliminate references to the supernatural than to incorporate Hiromichi's interpretive insights into a new, popular edition of the text.

CULTURAL ANXIETY AND THE FIRST TRANSLATION OF *GENJI* INTO ENGLISH

The previous examples establish that Hiromichi's challenge to the preeminence of Norinaga's *mono no aware* theory was not well received among the leading scholars in the early modern era. The response of those outside the *kokubungaku* faction provides even clearer evidence of how profoundly Hiromichi's ideas challenged the connection between *Genji*, nativism, and nostalgia. In 1890, the same year the *Nihon bungaku zensho Genji* came out, a scholar of Chinese studies, Yoda Gakkai (1830–1909), found himself embroiled in a heated debate with the first translator of *Genji* into English, Suematsu Kenchō (1855–1920). The focus of their debate was the relative merit to be found in Hiromichi's *Appraisal of Genji*. This debate provides a clear articulation of the clash between two influential yet diametrically opposed perspectives on the place of *Genji* and traditional literature in the building of a modern nation-state.

Gakkai was a highly respected scholar of Chinese fiction who had also written extensively on the works of Takizawa Bakin. He recorded his activities and thoughts on an almost daily basis from 1856 to 1901. His diary is an invaluable resource for studying the events and ideas that forever altered the intellectual and cultural landscape of Japan during the Meiji period. Although he tried his hand at writing modern fiction he is best known for his role as a mentor to some of the most successful and influential literary figures of the Meiji period, including Mori Ōgai (1862–1922) and Tsubouchi Shōyō. Gakkai tutored Mori Ōgai in classical Chinese when Ōgai was a teenager. Gakkai was also an advocate of "new theater" (*shingeki*) and actively participated in the promotion and development of a modern theater in Japan. It was through his connection with the promotion of new theater that Gakkai first clashed with Suematsu Kenchō. Kenchō sought to directly impose Western theatrical conventions on the production of a new theater in Japan. Gakkai and others rejected this notion in favor of a model in which traditional theatrical methods could be modified to incorporate foreign conventions while maintaining the character of traditional theater.

Among the wealth of information to be found in his diary, Gakkai's comments on *Genji* and its first translation into English are particularly informative. Through his remarks, we are able to observe an initial frustration in reading the tale evolve into a fascination with the story and an appreciation for the complexities of the text. After more than two decades of reading *Genji*, he emerges its champion and passionately argues against those who claimed that young writers in Japan should turn away from such works as *Genji* and look to the West for models of literary inspiration. Gakkai's stance particularly stands out because it came just four years after Tsubouchi Shōyō's influential critique of traditional literary models in his *The Essence of the Novel*.

Gakkai first mentions *Genji* in the entries for the year he began his diary, 1856. After noting that he has borrowed a copy of the *Kogetsushō*, he writes: "Despite its reputation as a generally licentious work, I have heard it said that a man of virtue ought to have read the *Genji monogatari*."[39] This remark characterizes the diligence with which he approached *Genji* and would continue to read it over the next two decades. For the first few years his progress through *Genji* is slow. In 1883, he notes that he has read up to the twenty-fourth chapter, "*Kochō no Maki*" ("The Butterflies"). He also mentions that of all the commentaries he has relied upon in his reading so far, Hagiwara Hiromichi's *Hyōshaku* has proven to be the best.[40] Finally, in 1889, he notes with a great sense of pride that he has read all fifty-four chapters of *Genji* and now intends to begin rereading the text from the beginning.[41] The following year, as he is about halfway through his second reading of *Genji*, he notes in his diary that he has been invited to speak at the next gathering of the literary society to which he belongs. Gakkai chose to promote Hiromichi's *Hyōshaku* at this meeting because of the compelling interpretive insights he believed it could provide readers of *Genji* and students of literature in general. In rebuttal to these positive remarks at the literary society Kenchō condemned the *Hyōshaku*. He found Hiromichi's emphasis on the aesthetic value of ambiguity completely misplaced. In particular, he argued that Hiromichi's interpretive strategy robbed *Genji* of its sense of mystery and beauty. After returning home from the debate with Kenchō, Gakkai recorded the following remarks in his diary:

> Following my talk on the *Genji monogatari hyōshaku*, Kenchō remarked: "*Genji* is well written, but whether such complicated principles are present or not is beside the point. Rather, what is important is that it is written in an engaging manner. For later generations to interpret the text in this way produces precisely the opposite effect, destroying its sense of mystery." . . . Kenchō and I were not in agreement. Concerning the ambiguous passages in *Genji*, he argued that the text did not strictly conform to any compositional principles. He related that when he translated *Genji* into English and showed it to foreigners, they often found this aspect of the text to be vexing. "Each chapter in *Genji* has its own particular aura of mystery, but it is not a continuous narrative from beginning to end. It is not necessary to delve into such things as chronological discrepancies [within the text]." He said one should take pleasure in the delicate nuances to be found in each volume and the work as a whole without theorizing about this and that. There were some points I wanted to make in response, but in the end I turned to Kenchō and said that because I had not spent enough time reading the work in its entirety I would leave my comments at that.[42]

He later added a headnote to this entry, indicating that an article on his talk appeared in a popular daily gazette of the time, the *Kokumin shinbun* (The Nation). Five days after making this entry he notes that he visited the offices of the *Kokumin shinbun* to request a correction about his remarks on *Genji* as reported in the paper.[43]

To gain a better understanding of Gakkai's thoughts on *Genji* at the time, we can turn to the newspaper's account of his lecture and debate with

Suematsu Kenchō, which appeared under the title "Current Events at the Literary Society."

> The literary society held its regular meeting on the thirteenth.... About twenty-eight members were gathered, as if a constellation of smiling faces all gazing in the direction of a single star, none other than Mr. Suematsu Kenchō. Yoda Gakkai moved to the center of the room and lectured on *Genji monogatari*. He then returned to his seat, smiling all the while, and Kenchō, who had a wry expression on his face for most of the lecture, rose to rebut, glancing alternately at the assembled crowd and at Gakkai.[44]

In keeping with the sensationalist tone of the newspapers of the day, the article focused on what was assumed to be the most captivating news for readers. Other than a brief summary of Gakkai's opening remarks, the substance of both talks was overlooked. The article immediately moved to an account of the most dramatic event of the evening under the heading "Verbal Sparring between Gakkai and Kenchō."

> Yoda Gakkai: (laughing) "According to Kenchō, *Genji* is a thoroughly sloppy piece of writing, but to those of us who struggle to write novels it hardly seems appropriate to say that simply because something was written by someone in a past age it is poorly written."
>
> Suematsu Kenchō: "But the Japanese do nothing but praise *Genji* and overlook its flaws."
>
> YG: "You yourself have failed to look at the flaws in your own argument. In short, I am forced to say that without understanding *Genji*, or failing to appreciate it, you recklessly attempt to criticize it with destructive and impetuous argument."
>
> SK: "Yet you, Sensei, rely on this commentary that argues for the importance of passages in which the name of a character is ambiguous leaving you to wonder which character is which in the story. If I'm not mistaken, you are the one who has read this work without understanding it."
>
> YG: "Ha ha, my friend, this is probably beyond your comprehending, but some of us can read *Genji* without commentary and understand it perfectly well. It is precisely those points of ambiguity that make reading a pleasure. For us, works in which chronology and character names are spelled out all too clearly are the poorly written ones. It is no different with poetry. In poems such as those of Mori Kennan, who is here with us this evening, and in the Chinese poems of Li Changji we find pleasure in the passages which defy instant comprehension. You, on the other hand, having translated *Genji* in order to show it to the Europeans [*akahige*; literally, "red beards"]

> without really understanding it find yourself unable to praise the work."
>
> SK: "I have praised it extensively . . ."
>
> YG: "Having grudgingly and imprecisely translated it you find words of praise. One can only imagine how much greater your praise would be had you translated it properly! Kenchō, do you have so little respect for our literary society? Do you treat us as you would some low-ranking bureaucrat? The likes of you wouldn't dare show his face at the meeting of our literary society a second time. To say more will lead to personal attacks, so I shall leave it at that!"
>
> SK: "But Sensei, these are not ideas to which I have arrived in haste!"
>
> YG: "Were they ideas at which you had arrived in astonishing haste one might be able to overlook them, but one can only marvel at the fact that you have arrived at such a position over the course of several years. Indeed, your lecture is completely lacking in merit. . . ."
>
> So continued the heated debate between the elderly scholar and Kenchō, in which neither party was willing to concede defeat, making for a remarkably entertaining event.[45]

The clash of differing worldviews held by Gakkai and Kenchō could hardly be more palpable than in this exchange. Gakkai is struck by the sophistication of *Genji* and the rational, consistent manner in which Hiromichi's commentary reveals its complex structure and literary style. He admires Hiromichi's articulation of an overall structure in *Genji* and cites it as evidence that ambiguous passages should be understood as an aspect of the text contributing to the artistic value of the work. On the other hand, Kenchō claims that *Genji* lacks sophistication and intelligible structure based on the very same details. For Kenchō, Hiromichi's theory is a prime example of the enduring influence of Edo-period traditions and backward ways that the proponents of enlightened civilization have been struggling to rid Japan of since the beginning of the Meiji period. By extension, he sees *Genji* as a relic of a bygone era with little to offer modern Japan.

In 1881, while a student at Cambridge University, Kenchō translated selections from *Genji* into English to provide Western readers with tangible evidence of Japan's great literary heritage. In his introduction he draws the reader's attention to the fact that this "national treasure" dates to the Heian period, when the Japanese had "made remarkable progress in our own language quite independently of any foreign influence."[46] For Kenchō, *Genji*'s greatest value is as a relic of primitive yet pure Japanese genius with many "faults" and "peculiarities" that he asks the Western reader to kindly forgive in reading this treasure of Japan's literary tradition. Since he had only a few months earlier won a seat in Japan's first Diet elections of 1890 the views

Kenchō expressed at the literary society meeting would certainly have been seen as carrying much weight. It must have been particularly unnerving for Gakkai to have his hard-earned views on *Genji* flatly dismissed by such a prominent figure.

Gakkai visited the offices of *Kokumin Shinbun* after the account of his debate with Kenchō was published. He was so disturbed by the characterization of his lecture and the ensuing debate that he submitted a corrected copy of his lecture and demanded that the paper print a revised account of the evening's events. Over the following three days, *Kokumin Shinbun* ran a revised summary of Gakkai's speech, followed by Kenchō's rebuttal. This detailed account of both lectures elaborates upon the particular points of Gakkai's and Kenchō's disagreement. In responding to Gakkai's lecture, Kenchō attempts to dismiss each point Gakkai has raised. In particular, he criticizes Gakkai for endorsing Hiromichi's application of Chinese interpretive theory to *Genji*. He rejects the validity of such theories because, he argues, they must have arisen in China after *Genji* was composed. How, he asks, can these theories shed light on the author's intentions when such ideas were not introduced to Japan until after she had already composed *Genji*? Gakkai's appreciation of Chinese interpretive theory is clearly incompatible with Kenchō's agenda to promote *Genji* as Japan's national treasure, untainted by Chinese influence.

In concluding his rebuttal, Kenchō argues that his views ultimately triumph, because *Genji* is not as masterfully composed as Hiromichi, or Gakkai, would have us believe.

> On the whole *Genji* is well written. I say "on the whole" because when I translated it into English there were places where the meaning would not have been clear had I not supplemented what was in the original Japanese. I find it difficult to say that the prose is truly beautiful. I fear that if *Genji* is unconditionally protected from critical review it may contribute to a stagnation of Japanese literature. I might venture to say that theories concerning *Genji*'s compositional principles, such as its structural warp and woof as we just heard in the previous lecture on Hagiwara Hiromichi, are not necessarily desirable.[47]

He goes on to draw an analogy between Hiromichi's commentary and Buddhist lore concerning the interpretation of natural images to be found in a limestone cave. The analogy is meant to suggest that there is no more rational meaning behind Hiromichi's identification of specific principles of composition at work in *Genji* than there is in the random rock formations to be found in a limestone cave. Kenchō is attempting to underscore what he considers the irrational, and ultimately unenlightened, nature of Hiromichi's theory. He goes on to list the various ways in which *Genji* pales in comparison to Western works of literature, to conclude that "*Genji* should not serve as a guide to future literary efforts."

From his careful reading of *Genji* for nearly three decades, Yoda Gakkai acquired a profound appreciation for the structure and language of the text. At the same time, he was well versed in current discussion of theories of the novel and Western literature in Japan. Hagiwara Hiromichi's *Hyōshaku* provided an interpretive framework that he believed would allow readers to favorably consider *Genji* within the context of modern novels. For this reason he brought it to the attention of the literary society. Kenchō's critical reception of Gakkai's lecture is revealing on several levels. After having translated *Genji* into English, Kenchō's denial of its literary value suggests that the process of translation resulted in his heightened awareness for how different *Genji* is from the norms of European literature. In large part, we can attribute this to the fact that he was translating into a language and literature whose norms were still new to him. The translation itself confirms that he was more concerned with producing an English text that met with the approval of Westerners than with producing an accurate rendering of the tale. At one point in the debate Kenchō even admits that he had never bothered to read *Genji* in its entirety.

Kenchō's response also illustrates the extent to which the broader political and cultural issues of the day entered into discourse on native literature. His concern that *Genji* fails to meet the standards of Western literature is similar to the stance taken by scholars in previous eras who emphasized *Genji*'s failure to embody the ideals of Buddhism and Confucianism. His rejection of Hiromichi's interpretive theory because it is derived in part from traditional Chinese literary criticism speaks to his motivation for translating *Genji* in the first place. Hiromichi's notion that Chinese interpretive theory might be useful in appreciating *Genji* contradicts his goal of establishing the superiority of Japanese sentiment.

Although Gakkai's admiration for Hiromichi's interpretation of *Genji* met with flat rejection by one of the most influential political figures of his day, anecdotal evidence suggests that his appreciation for what Hiromichi had to offer was handed down to his students and admirers in the field of literature, including Mori Ōgai and Tsubouchi Shōyō.

In his novel *Vita Sexualis* (*Ita sekusuarisu*, 1909) Ōgai includes a semi-autobiographical account of his lessons as a teenager in classical Chinese with a certain Professor Bunen (*Bunen Sensei*), who is also referred to by the nonsense name "Echi Tofu."[48] When Professor Bunen leaves the room, the student curiously peeks at the book the teacher is hiding under his writing table to discover a copy of what we understand to be a rather racy text written in Chinese. While Gakkai's diary does not refer specifically to having tutored Ōgai in classical Chinese, it does mention his reading the *Dream of the Red Chamber* at about the same time that Ōgai would have studied under him. In fact, it is during this period that Gakkai is completing his reading of *Genji* and notes that he has decided to read *Genji* and the *Dream of the Red Chamber* concurrently. Given his expression of admiration for Hiromichi's interpretive strategy, it is likely that Gakkai chose to read the *Dream of the Red Chamber* to apply Hiromichi's interpretive strategy from *Genji* to another long and complex work of prose fiction. In an article published years later, he makes reference to the fact that he approaches both *Genji* and the *Dream of the Red Chamber* as if they are novels (*shōsetsu*).[49]

Articles appearing in the literary journal *Shigarami sōshi* (The Weir), which Ōgai founded and closely oversaw in its early years of publication, indicate that Ōgai held Hiromichi's work in high esteem. An article in an early issue of the journal describing a trip to Hiromichi's grave in Osaka is signed by one "Echi Tofu." A follow-up article continues to describe at some length Hiromichi's accomplishments as a scholar of literature. It is possible that the fictitious Echi Tofu was either Gakkai writing under the pseudonym Ōgai had given him in *Vita Sexualis* or Ōgai himself, using the pseudonym he had given to the teacher who introduced him to the writings of Hiromichi. In either case, anecdotal evidence suggests that Ōgai shared Gakkai's admiration for Hiromichi's work on *Genji*.

GENJI AND THE ESSENCE OF THE MODERN NOVEL

Tsubouchi Shōyō is best known for his translation of the complete works of Shakespeare into Japanese between 1884 and 1928. His *The Essence of the Novel* is widely considered the first substantial treatise on contemporary literary criticism in Meiji Japan. Shōyō's complete works contain an account of his efforts to mature as a writer, translator, and literary critic. In this essay, composed in 1920, Shōyō also reveals a number of details concerning the setbacks he experienced in seeking to master Western literature and to contribute to the development of a new language for the novel in Japan. At the beginning of the essay he condemns his childhood fascination with popular fiction in general, and the works of Takizawa Bakin in particular, as a "pernicious infection" and a debilitating intoxication. After attending lectures in philosophy from American instructors at Tokyo University and studying Shakespeare, he attempts to write a Japanese version of *Hamlet* in novel form. To develop his story depicting the inner struggle of the individual, he turns to more familiar material by borrowing plot devices and characters from his favorite work of historical fiction by Bakin, *Daring Adventures of Chivalrous Men*. An analysis of Shōyō's *Essence of the Novel* indicates that many of the terms he uses to develop his systematic theory of the modern novel, which he attributes to Bakin's *Hakkenden* and Motoori Norinaga's *Genji monogatari tama no ogushi* in terms of Japanese sources, are actually taken from Hiromichi's postscript to the final volume of *Daring Adventures of Chivalrous Men*.[50] Hiromichi's postscript discusses many of these terms with the same complexity and distinction of terminology Shōyō includes in his *Essence of the Novel*. Shōyō's argument concerning the modern novel in this essay also contains many references to *Genji* that also suggest he must have been familiar with Hiromichi's *Appraisal of Genji*. A particularly telling example of Hiromichi's influence comes in Shōyō's reference to the "Kumogakure" chapter, which appears only as a title in *Genji*. In suggesting models of exemplary technique in the composition of fiction, Shōyō writes:

> In the "Kumogakure" chapter of *The Tale of Genji*, Murasaki Shikibu informs the reader of Genji's death merely by alluding to his passing. Ultimately, the attention paid to technique in this way is what characterizes the elegance of this great female literary talent.[51]

Shōyō could not have arrived at such a conclusion from reading Norinaga's *Tama no ogushi* alone. At no point does Norinaga praise the compositional style of *Genji* in terms of textual ambiguity or the ellipsis of chapters. This point is surprisingly similar to the comments made by Hiromichi in his *Appraisal of Genji*.

Despite this evidence indicating an indebtedness to Hiromichi's literary theories, Shōyō makes no reference to Hiromichi by name or to his work in any of his most famous literary treatises. This failure is especially telling in the essay that follows in which he refers to *Daring Adventures of Chivalrous Men* as his favorite literary work from his childhood. What he does not note here, or in his treatise on the modern novel, is that *Daring Adventures* was actually completed by Hagiwara Hiromichi in 1849, following Bakin's death the previous year.

A clearer understanding of Shōyō's deep love of Edo period fiction and his efforts to distance himself from its influence in becoming a modern writer and critic may provide insight into his reluctance to attribute some of his interpretive innovations to Hiromichi. In the essay in which he describes his love of *Daring Adventures of Chivalrous Men*, Shōyō confesses that he repeatedly sought to integrate what he loved from traditional fiction with what he believes to be important in modern literature, but he is merely appalled by the results. These failures result in the wholesale rejection of the traditional and familiar. An initial impulse to criticize Bakin's moral didacticism eventually results in the sweeping rejection of known conventions of prose composition in Japanese at the time. Shōyō then condemns the language in which he composed his own most famous translations and critical essays for their "intolerable phrasing in the style of Bakin." This radical rejection of the familiar leads to an unbearable sense of alienation. Even conscious efforts to alter the way he writes fail to produce the desired result. As a result, he temporarily becomes unable to write in Japanese. He confesses that the decision at the height of his career to abandon all hope of becoming a modern novelist is rooted in this lifelong infatuation with Edo period melodramas and lyric prose rich in Confucian and Buddhist morality and his inability to exorcise "Bakin's ghost" from his literary imagination.

At the end of the essay he explains how the "struggle" (lit. *sutoragguru*) he has just described led to his role in contributing to the development of a modern vernacular style of prose (*gembun itchi*) in Japan. He argues that other influential authors and critics of the time, including Ozaki Kōyō (1868–1903) and Futabatei Shimei (1864–1909), experienced a similarly painful process of linguistic, spiritual, and intellectual conversion. He then suggests that anyone setting out to become a novelist in Japan today can hardly imagine how fortunate he is to not have to endure this painful conversion.

The engaging description of his struggle to reject traditional literary models provides us with valuable insight into the process of modernization and Westernization prominent in Japan at this time. Shōyō's account is particularly useful in illustrating how authors and critics of the time felt compelled to distance themselves from things associated with the Edo period. Shōyō's own struggle to distance himself from Edo culture was manifest in the form of his complete rejection of Bakin's literature and literary style. Norinaga's *mono no aware* theory was perceived as a precociously modern rejection of Edo period didacticism. For this reason, Shōyō avoids any reference to Hiromichi and traces his own innovations in the *Essence of the Novel* back to Norinaga's interpretation of *Genji*.

This abstract discussion of intellectual history and cultural anxiety is perhaps best brought to a close by turning to a more concrete example. The literary and cultural concerns Shōyō touches upon in his personal essay of 1920 are closely related to factors that influenced the reception of Hiromichi's work. The essay is particularly revealing in the way it connects literary criticism, national identity, and nostalgia. Therefore, a number of parallels exist between Shōyō's efforts to distance himself from Edo literary aesthetics and the broader trend of his contemporaries to dismiss Hiromichi's work on *Genji*. The essay also spans the period of Shōyō's early childhood, the final decades of the Edo period, through the Taishō period, which coincides with a crucial time in the reception of the *Hyōshaku*. Shōyō begins with his arrival in Tokyo as a scholarship student from the less urbane city of Nagoya some eight years after the Meiji Restoration:

> I came to Tokyo the summer of 1876 as a scholarship student from Aichi prefecture. I had already turned eighteen at the time but was far from being mature for my age. I was probably no more mature than your average fifteen year old of today. One of my classmates, Katō Takaaki (1860–1926), had been sent to Tokyo on a scholarship a few years before me and had already begun studying at Tokyo Kaisei Gakkō, which became part of Tokyo Imperial University the following year. Katō was a year younger than me, but I looked up to him as if he were my senior of five or six years. On our trips back home Katō was always the one to take charge of things. Another classmate, Rokurō Taishō (1860–1930), had been in Tokyo just as long, was also a year my junior, and he too outstripped me in terms of height, scholarship, intelligence, and judgment. He was better than me at everything we did. What, might you ask, was the cause of my immaturity? The obvious answer is simply that I was endowed with traits inferior to my contemporaries. However, an even more precise reason exists. From an early age I had suffered from an infectious disease.

At the age of seven or eight I had become contaminated by an all-consuming passion for popular literature. Unlike the novels of today, the illustrated story books (*kusazōshi*) and popular novels (*yomihon*) back then were completely lacking in practical value. In particular, my infection from the most pernicious writer of all, Takizawa Bakin, rendered me a feeble-minded child of sorts for some time. Quite probably, the poison still lingers somewhere in my brain. At a time when most children my age had already begun to read *The Records of the Grand Historian* and *The First Selection of Imperial Poetry and Prose*, I had failed to even begin learning the rudiments of the *Five Confucian Classics*, because every free moment available I indulged in the reading and re-reading of such works as Bakin's *Legend of the Eight Dog Warriors* and *Daring Adventures of Chivalrous Men*.[52]

My association with Bakin now stretches back four or five decades. I think I first became a devout follower of Bakin around the age of nine, when my family still lived in the village of Mino Ōta in Gifu prefecture, where I was born.[53] At home the book anyone capable of deciphering even the simplest writing could read was an abridged version of Bakin's *Legend of the Eight Dog Warriors* in about 20 fascicles. It was charmingly illustrated and free of any embellishments, argumentation, and extraneous text so as to appeal to even the least sophisticated reader. Reading the *Legend of the Eight Dog Warriors* inspired my first love of Bakin. After I turned eleven and we moved to Nagoya, I visited book lenders every day and read mindless fiction with total abandon. I made my way through anything by Bakin I could find. So it is that I came to worship him with blind devotion. This fascination and intoxication continued up to the very moment I was sent to Tokyo to study. Until that time I remained completely unaware of my own immaturity and mental deficiency.

I was so consumed by Bakin's mechanical, mindless style of repeatedly phrasing things in seven and five syllables combined with his excessive pedantry and dramatization that I lost interest in reading anything else. If it wasn't Bakin it seemed watered down and flavorless, the way traditional Kyoto cuisine tastes bland or country cooking tastes too salty after one has grown accustomed to eating Chinese food. When I was in Nagoya I almost completely ignored puppet theater productions, works by Saikaku and Chikamatsu, Hachimonjiya comedies, chapbooks, and various works of pulp fiction.[54] On the rare occasion when I did go to the theater I paid so little attention I might as well not have gone at all. Not only had my senses become dulled, but also my intoxication had sunk to the level of addiction. Bakin's works were quite popular at the time, and most people could recite some of his more famous lines by heart. But the range of my own memorization was far from average. Foolish as this may sound, even today with my terribly diminished powers of recall, I can recite a good portion of his works from memory.

As the summer I was to set off for Tokyo approached, I recall two occasions on which I dreamed of meeting Bakin at some house in Tokyo. At the time I felt so pleased to see "my teacher" still alive, though I knew he had died several decades earlier. How foolish I was. My fantasy was to become Bakin's disciple and receive the precepts from him so that I too might become a great novelist.

I grew up during the Meiji Restoration with the warrior Kusunoki Masashige [d. 1336] as my ideal hero. Naturally, my favorite work by Bakin when I was fifteen or sixteen was *Daring Adventures of Chivalrous Men.*[55] In an attempt to imitate the central theme of *Daring Adventures* I tried dashing off something in the style of a novel based on the first work by Shakespeare everyone reads, *Hamlet.* Naturally, the plot I concocted centered on the great-great grandchildren of the imperial loyalists Kusunoki and Nitta Yoshisada. My attempt to produce five or ten pages resulted in something inexplicably strange.[56] Needless to say, my skills, in particular my intellectual command of the material, were hardly up to the task. Never before in my twenty years had I attempted anything like it. . . .

My contact with Western novels—primarily the works of late-eighteenth-century English writers such as Scott, Bulwer-Lytton, and Dickens, as well as Dumas, among the French writers—was relatively early in Japan, so that my own passion for Bakin cooled rather early as well. As such, I was probably the first to publicly criticize Bakin's works. My infatuation with Bakin being as strong as it was, I found the task of reacting against his style to be particularly challenging. My *Essence of the Novel* does not bear my remarks on this in great detail, but in the preface to my translation of Lytton's *Reinze*, I devote a great deal of space to a critique of Bakin's written style which had been the object of veneration for so long.[57] Despite my critical stance, I was unable to escape the long-ingrained habit of phrasing things in seven and five syllables using Bakin's awkward, imprecise style. Everything I wrote—whether it is a critical treatise, a translation, or fiction—came out in this dreadful, intolerable, seven-five meter. My *Essence of the Novel* suffers from being written in this style, as do my translations of Bulwer-Lytton and Scott, and my other attempts at writing prose narrative for popular literature.

My initial dissatisfaction with the content of Bakin's works grew into a sense of antipathy for everything about his writing. In particu-

> lar, his seven-five meter began to seem unpleasant to me. I had finally reached the point where I was ready to make my first attempt at wanting to write without resorting to this bad stylistic habit, but I was like a small bird ensnared in a net with no means of escape. I suffered terribly from this lingering evil until 1902 or 1903.
>
> To people today, this must seem like nothing more than a matter of choosing a style in which to write. However, for about a decade, from approximately 1877 to 1887, the literary world struggled in part to come to terms with this issue. At the time it was referred to as "*gembun itchi*"—unification of the spoken and written language. It was a difficult process giving birth to what has matured into today's vernacular style of literature. I will avoid going into a lengthy historical explanation here, but I should like to note that even Ozaki Kōyō and Futabatei Shimei struggled with this same idea and wasted countless hours in its resolution. Those trying to get started today as writers should consider themselves fortunate that they do not have to think about such things. The struggle to emancipate myself from this mock-Bakin style was one part of this painful process. In all matters, it is easiest to follow one's habitual way of doing things. That way everything just seems to fall into place. Especially for a writer, there is nothing harder than trying to write in a new way using a different style after becoming accustomed to a particular way of writing over the course of so many years. When I wrote *Tōsei Shosei katagi* (*The Character of Today's Students*, 1885–1886), I thought of myself as an author of fiction and devoted whatever time I wasn't teaching at Waseda University—which was over 40 hours per week—working for a magazine or newspaper, preparing for my classes, or reading for myself—to writing what amounted to a spectacular literary failure. At any rate, once I began to reflect on my failure and the shame I felt at my own lack of sincerity and good judgment and my inability to write except in the style I had become accustomed to over the years, it should come as no surprise that I was no longer able to write. I had become so inwardly focused on my habitual style that I found myself unable to move even a few steps beyond it. Around 1888–89 I completely gave up on writing novels. Among the various reasons for giving up writing the foremost was that I continued to be possessed by Bakin's ghost.[58]

Distinguishing the romance from the reality of Shōyō's narrative based solely on this account is no easy task. While he divulges some of his most heartfelt secrets and is brutally honest in his confession, one is left to wonder whether this is simply a tale of youthful ignorance or a narrative of profound cultural conversion. In either case, the specter of Bakin's ghost, which gave Shōyō such cause for concern, helps to explain why he traces his innovations in literary criticism back to Norinaga while avoiding any reference to Hiromichi in his *Essence of the Novel.* For Shōyō and many of his contemporaries Norinaga's *mono no aware* was like a charm capable of warding off the anxieties of cultural difference. When appraising *Genji* this theory made it possible to imagine that the most cherished object of native literature was somehow immune to unflattering comparison.

CONCLUSION

To refer to Hiromichi in the Meiji period was to risk associating oneself with scholarship that failed to embrace modernity. This chapter has established that the stigma of Edo backwardness was strong enough to force at least two influential scholars of the Meiji period to avoid promoting Hiromichi's *Appraisal of Genji*: Shōyō was certainly aware of the benefits Hiromichi's critical innovations offered but silently applied them to his own articulation of what the novel should become in modern Japan. Only a few years after Shōyō published his *Essence of the Novel*, Kenchō sought to ridicule Gakkai for promoting the *Hyōshaku.* Despite the apparent merits of Gakkai's argument and the failings of Kenchō's in terms of the literary value of *Genji*, the overwhelming force of Kenchō's position silenced Gakkai and caused this attitude to be perpetuated by subsequent generations of scholars in the Taishō and early Shōwa periods. At the same time, the preeminence of Norinaga's *mono no aware* theory remained relatively unchallenged. Orikuchi Shinobu, Kobayashi Hideo and their contemporaries continued to find inspiration in Norinaga's work for their own exploration of the roots of Japanese culture well into Japan's modern era. The painful changes wrought by World War II and the postwar economic boom provided enough distance from the anxiety of Edo influence that intellectuals no longer felt compelled to turn away from the work of Hagiwara Hiromichi. Since the 1980s, scholars have increasingly turned to Hiromichi's *Appraisal of Genji* in discussing the development literary analysis in the Edo period. Noguchi Takehiko's study of *Genji* commentary in the Edo period (*Genji monogatari o Edo kara yomu*, 1985) brought Hiromichi's innovative use of interpretive terminology to the attention of a wider audience.

The absence of Hagiwara Hiromichi's name and references to his scholarship in works of the Meiji period speaks volumes. This rejection serves as a testament to the power of his interpretive insights to challenge the values of a generation bent on bolstering national pride at all costs. The silencing of Hiromichi's voice illustrates in only a small way the enormous intellectual price that was paid for such intense devotion to the promotion of national identity during the Meiji and Taishō periods. Hagiwara Hiromichi devoted the final years of his life to crafting an interpretive strategy that made possible an appraisal of *Genji* as a masterpiece of prose fiction. However, the notion that *Genji* is primarily about transporting us to a time and place that reveal the unique roots of Japan's cultural identity continues to be an appealing fantasy, both within Japan and to readers beyond its borders. As the examples of *Genji's* reception in the modern era provided in chapter 1 illustrate, the link that Norinaga promoted between *Genji* and nostalgia remains surprisingly intact.

Hiromichi sought to transcend interpretation that catered to the attraction of nostalgia. He believed any reader was capable of appreciating *Genji* on a more sophisticated level. The close examination of a passage from his *Appraisal of Genji* succinctly illustrates why his scholarship merits greater recognition as a landmark in the reception and interpretation of *Genji*.

In the opening chapter of the tale, Genji's mother, Kiritsubo, falls ill. Genji's father, the Emperor, is overcome with grief when he realizes how serious her illness has become. Reluctantly, he accedes to Kiritsubo's wishes and allows her to return home to die. News of her death soon reaches the Emperor. This scene begins as follows:

> Hearing of Kiritsubo's death, the Emperor was so heartbroken he could think of nothing else and retreated to the solitude of his chambers.
>
> He wanted their son to remain with him, but children this young were still expected to observe mourning for a parent. Kiritsubo's son had to leave the palace. The little boy could not understand what was happening. *He looked on in surprise* at the attendants as they sobbed and at the tears streaming down his father's face. Such a separation would be immensely sorrowful under the best of circumstances, but in this case the parting was poignant beyond description [*mashite, aware ni iukai nashi*].[59]

The *Hyōshaku* directs our attention to an aspect of this passage that appears to have been overlooked by other commentaries.[60] Hiromichi focuses on the line in the original text that reads *ayashi to mimatsuri tamaeru*. This is translated above as *He looked on in surprise.* For this passage, Hiromichi provides the following interpretation:

> This expression so fully captures the profound sadness of the scene that it is painful and upsetting simply to read it.[61]

Hiromichi's comment draws our attention to the literary style and sophistication of the tale in a way that no other commentary of his time ever did. His interpretation urges us to read the text as closely as he did and appreciate the power of this description. He draws our attention not only to the fact that it is beyond the ability of a child so young to comprehend the traumatic events that have just unfolded, but also how the author conveys this information to us and how it influences our reading of the tale. His footnote invites readers to appreciate the capacity of this specific phrase to succinctly convey Genji's innocence and vulnerability. This sadness is intensified because the

Emperor's own grief is compounded in seeing the perplexed expression on his son's face. The loss experienced by both father and son conveyed by this sentence is so profound that it will remain with them both for the rest of their lives. The helplessness and piercing sadness of this moment resonate throughout Genji's life and the decisions he makes in the remaining chapters of the tale.

Looking back on Hiromichi's biography, one might argue that the death of his mother when he was six and the subsequent loss of his stepmother were personal experiences that made the tale especially meaningful to him. The footnote he provides for this passage conveys how profoundly moving this scene must have been for him. Hiromichi sought to bring *Genji* to life for others in a way that was faithful to his own close engagement with the text. He urges readers to understand that the sense of loss and nostalgia in the tale can teach us something about the way people experience the world. Hiromichi's *Appraisal of Genji* offers this insight to any reader, regardless of nationality or ideology, who wishes to understand what makes *Genji* a great work of fiction. Despite the enormity of change since the age of the last samurai, this interpretive approach has not diminished in significance as we continue to search for ways to explain and understand cultural difference.

Notes

INTRODUCTION

1. *GMH*, 57. Hiromichi's general remarks (*sōron*) on *Genji* were reprinted in Akiyama Ken, ed., *Hihyōshūsei Genji monogatari* (Tokyo: Yumani Shobō, 1999). The passage translated here appears in *Hihyōshūsei Genji monogatari* 2: 347. Most references in this book are to the complete, typeset edition of the *Genji monogatari hyōshaku*, abbreviated as GMH. In correspondence prior to publication of the *Appraisal of Genji*, Hiromichi specifically mentions that he expects his work on *Genji* to "topple" the dominant edition of the text at the time, Kitamura Kigin's *Kogetsushō* (1673). This point is discussed in chapter 2. Portions of this introduction were presented at the symposium titled, "*The Tale of Genji* in Japan and the World: Social Imaginary, Media and Cultural Production" held at Columbia University on March 25 and 26th, 2005.

2. Kōda Rohan, *Rohan zenshū* (Tokyo: Iwanami Shoten, 1978), 32: 207.

3. See, for example, Nakamura Mitsuo, *Japanese Fiction in the Meiji Era* (Tokyo: Kokusai Bunka Shinkokai, 1966), 39. Nakamura characterizes Shōyō as promoting a "revival of the thought of Motoori Norinaga."

4. Kobayashi Hideo, *Motoori Norinaga* (Tokyo: Shinchōsha, 1977), 1:7. The quotation in Japanese emphasizes Orikuchi's familiarity with Norinaga by using the expression "Norinaga-san" to refer to the historical figure as if he were a personal acquaintance.

5. Takahashi Tōru, *Genji monogatari no taihō* (Tokyo Daigaku Shuppankai, 1982), i.

6. In English, see T. J. Harper, "Motoori Norinaga's Criticism of the 'Genji monogatari' " (Ph.D. dissertation, University of Michigan, 1971); H. Harootunian, *Things Seen and Unseen: Discourse and Ideology in Tokugawa Nativism* (Chicago: University of Chicago Press, 1988); S. Burns, *Before the Nation: Kokugaku and the Imagining of Community in Early Modern Japan* (Durham, NC: Duke University Press, 2003).

CHAPTER ONE

1. J. Robinson, *Takarazuka* (University of California Press, 1998), 152–59.

2. Tanizaki Jun'ichirō is given credit as editorial supervisor and the noted scholar of classical literature Ikeda Kikan is billed as having reviewed the script, emphasizing

the film's historical authenticity. Fujita Masayuki, *Eiga no naka no Nihonshi* (Tokyo: Chirekisha, 1997), 36.

3. J. Anderson and D. Richie, eds., *The Japanese Film* (Princeton, N.J.: Princeton University Press, 1982), 225.

4. Similar sections of Tanizaki's first *Genji* translation were expunged by military censors. See Gaye Rowley, *Yosano Akiko and* The Tale of Genji (Ann Arbor, MI: Center for Japanese Studies University of Michigan, 2000), 154.

5. *NKBZS* 4.503–04: R. Tyler, trans., *The Tale of Genji* (New York: Viking, 2001), 763.

6. Egawa's *Genji monogatari* was so successful that the publisher, Shūeisha, quickly released a bound print edition of all of the magazine installments from "Ultra Jump" for the first chapter of *Genji* in 2001. Other adaptations of *Genji* published since the 1980s include: Yamato Waki's illustrated comic *Asakiyumemishi* ("*The Tale of Genji* seen in a Shallow Dream"), first published by the women's magazine *Gekkan mimi*. *Asakiyumemishi* began in 1979 and continued in serialized publication for over a decade. Setouchi Jakuchō published a translation of *Genji* into modern Japanese between 1996 and 1998. Setouchi's translation, published by Kodansha, continued to sell well into 2000.

7. Takarazuka Flower Troupe, program (4/7–5/15/2000), *Takarazuka myujikaru roman Genji monogatari asaki yumemishi*, published by Hankyu Corporation. No page numbers or publication date. Tanabe revised her *Shin Genji monogatari* in composing the script for the two prior productions of *Genji* at Takarazuka in 1981 and 1989.

8. The 2,000 yen note bearing a portrait of Murasaki Shikibu and a scene from an illustrated *Genji* hand scroll, to which Tanabe refers, was issued by the Japanese Ministry of Finance in 2000.

9. For an interesting discussion of *Genji* as gossip, see the chapter "Miyabi to skyandaru" in Tōru Takahashi, *Monogatari no sen'nen* (Tokyo: Shinwasha, 1999), 10–12. Roundtable participants suggest that fascination with the Princess Diana scandal and tragedy is similar to the Heian fascination with *Genji*.

10. *Murasaki Shikibu nikki*, *SNKBT*, 24: 285, Cf. R. Bowring, *The Diary of Lady Murasaki* (Cambridge: Cambridge University Press, 1988), 33.

11. *SNKBT*, v. 20, 439. Cf. Tyler, trans., *The Tale of Genji*, 461.

12. *Shakkyōka* (*waka* that take Buddhist teachings or material from Buddhist literature as their subject matter) represent an important exception to this generalization. Beginning with the *Goshūishū* (completed 1086), *shakkyōka* appear as a category of *waka* in Imperial anthologies. Such poems take Buddhist concepts, language, or symbols as their inspiration, but they are not necessarily evaluated in terms of Buddhist philosophy. Poetry centering on Confucian and Taoist themes appears briefly in the *Man'yōshū* as a form of experimentation with new concerns learned from China, but as R. Brower and E. Miner observe, "from the perspective of literary history, they remain only curiosities, evidence of experimentation briefly attempted by single poets in one generation and then abandoned forever" (*Japanese Court Poetry* [Stanford, CA: Stanford University Press, 1961], 91).

13. See T. J. Harper's dissertation, "Motoori Norinaga's Criticism of the 'Genji Monogatari'" (chapter 4), where he provides a valuable discussion of the relationship between poetry and early *Genji* criticism.

14. *SNKBT*, v. 19, 227. Cf. Tyler, *The Tale of Genji*, 157.

15. Setsuko Ito, *An Anthology of Traditional Japanese Poetry Competitions* (Bochum: Brockmeyer, 1991), 237, note.

16. Konishi Jin'ichi, *Shinkō roppyakuban utaawase* (Tokyo: Yūseidōshuppan, 1976), 188.

17. Konishi Jin'ichi, *Shinkō roppyakuban utaawase*, 557 (*kaisetsu*).

18. Had Toshinari been more concerned about an appreciation of *Genji* as prose fiction, there are other references to "barren fields" in *Genji* to which he would probably have seen fit to refer. Particularly in the later chapter, "Minori" (*SNKBT* 4, 503) this image is used with great poignancy.

19. See corresponding entry in Ikeda Kikan, *Genji monogatari jiten* (Tokyo: Tōkyōdō Shuppan, 1965), 2: 43. Ikeda states that the *Kakaishō* is a compilation of the results of the early period of *Genji* studies and therefore had an impact on all subsequent commentaries.

20. Kadokawa, *Nihonshi jiten*. See entries "An'na no hen" and "Minamoto no Takaakira."

21. Noguchi Takehiko, *Genji monogatari o Edo kara yomu* (Tokyo: Kōdansha, 1985), 215.

22. See Zeami, *On the Art of Noh Drama* (Princeton, N.J.: Princeton University Press, 1984), 153–54. See also J. Goff, *Noh Drama and* The Tale of Genji (Princeton, N.J.: Princeton University Press, 1991), 1 10.

23. J. Goff, *Noh Drama and* The Tale of Genji, 7.

24. Noguchi Takehiko, *Genji monogatari o Edo kara yomu*, 215.

25. J. McMullen, *Genji Gaiden* (Reading: Ithaca Press, 1991), 38–41.

26. See Noguchi Takehiko, *Genji monogatari o Edo kara yomu*, 212–13.

27. Ikeda Kikan, *Genji monogatari jiten* 2: 100.

28. For example, Kamo no Mabuchi's *Genji shinshaku* and Motoori Norinaga's *Tama no ogushi* were both based on editions of the *Kogetsushō*.

29. P. Nosco, *Remembering Paradise* (Cambridge, MA: Harvard University Press, 1990), 53. This was not a notion unique to Mitsukuni. As Brower and Miner note in *Japanese Court Poetry*, the *Man'yōshū*, *Kojiki*, and *Nihonshoki* reflect the desire of early Japanese scholars "to possess their own equivalents of the Chinese books that were known to them" (84).

30. The extant version of the *Genchū shūi* contains eight fascicles. The eighth fascicle on general themes and the author's intention is believed to have been appended to the *Genchū shūi* by later scholars. See Ikeda Kikan, *Genji monogatari jiten* 2: 97.

31. See Nosco, *Remembering Paradise*, 55–56. In particular, note 29 refers to *Genchū shūi* (Hisamatsu Sen'ichi, ed.), 6: 294.

32. See Nosco, *Remembering Paradise*, 55, 64.

33. The expression "poignancy of things" as a translation of the term *mono no aware* requires two points of caution. First, the term *poignancy* should be considered in both its negative sense associated with pain and sorrow and its positive sense associated with pleasure and amusement. Norinaga did not limit the range of emotions associated with *mono no aware* to matters of sadness and sorrow. Second, the term *things* should be

taken in the broader context of event, circumstance, and matter of concern rather than simply "things" as inanimate objects.

CHAPTER TWO

1. See Tsuji Tatsuya, "Politics in the Eighteenth Century," in *The Cambridge History of Japan*, ed. vol. 4 (Cambridge : Cambridge University Press, 1991), 425–77, especially the section on Kyōhō reforms, 441–56.

2. Uno Shun'ichi, *Nihon zenshi* (Tokyo: Kōdansha, 1991), 654.

3. Morikawa Akira, "Hagiwara Hiromichi *no jijōden*," *Konton* 8 (1982): 11–12.

4. See "Part II: A Warrior's Life," in McMullen's *Genji Gaiden.*

5. See Kudō Shinjirō, *Fujii Takanao to Matsunoya-ha* (Tokyo: Kazama Shobō, 1986) for a detailed discussion of Fujii Takanao's life and study of *kokugaku.*

6. Fujii Manabu, *Okayama ken no rekishi* (Tokyo: Yamakawa Shuppansha, 2000), 251.

7. Morikawa Akira, "Hagiwara Hiromichi *no jijōden*," 19–20. Keichū was credited with memorizing the *Hyakunin isshu* in the span of only ten days at the age of five (Mostow, *Pictures of the Heart*, 34.). Such legends and his own respect for Keichū's work may have reinforced Hiromichi's fondness for this childhood memory.

8. Yamazaki Katsuaki, *Ashi* 2 (1997): 24. Cf. *Jijōden ka*, 14.

9. Yamazaki Katsuaki, *Ashi* 2 (1997): 24.

10. Morikawa Akira, "Hagiwara Hiromichi *no jijōden*," 21–22.

11. Morikawa Akira, "*Genji monogatari hyōshaku* no shuppan," *Konton* 5 (1978): 33.

12. Yamazaki Katsuaki, "Hagiwara Hiromichi *ryakunenpukō*," *Kokubun ronsō* 17 (March 1990): 66–72.

13. See Nakamura Yukihiko, "*Jinseiha no shijintachi*," in *Nihon bungaku no rekishi* 8: 466. Also see entry on Hiraga Motoyoshi in San'yō Shinbunsha, *Okayama-ken rekishi jinbutsu jiten.* (Okayama-shi: San'yō Shinbunsha, 1994), 844. Motoyoshi's distinctive poetry and his intense devotion to a *Man'yōshū* style of composition later attracted the admiration of modern writer Masaoka Shiki (1867–1902).

14. Yamazaki Katsuaki, *Ashi* 6 (2000): 97–98. Motoyoshi comments that he counted Hiromichi among his lifelong friends, but no comments by Hiromichi remain beyond his recollection of this first encounter.

15. Morikawa Akira, "Hagiwara Hiromichi *no jijōden,*" 23.

16. For reference to Hiromichi's contact with Ōkuni, see Yamazaki Katsuaki in Ichinichi kai, *Hagiwara Hiromichi shokan*, 235–37. For a discussion of the difficulty in establishing the exact details of their relationship, see Yamazaki Katsuaki's article "Ōkuni Takamasa to Hagiwara Hiromichi," *Kokubun ronkō* 20: 3 (1993): 52–66. The previous term philology is a translation of the phrase "*te-ni-wo-ha no kaku*," which Hiromichi uses in reference to the instruction he received from Ōkuni. Ōkuni in turn uses the same phrase to refer to what Motoori Norinaga contributed to the development of nativist studies in Japan. See the *kaisetsu* to Ōkuni's work in *Nihon shisō taikei*, vol. 50, p. 629.

17. M. McNally, "Phantom History: Hirata Atsutane and Tokugawa Nativism" (Ph. D. dissertation, UCLA, 1998) p. 536 from Ōkuni's *Gakuto benron*, n. 54.

18. J. Mostow, *Pictures of the Heart* (Honolulu: University of Hawaii Press, 1996), 34–38. Quotation from *Hyakunin ishhu shinshō,* as cited by Ōtsubo Toshikinu in Kagawa Kageki, "*Hyakushu iken*," (Osaka: Izumi Shoin, 1999), 10.

19. Kagawa Kageki, "*Hyakushu iken*," 10–11. On Kageki, see also Keene, *World within Walls*, (New York: Holt Rinehart and Winston, 1976), 486–97.

20. See entry on Nariai Ōe in San'yō Shinbunsha, *Okayama-ken rekishi jinbutsu jiten*, 727.

21. Kagawa Kageki, *Hyakushu iken* (1826). The manuscript by Hiromichi is titled *Hyakushu iken tekihyō* (an outline and critique of the *Hyakushu iken*, 1840). Hiromichi signed this manuscript with the name Fujiwara Hamao. See Yamazaki Katsuaki's note in Ichinichi kai, *Hagiwara Hiromichi shokan* 272.

22. Quoted in Yamazaki Katsuaki, "Ōkuni to Hagiwara Hiromichi," 54.

23. Yamazaki Katsuaki, "Naoyō to Hiromichi," *Nihon bungaku* 40: 9 (1991): 59.

24. See Mostow, *Pictures in the Heart,* 319 for a translation and analysis of this poem (*Hyakunin isshu*, 60).

25. From Hagiwara Hiromichi, *Tamazasa*, vol. 1, section 1, as transcribed by Yamazaki Katsuaki in "Hagiwara Hiromichi to *Kyōkakuden* daigoshū," in *Konton* 24 (2000): 6.

26. Yamazaki Katsuaki, "Hagiwara Hiromichi *ryakunenpukō*," 67.

27. Yamazaki Katsuaki, "Naokai to Hiromichi," 44.

28. Yamazaki Katsuaki, "Hagiwara Hiromichi *ryakunenpukō*," 76.

29. See Najita Tetsuo, *Visions of Virtue in Tokugawa Japan* (Chicago: University of Chicago Press, 1987), for a detailed discussion of Kaitokudō.

30. See Najita Tetsuo, "Ambiguous Encounters: Ogata Kōan and International Studies in Late Tokugawa Osaka," in J. McClain *Osaka*, (N.Y.: Cornell University Press, 1999), 218–19.

31. See Najita Tetsuo, "Ambiguous Encounters," 214–15.

32. Yamazaki Katsuaki, "Hagiwara Hiromichi *ryakunenpukō*," 82.

33. Hagiwara Hiromichi, *Seijū on'yakujiron*. See unpublished manuscript, preface dated 1845, from the holdings of the library of the department of the faculty of letters, Kyoto University. Pages 7–10 in manuscript (not numbered).

34. Hagiwara Hiromichi, *Seijū on'yakujiron*. Page 34 in manuscript (not numbered).

35. Hagiwara Hiromichi, *Seijū on'yakujiron*. Page 54 in manuscript (not numbered).

36. Hagiwara Hiromichi, *Seijū on'yakujiron*. Page 61 in manuscript (not numbered).

37. Hagiwara Hiromichi, *Seijū on'yakujiron*. Page 60 in manuscript (not numbered).

38. Hagiwara Hiromichi, *Genji monogatari hyōshaku: kōsei yakuchū*. This preface was not included in the typeset edition of the *Hyōshaku* printed in 1909.

39. Yamazaki Katsuaki in Ichinichi kai, *Hagiwara Hiromichi shokan*, 16. Watanabe's comments were written in the context of an account to a friend back in Nagasaki and should be taken merely as a sign of Hiromichi's reputation among the *kokugakusha* Watanabe encountered in passing through the area rather than as a systematic evaluation of his scholarship.

40. Satō Kiyoharu, ed., *Kokugogaku kenkyū jiten* (Tokyo: Meiji shoin, 1977), 163.

41. Yamazaki Katsuaki, "Hagiwara Hiromichi ryakunenpukō," 67–69.

42. See S. Katō, "Tominaga Nakamoto: A Tokugawa Iconoclast," *Monumenta Nipponica* 22 (1967): 1–2.

43. Nakamoto Tominaga, *Emerging from Meditation*. See Michael Pye's "Introduction," (Honolulu: University of Hawaii Press, 1990), 9.

44. Kuwayama Ryūhei, "Hagiwara Hiromichi to *Kyokakuden* no hon'yaku," *Biblica* 69 (June 1978) 27.

45. A brief entry on Hiromichi's continuation of Bakin's work can be found in Mori Ōgai, ed., *Shigarami–zōshi*, vol 5 (Tokyo: Shinseisha, 1889–1894), 29. See also Mizuno Minoru, *Edo shōsetsu ronsō* (Tokyo: Chūō Kōron Sha, 1974). Yoda Gakkai also praises Hiromichi's continuation of Bakin's novel in an essay on *Nansō Satomi hakkenden* (see Kuwayama, "Hagiwara Hiromichi to *Kōkyūden*," 28).

46. Kuwayama Ryūhei, "Hagiwara Hiromichi to *Kyōkakuden* no hon'yaku," 28.

47. Kōda Rohan. *Rohan zenshū*. 32:148.

48. *SNKBT* 87:708.

49. This document has received little scholarly attention, and the thesis that Hiromichi provided a rough translation into Japanese is speculative at best. See Kuwayama, "Hagiwara Hiromichi to *Kyōkakuden* no hon'yaku," 27.

50. Morikawa Akira, "*Genji monogatari hyōshaku* no shuppan," 33. The last line quoted is ambiguous. I translate *Kogetsushō wa taore* ("The *Kogetsushō* will be toppled/ collapsed") to convey the sense that "the *Hyōshaku* will surpass the *Kogetsushō*." However, it is unclear whether Hiromichi imagined that the *Kogetsushō* would collapse in terms of sales or simply reputation.

51. Morikawa Akira, "*Genji monogatari hyōshaku* no shuppan," 34–35.

52. Hagiwara Hiromichi, *Genji monogatari hyōshaku*, "Preface," iix. This preface is not included in the 1909 typeset edition of the *Hyōshaku*. A transcription and translation of this preface were included in the appendix to my dissertation (Yale, 1998). Ii Haruki has since published a transcription in his *Genji monogatari chūshakusho kyōjushi jiten* (Tokyo: Tōkyōdō Shuppan, 2001), 318. The reference in this passage to having written the *Hyōshaku* to guide "women and children" eager to become versed in *Genji* should not be taken too literally. As a conventional expression of the time, it was probably understood as a reassurance to potential readers—and buyers—that the *Hyōshaku* was written in a less than intimidating style that required little specialized knowledge. In the letter to Kōrai, where he was not addressing his intended audience directly, Hiromichi refers to these readers simply as "amateurs."

CHAPTER THREE

1. Noguchi Takehiko, "Hagiwara Hiromichi '*Genji monogatari hyōshaku' no bungaku hihyō*," *Kōza Genji monogatari no sekai* 7: 322.

2. Ibid. Noguchi expanded upon this point in a subsequent book, *Genji monogatari' o Edo kara yomu* (see part II, sections 1 and 2, 137–64).

3. Several scholars have suggested that additional text for the *Hyōshaku* must have existed in draft form. Their argument is supported by the fact that Hiromichi frequently refers the reader to a comment that is to appear in a later chapter of *Genji*. To date, no manuscript has been found for unpublished portions of the *Hyōshaku*. See Morikawa Akira, "*Hyōshaku* no shuppan," and Yamazaki Katsuaki, "Hagiwara Hiromichi *ryakunenpukō*."

4. Hiromichi's "Preface" precedes his "General Remarks" in the original work. The Preface was omitted from the typeset edition of the *Hyōshaku*. Two sections of explanatory notes and miscellaneous remarks follow his "General Remarks" in the second volume. These sections are discussed at the end of this chapter.

5. In a section following the "General Remarks," Hiromichi notes that in preparing the main text for the *Hyōshaku* he compared various editions of *Genji* to provide a corrected version. He remarks that he consulted five extant versions of the *Bansui ichiro* (1575) and *Kogetsushō*, three extant versions of *Genji* in old manuscript form (*koshahon*, owners of these manuscripts remain unidentified), and the corrections found in a *Genji* commentary titled *Genchū yoteki* (1818). See *GMH*, 67.

6. *GMH*, 20. Cf. *MNZS* 4: 201.

7. *GMH*, 20.

8. Saibara: a form of early song from the eighth and nineth centuries; note, that the printed version of the *Hyoshaku* contains a misprint. This should be read as ***Saibara*** not ***Saibashū***. See Hagiwara Hiromichi, *Genji monogatari hyōshaku* 22.

9. *GMH*, 20.

10. *GMH*, 20–21. Hiromichi omits large portions of *Tama no ogushi* in this section. Cf. *MNZS* 4: 203, 214–15. Ellipsis marks are mine.

11. Azuchi-Momoyama period soldier, poet, and scholar of Japan studies (*wagaku*). Hiromichi refers to Yūsai by his religious name, Genshi Hōin. This quotation can be found in the *Zokumumyōshō*, *NKBDJ* 5: 457–58.

12. *GMH*, 21–22. It is unclear whether this critique is directed specifically toward scholars of Chinese studies or toward all of those involved in scholarly endeavor. According to Harper, Motoori Norinaga protested against the term *gakumon* being used to specify Chinese studies while requiring a different designation for the field of nativist studies (*kokugaku*). (See T.J. Harper, "*The Tale of Genji* in the Eighteenth Century, in *Eighteenth-Century Japan*, ed. C. Andrew Gerstle [Sydney: Allen & Unwin, 1989], 117). In this case I have taken *gakumon* to refer to scholarship in general and have translated the expression simply as "scholars." I base this decision on the fact that Hiromichi refers to scholarship related to "*inishie no michi*," which is a nativist term for the Ancient Way, as opposed to the Confucian term *kodō*.

~~13. *GMH*, 24. Cf. *Shikashichiron*, 433.~~

14. *GMH*, 24. Cf. *Shikashichiron*, 433. Tameakira also quotes from the "Momiji no ga" chapter. Hiromichi, intending to bring these passages to the reader's attention in his commentary on the main text, simply refers to the various chapter titles in which these events occur rather than quoting extensively from the *Shikashichiron*.

15. Empress Nijō (Nijō no Kisaki): Fujiwara Takaiko (842–910), a consort to Emperor Seiwa (858–876), who was later granted the title of empress. She is largely

known for the story of her love affair with the poet and romantic hero of the *Ise monogatari*, Ariwara Narihira. This story is related in the *Ise monogatari* and the *Yamato monogatari*. See *NKBDJ* 1: 99 and *Heian jidaishi jiten* 2: 2117.

16. Kyōgoku Miyasundokoro: Fujiwara no Yoshiko (dates unknown). Consort to the retired Emperor Uda (887–897) as indicated by her title "Miyasundokoro" (lit. Imperial sleeping chambers). Legend has it that she fell in love with an elderly monk while at the Shiga Temple for religious observances (*Nihon setsuwa bungaku sakuin*, 288. The poem referring to this event can be found in *Gosenshū* number 960). See *NKBDJ* 2: 195 and *Heian jidaishi jiten* 2: 2211.

17. Lady Kazan: Kazan no nyōgō. In the *Eiga monogatari* (*A Tale of Flowering Fortunes*), a middle counselor reportedly has an affair with one of Emperor Kazan's consorts. This prompts the dispatch of romantic poems to the consort from another member of the court. At this point, Emperor Kazan had already renounced his title and all worldly affairs. See *Eiga monogatari*, chapter 4 in Matsumura Hiroji, *Eiga monogatari: Nihon koten bungaku taike*, 75: 153. Cf. McCullough translation in 1: 179. The *Eiga monogatari* is thought to have been composed after *Genji*, but the event referred to here transpired between 991 and 996.

18. *GMH*, 24–25. Cf. *Shikashichiron*, 434.

19. *GMH*, 25. Tameakira refers to certain "incidents" involving Emperor You (J: Yūō) of Chu (J: So) and a former emperor of the Jin dynasty (J: Shin). The story of Emperor You can be found in the *Doushiguanjian* (J: *Dokushikanken*: Song dynasty (A.D. 960–1269) work, thirteen fascicles. Cf. Morohashi, Tetsuji. *Taishūkan shin Kan-Wa jiten* [Tokyo: Taishūkan Shoten, 1988] 10: 611) Emperor You's parentage was brought into question leading to an insurgency that brought down the dynasty. Tameakira also cites two stories from the *Helinyulou* (J: *Kakurin gyokuro*: Song dynasty work in sixteen fascicles, divided into three sections: Heaven, Earth, and Man. See Morohashi, *Taishūkan shin Kan-Wa jiten*, 12: 862.). The parentage of the Emperor of Qin (J: Shin) as well as that of the son of the former emperor of Jin (J: Shin) came into question. Suspicion that the Imperial lineage had been disrupted ultimately contributed to the downfall of both dynasties. See *Shikashichiron*, 434 for original quotation.

20. *GMH*, 25. Cf. *Shikashichiron*, 434.

21. This story can be found in the *Shiji*. Lu Zhonglian went to the eastern sea and drowned himself rather than remain in the kingdom under a false emperor. See Morohashi 12: 729; *Kokugo daijiten* 10, 1289.

22. *GMH*, 25. Cf. *Shikashichiron*, 434 *GMH* 435. Ellipsis marks are mine. I omit some of Hiromichi's quotation from *Shikashichiron*.

23. Hiromichi's interpretation of these terms is similar to definitions provided by current dictionaries such as the Nihon Daijiten Kankōkai's *Nihon kokugo daijiten* (Tokyo: Shōgakkan, 1972). In the *Nihon kokugo daijiten, kanzen chōaku* is defined as "the encouragement of good and chastisement of evil" (v. 3, 384), and *fūyu* is defined as "to indirectly make a point or to make it subtly or to cause a person to deduce something by means of an example" (v. 9, 274). As Hiromichi attempts to illustrate, *fūyu* is much less direct and precise than *kanzen chōaku*.

24. Cf. *MNZS* 4: 228.

25. *GMH*, 25. Cf. *MNZS* 4: 228–29.

26. *GMH*, 26. Cf. *MNZS* 4: 229.

27. *GMH*, 30.

28. *GMH*, 29.

29. Ibid.

30. *GMH*, 30.

31. *GMH*, 26. Cf. *MNZS* 4: 229.

32. *GMH*, 31.

33. Hiromichi refers to two events that profoundly influenced the economic, political, and social conditions of the aristocracy. Following the Jyōkyū disturbance, the shogunate confiscated land belonging to the nobility who had sided with the retired Emperor Go-Toba and redistributed it among loyal factions. The Kemmu Restoration led to the promulgation of the Kemmu Code (*Kenmu shikimoku*), which consists of seventeen articles governing the property rights and behavior of the aristocracy.

34. *GMH*, 36. This passage is also translated by T. J. Harper in "*The Tale of Genji* in the Eighteenth Century" in *Eighteenth-Century Japan*, ed. C. Andrew Gerstle, 113–14. I provide my own translation here.

35. See Harper, "*The Tale of Genji* in the Eighteenth Century, in *Eighteenth-Century Japan*, ed. C. Andrew Gerstle, 114–16 for comments by Keichū, Mabuchi, and Norinaga on this subject.

36. Hiromichi discusses his methodology in greater detail in a section following the "General Remarks." In cases where the commentary does not differ in substance from one commentary to the next, he cites from the earliest source. He notes that this is the method advocated by Norinaga in his criticism of the *Kogetsushō*, which tended to cite the most recent source. He adds that in cases where the substance does not vary, but one commentary provides a clearer explanation, he refers to the commentary providing the clearest explanation. See *GMH*, 62.

37. *GMH*, 36–37. My translation overlaps in part with Harper's translation. See Harper, "*The Tale of Genji* in the Eighteenth Century, in *Eighteenth-Century Japan*, ed. C. Andrew Gerstle, 107–108.

38. Motoori Norinaga, "*Shibun yōryō*" 1: 37 (*Shinchō nihon koten shūsei*, Motoori Norinaga shū), as quoted by Inoguchi Takashi in *Keichūgaku no keisei* (Tokyo: Izumi shoin, 1996), 77–78. A similar passage appears in Norinaga's discussion of commentaries in volume 1 of *Tama no ogushi*.

39. See *Encyclopedia Nipponica 2001* 8 (Shōgakukan, 1986), 739–40; *Kodansha Encyclopedia of Japan* 3, 155–56. See also Benjamin A. Elman, *From Philosophy to Philology: Intellectual and Social Aspects of Change in Late Imperial China* (Cambridge, MA: Harvard University Press, 1984) for a detailed account of the development of evidential scholarship in China. For an account of evidential scholarship in *bakumatsu*, Japan see Nakaya Osamu's article "Nihon kōshōgaku no seiritsu" (38–88) in *Edo kōki no hikaku bunka kenkyū*, ed. Minamoto Ryōen (Tokyo: Perikan sha, 1990).

40. Inoguchi Takashi, *Keichūgaku no keisei*, 89–91.

41. The large number of commentaries on *Genji* make it impractical to prove empirically that Hiromichi was the first scholar to refer to certain commentaries as "new." However, a cursory examination of *Genchū shūi*, Mabuchi's *Shinshaku*, and *Tama no ogushi* yields no use of the term "new commentaries" to predate its use in the *Hyōshaku*. In addition, the language that Hiromichi uses in this section gives the

impression that he is introducing readers to a category now labeled "new commentary." In the passage quoted earlier he specifically "distinguishes works from Keichū on as being 'new commentaries' " (*shinchū to nazukete wakateri*). See also Harper's note 6 regarding the term "new commentaries," in *Eighteenth-Century Japan*, 121.

42. *KMZS* 5: 4425–26.

43. Tsutsumi Yasuo, *Genji monogatari chūshakushi no kisoteki kenkyū*, 169–70.

44. Tsutsumi Yasuo, *Genji monogatari chūshakushi no kisoteki kenkyū*, 211, 223–24.

45. *GMH*, 40.

46. *GMH*, 40.

47. *GMH*, 59. See *MNZS* 4: 204–205. Hiromichi paraphrases portions of Norinaga's discussion in his quotation from *Tama no ogushi*

48. *GMH*, 59.

49. *GMH*, 59.

50. Earlier commentaries by nativist scholars may also be said to follow this practice, but they provide annotation for isolated lines of text rather than a complete version of the text that can be read as literature.

51. *GMH*, 70.

52. *GMH*, 77; *NKBT* 12: 97; *SNKBT* 19:5; Seidensticker, *The Tale of Genji*, (New York: Alfred A, Knopf, 1983), 4; Tyler, *The Tale of Genji*, 3–4.

53. *GMH*, 70.

54. For example, see the analysis of the term "key word" (*kagigo*) in Hiyashida's *Genji monogatari jiten* (Tokyo: Daiwa Shobō, 2002), 122.

55. *GMH*, 69.

56. See *NKBDJ* entries on *gikobun* (2: 124–25) and *Tama arare* (4: 184). I argue that Hiromichi rejects this interpretive approach in his treatment of prose. On the other hand, his own linguistic treatise on ancient language and poetic composition, *Sayoshigure* (1849), was heavily influenced by Norinaga's arguments in *Tama arare*. See *NKBDJ* 3: 81. See also Lawrence Marceau, "The Emperor's Old Clothes: Classical Narratives in Early Modern Japan," *Proceedings of the Midwest Association for Japanese Literary Studies* 3 (1997), for a discussion of classical-style prose composed during the Edo period.

57. Rita Copeland, *Rhetoric, Hermeneutics, and Translation in the Middle Ages* (New York: Cambridge University Press, 1991), 51.

58. Yosano Akiko's translation is generally considered the first complete, literary translation of *Genji* into vernacular Japanese. See Oka Kazuo, *Genji monogatari jiten* (Shunjūsha, 1964), 460. Akiko's first translation was an abridged version published under the title *Shin'yaku Genji monogatari* (Tokyo: Kanao Bun'endō, 1912–1913). She later published a complete and more accurate version of this work under the title, *Shinshin'yaku Genji monogatari* (1938–1939). See G. G. Rowley, "Textual Malfeasance in Yosano Akiko's *Shin'yaku Genji monogatari*," *Harvard Journal of Asiatic* Studies 58: 1 (1998): 202.

59. Henry James, *Selected Literary Criticism* (New York: McGraw-Hill, 1965), 50.

60. Henry James, *Selected Literary Criticism of Henry James*, 66.

61. R. W. Leutner, *Shikitei Sanba and the Comic Tradition in Edo Fiction*, (Cambridge, MA: Harvard University Press, 1985), 2.

CHAPTER FOUR

1. Morikawa Akira, "*Genji monogatari hyōshaku* no shuppan," 33. This phrase is from a letter Hiromichi wrote prior to his publication of the *Hyōshaku*, in 1851. In the letter he further describes his goal to "provide guidance to women and children who are eager to become versed in *Genji*."

2. The expression *sakusha no fudezukai* along with the related terms *imijiki fude nari* and *fude no takumi* appears more than seventy times in the "General Remarks" and "Main Text" of the *Hyōshaku*. For examples, see *GMH*, 56, 74, 76 (*fudezukai*), and 375 (*fude no takumi*).

3. *GMH*, 47–48.

4. In the previous chapter, I quote from Hiromichi's discussion of Confucian attempts to interpret the text as a product of the author's intention to produce a moral allegory. Hiromichi concludes this discussion by stating that because the author lived in a period so remote from his own time, it is impossible to know the mind of the author, and such theories could only end in idle speculation. He also points to this limitation in his own comments where they are based on the intentions of the author.

5. Conclusions concerning Hiromichi's interpretive approach cannot be made solely on the basis of his application of a specific reading to Chinese characters. Orthography remained unstandardized during the Edo period, and Hiromichi's assigned reading of *nori* would probably not have been seen as particularly significant by Edo readers. In fact, contemporary scholars often overlook Hiromichi's unorthodox reading and refer to the term as *hōsoku* rather than *nori*. See Noguchi Takehiko, *Genji monogatari o Edo kara yomu*, 169–70, and Yamazaki Fusako, "*Genji monogatari hyōshaku no hōhō*," *Kokugo Kokubun* 51: 3 (1982): 29–30.

6. *GMH*, 48.

7. Itasaka Noriko, "*Haishi shichi hōsoku*," *Kokugo to Kokubungaku* 55: 11 (November 1978): 80. Itasaka gives the date of 1835 for the installment of *Hakkenden* in which Bakin published his "*Haishi shichisoku*" theory. The full title of Bakin's work is *Nansō Satomi hakkenden*. It was published between 1814 and 1842 with a total of 181 chapters. *Hakkenden* is a historical romance set in mid fifteenth-century Japan. The story centers on the restoration of the Satomi family's fortunes, due to the efforts of eight warriors, each of whose surnames contains the word for dog. See L. M. Zolbrod, "Tigers, Boars, and Severed Heads," *The Chung Chi Journal* 7: 1 (November 1967): 30–39.

8. The full title of this work is *Diwu caizi shu Shi Nai-an Shuihu zhuan* (The Fifth Book of Genius, Shi Nai-an's *The Water Margin*). See D. L. Rolston, *How to Read The Chinese* Novel (Princeton, NJ: Princeton University Press, 1990), 413–28, for extensive bibliographic information on this work. Possible sources for Bakin's critical terms are discussed by Hamada Keisuke in his article "Bakin no iwayuru haishi shichi hōsoku ni tsuite," *Kokugo Kokubun* 28: 8 (1959): 31–43. Hamada refers to this text as Jin Shengtan's *The Fifth Book of Genius*.

9. Rolston, *Traditional Chinese Fiction and Fiction Commentary* (Stanford, CA: Stanford University Press, 1997), 30–31.

10. Rolston, *Traditional Chinese Fiction*, 2.

11. *GMH*, 6.

12. *GMH*, 48.

13. Nosco, *Remembering Paradise*, 137.

14. Nosco, *Remembering Paradise*, 198.

15. Hiromichi was certainly not the first to suggest that works of Chinese literature influenced the author of *Genji*. Commentaries such as the *Sairyūshō* (1528) and the *Mingō nisso* (1598) refer to the influence of the *Shiji*, *Hanshu*, *Changhenge* ("Song of Everlasting Sorrow"), and *Zhuan-zi* on the style and content of *Genji*. In fact, such comments probably served to confirm for Hiromichi that *pingdian* commentary addressed many of the same compositional techniques that had inspired Murasaki Shikibu's composition of *Genji*.

16. *Norito* is a sacred form of speech used to address deities in a Shinto ceremony. Due to the early Japanese belief in the spirit that resides in words (*kotodama*), the words themselves were believed to possess a sacred quality. *Senmyō* convey mandates decreed by the emperor (*shōchoku*). *Norito* and *senmyō* texts, or *senmyōgaki*, are recorded according to a unique orthographic system in which Chinese characters (*man'yōgana*) are used to signify the sounds corresponding to such lexical elements as verbal endings and particles. While Chinese characters are used to signify these sounds, the text is structured according to the rules of Japanese grammar (*kokubuntai*). The earliest surviving collection of *norito* is found in the *Engi Shiki* (927).

17. *GMH*, 48–49.

18. In modern Japanese, *bunshō* has come to be translated as "sentence." However, it retains the nuance that Hiromichi amplifies here of being related not only to grammatical structure, but style—buntai—as well. Cf. Morohashi, *Taishūkan Shin Kan-Wa Jiten* 5: 579 and Kenkyusha's *New Japanese-English Dictionary* entries for *bunshō*.

19. *GMH*, 49.

20. *GMH*, 50. As indicated by the large number of parenthetical brackets, Hiromichi's language in this paragraph does not lend itself to smooth translation into English. Takahashi Tōru also quotes the final lines of this passage in his discussion of the "grammar" of *The Tale of Genji*. Rather than attempting to translate the text into modern Japanese, he summarizes the point Hiromichi makes here. I have relied on Takahashi's summary of this paragraph in my interpretation and translation of this passage. See Takahashi Tōru, "*Genji monogatari* tekusuto no "bunpō" josetsu," in *Genji monogatari* no tankyū 12 (Kazama shobō, 1987): 18–19.

21. *GMH*, 59. This quotation, which continues from the passage quoted above, is from the section that directly follows Hiromichi's introduction to the "principles of composition."

22. *GMH*, 60.

23. *GMH*, 50. Cf. *Shikashichiron*, 430–31. Note, *GMH* contains a typographical error for this passage on 50, l. 6. The character *kei* should be *kan* according to the *Shikashichiron*.

24. *GMH*, 50. Cf. *Shikashichiron*, 431. See also Harper's "Motoori Norinaga's Criticism of *The Tale of Genji*," 94. My translation overlaps portions of the *Shikashichiron* translated by Harper.

25. *Shikashichiron*, 431. See also Harper's "Motoori Norinaga's Criticism of *The Tale of Genji*," 95, concerning this point.

26. Rolston, *How to Read the Chinese Novel*, 10.

27. Morohashi, *Taishūkan Shin Kan-Wa Jiten* 5: 579. Cf. Rolston, *How to Read the Chinese Novel*, 25.

28. Yamazaki Fusako, "*Genji monogatari hyōshaku* no hōhō," 41.

29. The list of classical texts and authors he provides closely parallels the works represented in the *Wenzhuang guifan*. Tameakira's synecdoche for Chinese classical texts is *Shiki-Sō-Kan-Ryū-Ou-Sō*. This list covers the major Chinese works of history, philosophy, and rhetoric. The texts represented in the *Wenzhuang guifan* are referred to collectively as *Kan-Ryū-Ou-Sō*. This combination of characters is translated as "the *Shiji*, the *Zhuan-zi*, and works by Han Yu (768–824), Liu Zong-yuan (773–819), Ou Yang-xiu (1007–1070), and Su Shi (1037–1101)."

30. One example would be the work of Confucian scholar and poet of classical Chinese Ogyū Sorai (1666–1728). See Suwa, *Edo bungaku to Chūgoku* (Tokyo: Mainichi Shinbunsha, 1977) 101–103.

31. I have not yet identified an edition of the *Wenzhuang guifan* printed in Japan early enough to be considered a possible source for Tameakira's comments on *Genji*. See entries under *Bunshō kihan* in Morohashi's *Taishūkan shin Kan-Wa jiten* and Iwanami's *Kokusho sōmokuroku*. Publication date for *Bunshō kihan hyōrin chūshaku* from the *Edo Printed Books at Berkeley, ed.* Oka Masahiko (Berkeley: East Asiatic Library, University of California Press, 1990), 429.

32. Emura Hokkai *Jugyōhen. Nihonkyōiku bunko: gakkōhen*, vol 8 (Tokyo: Dōkubunkan, 1911), 650–51. Hokkai's preface is dated 1781. The first printing appears to have been 1783. The *Jugyōhen* was reprinted as a part of several popular series on education, such as *Nihon kyōiku bunko*, widely available during the Edo and Meiji periods.

33. *GMH*, 50.

34. This is Mabuchi's note, not Hiromichi's.

35. *GMH*, 50. There are slight discrepancies between Hiromichi's quotation and the text as it appears in the *KMZS* (4427–28). Some discrepancies are simply errors generated in copying the quotation from the original to the typeset edition of the *GMH*. Others seem to have been caused by either slight copying errors on Hiromichi's part or use of a variant version of the *Shinshaku*. Note that character before *chōhon* should be *wa* not *shō* in the typeset edition. The first sentence also contains a variant. Hiromichi uses the character *mae*, where the *Mabuchi zenshū* edition uses the character *hoka*.

36. Hayashi Tsutomu, "Mabuchi no *Genji monogatari* kenkyū," in *Genji monogatari Koza*, vol 8, ed. Imai Takuji et al. (Tokyo: Benseisha, 1992), 210.

37. Rolston, *Traditional Chinese* Fiction, 309.

38. *KMZS*, 4423–24.

39. In her article on Hiromichi's interpretive approach to *Genji*, Yamazaki Fusako remarks, "One sees almost no indication in *Tama no ogushi* that Norinaga wished to draw attention to compositional technique [*bunshō no gikō*]." See "*Genji monogatari hyōshaku no hōhō*."

40. *GMH*, 51.

41. Ibid.

42. See Tokuda Takeshi's "*Yomihon to Chūgoku hakuwa shōsetsu*," in Suwa, *Edo bungaku to Chūgoku*, 55–57.

43. See Rolston, *How to Read the Chinese Novel*, 3–49, for a detailed discussion.

44. Rolston, *How to Read the Chinese Novel*, 20. Rolston notes that Li Yu "is supposed to have published volumes of examination essays with commentary, but no copies seem to have survived."

45. N. Mao and Liu Ts'un-yan, *Li Yu* (Boston: Twayne, 1977), 117.

46. Chen Duo, ed., *Li Li-weng quhua*, 26, as quoted in Rolston's *How to Read the Chinese Novel*, 88. This passage also cited by Hamada in "*Bakin no iwayuru haishi shichi hōsoku ni tsuite*," 32.

47. Rolston, *How to Read the Chinese Novel*, 89.

48. Rolston, *How to Read the Chinese Novel*. 13–14. Rolston notes that lengthy landscape paintings and narrative texts often shared a similar format. Both were recorded on scrolls that were unrolled as the painting or story progressed. This similarity helps explain how abstract spatial concepts that played a conspicuous role in the visual arts influenced the development of concepts such as composition and the balancing of major and minor elements in narrative fiction. Terms used in manuals for landscape gardening to describe the effective placement of objects were also adapted for use in *pingdian* criticism, (14, n. 40).

49. Rolston, *How to Read the Chinese Novel*, 32. Readings have been converted from Wade-Giles to *Pinyin* in Chinese, and readings in Japanese have been added to for consistency of formatting. The "Four Books" are *The Great Learning*, *The Doctrine of the Mean*, *The Confucian Analects*, and *The Mencius*. The phrase "filling in the pupils of the dragon" refers to an anecdote about a painter who painted four dragons without pupils. Putting the final touch on his painting, he filled in the pupils, and the dragons flew away. The phrase "adding the whiskers" refers to a similar anecdote in which attention to detail brought out the spirit of a painting.

CHAPTER FIVE

1. *GMH*, 51.

2. The term *fudezukai*, along with related terms, *imijiki fude nari* and *fude no takumi*, appears more than seventy times in the "General Remarks" and "Main Text" of the *Hyōshaku*. For examples see, *GMH*, 56, 74, 76 (*fudezukai*), and 375 (*fude no takumi*).

3. *GMH*, 55.

4. This section is discussed in greater detail at the end of chapter 3.

5. An index of specific interpretive terms as they appear throughout the *Hyōshaku* can be found in P. Caddeau, "Hagiwara Hiromichi's Theory of the Principles of Composition and Its Application to *The Tale of Genji*, Including an Index of Critical Terms," *Shirin* 21:4 (1997): 48–63.

6. *GMH*, 51.

7. Tamagami Takuya et al., eds., *Shimeisho Kakaishō* (Tokyo: Kadokawa Shoten, 1968), 233. The *Kakaishō* includes a brief quotation from the *Okuiri* on this point.

8. Ibid., 232. Hiromichi comments in the introduction to the "Kiritsubo" chapter that this chapter was considered a preface to the entire work and therefore is not included in the grouping of the "Hahakigi" and "Utsusemi" chapters. See *GMH*, 73.

9. Ii Haruki, ed., *Kachōyosei* (Tokyo: Ōfūsha, 1973), 38; Ii Haruki, ed., *Sairyūshō* (Tokyo: Ōfūsha, 1975), 35.

10. *GMH*, 226.

11. A. Preminger et al., eds., *The New Princeton Encyclopedia of Poetry and Poetics* (Princeton, NJ: Princeton University Press, 1993), 814. See Leonard Nathan's entry on "Narrative." Parentheses, abbreviation, and italics are as in the original.

12. See *GMH*, 478.

13. Ibid.

14. See *GMH*, 33.

15. Ibid.

16. *GMH*, 51.

17. Hiromichi quotes at length from the *Tama no ogushi* in his introductory remarks for the following chapters: "Kiritsubo," "Hahakigi," "Utsusemi," "Suetsumuhana," and "Momiji no Ga."

18. Hiromichi quotes from *Tama no ogushi* on this point. See *GMH*, 121–22.

19. See entry on "Kumogakure rokujō" in *NKBDJ* 2: 301.

20. *GMH*, 54. Theories concerning an additional chapter to which Hiromichi refers to earlier are thought to have come from the application of critical scriptural classifications particular to the Tendai school of Buddhism to an interpretation of *Genji*. According to this theory, teachings on the *Lotus Sutra* by the third patriarch of the Tendai school in China can be found in three major texts. Together these teachings comprise a total of sixty fascicles. At some point, the fifty-four chapters of *Genji* were supplemented with an additional six chapters, so that the sixty chapters of *Genji* might be associated with the sixty fascicles of scripture transmitted by the third patriarch. One of these chapters was the "Kumogakure" chapter. The remaining five chapters continue the story of the final "Uji" chapters. See entry on "Kumogakure rokujō" entry in *NKBDJ* 2, 301–302, and the "Hoke-kyō" entry in Mizuno, *Butten kaidai jiten* (Tokyo: Shunjūsha, 1977), 83.

21. *GMH*, 54.

22. Ibid.

23. *GMH*, 55.

24. Ibid.

25. *GMH*, 56.

26. This chapter is believed to be a thirteenth-century forgery.

27. *GMH*, 56.

28. In fact, the artistic vision of the author is so complete that there is relatively little disagreement among modern scholars concerning the correct sequence of events and order of chapters in *Genji*. See A. Gatten, "The Order of the Early Chapters in the Genji *monogatari*," *Harvard Journal of Asiatic Studies* 41: 1 (1981), 5–46: and Shirane, *The Bridge of Dreams* (Stanford, CA: Stanford University Press, 1987), 224 for related discussions.

29. *GMH,* 56–57.

30. Henry James, from the preface to "Daisy Miller," *The Art of the Novel* (New York: Charles Scribner's Sons, 1934), 278.

31. *GMH,* 63.

32. These terms are largely taken from Preminger, *Princeton Encyclopedia of Poetry and Poetics* and Bal, *Narratology: Introduction to the Theory of Narrative* (Toronto: University of Toronto Press, 1985).

33. *GMH,* 63.

34. Rolston, *How to Read the Chinese Novel,* 3.

35. *GMH,* 139.

36. *GMH,* 61.

37. *GMH,* 52.

38. *GMH,* 64.

39. *GMH,* 63–64.

40. *GMH,* 52.

41. Ibid.

42. *GMH,* 78.

43. Henry James, *The Art of the Novel,* preface to "Roderick Hudson," 18.

44. *GMH,* 64.

45. Takizawa Bakin, *Nansō Satomi hakkenden,* 6 (Tokyo: Iwanami Shoten, 1990.), 7.

46. *GMH,* 555.

47. Ibid. Specifically, Hiromichi refers to the recycling of images of flowers in bloom between the two festival scenes.

48. L. R. Williams, *Critical Desire: Psychoanalysis and the Literary Subject* (New York: St. Martin's Press, 1995), 132. An example of *nachträglichkeit* can be found in Freud's analysis of a young boy in the case known as the *Wolf Man.* At the age of one and a half, the boy witnessed his parents engaged in sex. He later had a traumatic dream at the age of four. Freud theorized that the frightening nature of the dream at age four brought out a deeper meaning that was not originally understood in relation to the trauma the boy experienced at the earlier age. See also Preminger, *The New Princeton Encyclopedia of Poetry and Poetics* (607) for a discussion of Freud's theory of *nachträglichkeit.*

49. *GMH,* 64.

50. *GMH,* 492, 496.

51. *GMH,* 480.

52. *GMH,* 64.

53. Takizawa Bakin, *Nansō Satomi hakkenden* (6), 7.

54. *GMH,* 108.

55. *GMH,* 273.

56. *GMH,* 65.

57. *GMH*, 77. See E. G. Seidensticker, *The Tale of Genji*, 4; Tyler, *The Tale of Genji*, 3.

58. *GMH*, 78.

59. *GMH*, 65.

60. Ibid.

61. Ibid.

62. *GMH*, 349.

63. *GMH*, 65.

64. Ibid.

65. *GMH*, 65–66.

66. *GMH*, 66.

67. Ibid.

68. Hiromichi often indicates when his interpretation relies on the work of a previous commentator. "Appendix D" in P. Caddeau, "Hagiwara Hiromichi's *Genji Monogatari Hyōshaku*: Criticism and Commentary on the *Tale of Genji*." (Ph.D. dissertation, Yale University, 1998) includes a comprehensive list of critical terms applied to *Genji* by Hiromichi as well as his notes indicating that his commentary is derived from a previous work.

69. *GMH*, 66.

70. *GMH*, 78.

71. *GMH*, 66.

72. *GMH*, 66. Hiromichi often indicates whether he has applied the term *yōi* to identify careful planning from the perspective of either the author or narrative character in individual notes. "Appendix D" in P. Caddeau, "Hagiwara Hiromichi's *Genji Monogatari Hyōshaku*: Criticism and Commentary on the *Tale of Genji*." includes a comprehensive list of the passages in which Hiromichi specifically applies the term *yōi* and indicates when he distinguishes between the perspective of author and narrative character.

73. Henry James, *The Art of the Novel*, preface to "Roderick Hudson," 14.

74. *GMH*, 66.

75. M. Enomoto, *Genji monogatari no sōshiji* (Tokyo: Chikuma shoin, 1982), 151–55.

76. *GMH*, 66–67.

77. Rolston, *How to Read the Chinese Novel*, 87, 186.

78. Fujita Tokutarō includes a schematic diagram of *Genji* commentaries in which the *Hyōshaku* completes a direct link between Norinaga's commentary and succeeding generations of commentary. See Fujita, *Genji monogatari kenkyū shomoku yōran* (Tokyo: Rikubunkan, 1932), 195–96.

CHAPTER SIX

1. *SNKBT*, 24: 385. See Ivan Morris translation in Sugawara, *As I Crossed a Bridge of Dreams* (London, New York: Oxford University Press; Dial Press, 1971), 55. Portions

of this chapter were presented at a symposium on *The Tale of Genji*, sponsored by Stanford University (April 25–26, 2003). I wish to thank my discussant at the symposium, Thomas Harper, for his helpful comments and suggestions.

2. *SNKBT* 24: 385. Cf. Sugawara, *As I Crossed a Bridge of Dreams*, 54–57.

3. *SNKBT* 24: 429–30. Cf. Sugawara, *As I Crossed a Bridge of Dreams*, 119.

4. See T. J. Harper's "Motoori Norinaga's Criticism of the 'Genji Monogatari'" 50–55 for a more detailed account of these early, Buddhist-inspired responses to *Genji*.

5. Genji takes Yūgao to the Nanigashi estate (*Nanigashi no In*) in the "Yūgao" chapter: *NKBZS* 1: 233; Tyler, *The Tale of Genji*, 64. Kaoru takes Ukifune to Uji in the "Azumaya" chapter: *NKBZS* 6: 86; Tyler, *The Tale of Genji*, 1002.

6. *GMH*, 55–56. Hiromichi's general remarks (*sōron*) have been reprinted in Akiyama Ken, et al, ed., *Hihyōshūsei Genji monogatari* (Tokyo: Yumani Shobō, 1999) 2: 342.

7. Most notably, the examples of spirit possession that stand in contrast to those of Yūgao and Ukifune are those of *the ikiryō* involved in Aoi's death and the *shiryō* that tormented Onna san no miya. See Abe Toshiko, "*Shukuse to mono no ke*," *Kokubungaku* 45: 5 (1980): 12.

8. *GMH*, 57. Cf. Akiyama Ken, ed., *Hihyōshūsei Genji monogatari*, 2: 347–48. The other five examples he cites are: (1) The "Kumogakure" chapter is not missing but omitted by design; (2) The "Yume no Ukihashi" chapter is not incomplete but is perfect as it is; (3) it is not a matter of oversight that characters are not assigned fixed names throughout the text; (4) readers only know that Genji is headed in the direction of Rokujō when introduced to the tragic story of Yūgao. The thread of the Rokujō Haven being implicated in the death of Yūgao is not revealed until several chapters later; and (5) readers are at first stunned by the opening of the "Makibashira" chapter in which Tamakazura has been married to Higekuro and the gap that exists between this scene and the end of the previous chapter. It is only after they read further into the chapter that they understand Higekuro's obsession with Tamakazura well enough to understand how he could have made this happen.

9. Tsutsumi Yasuo, "Genji *monogatari chūshakushijo ni okeru 'chūsei' to 'kinsei'*" *Kokugo to kokubungaku* 67: 1 (1990): 15–18.

10. Abe Toshiko, "*Shukuse to mono no ke*," *Kokubungaku* 45: 5 (1980): 11.

11. See Doris Bargen, *A Woman's Weapon: Spirit Possession in* The Tale of Genji (Honolulu: University of Hawaii Press, 1997).

12. See Tsutsumi Yasuo, "*Genji monogatari chūshakushijo ni okeru 'chūsei' to 'kinsei'*," 23–24.

13. Gaye Rowley notes that the editors of this series (Hagino Yoshiyuki, Ochiai Naobumi, and Konakamura Yoshikata) came to be seen as "Japan's first scholars of National Literature (*kokubungakusha*)." See Rowley, *Yosano Akiko and* The Tale of Genji, 60.

14. *NKBZS*, 6: 191; *SNKBT* 5: 264; Tyler, *The Tale of Genji*, 1047.

15. This quotation is taken from Inokuma Natsuki's supplementary comments to a revised version of Kitamura Kigin's *Kogetsushō* (Inokuma, *Zōchū Genji monogatari Kogetsushō* [Osaka: Kōbunsha, 1927]). Originally published in 1890–1891.

16. See Akiyama Ken, *Genji monogatari handobukku* (Tokyo: Shinshokan, 1996), 97, entry on *Kogetsushō* explains that annotation attributed to the *Kogetsushō shisetsu* within the *Kogetsushō* itself is derived from comments made during lectures on *Genji* by Minokata Joan.

17. Enomoto Masazumi, *Genji monogatari no sōshiji* (Tokyo: Chikuma shoin, 1982), 151–55.

18. Cf. "Novelists were the first storytellers to pretend that their stories had never been told before, that they were entirely new and unique, as is each of our own lives" (see David Lodge, *Consciousness and the Novel* [Cambridge, MA: Harvard University Press, 2002], 39.

19. See Rolston's *How to Read the Chinese Novel.*

20. "Hanrei," in Hagino, *Genji Monogatari, Nihon bungaku zensho* 1:1, as translated by Gaye Rowley in *Yosano Akiko and The Tale of Genji*, 61.

21. Rowley, *Yosano Akiko and* The Tale of Genji, 61.

22. Hagino, *Genji Monogatari, Nihon bungaku zensho*, 12: "Kagerō" 1.

23. Hagino, *Genji Monogatari, Nihon bungaku zensho*, 12: "Tenarai" 5 (*NKBZS* 6: 272; Tyler, *The Tale of Genji*, 1079).

24. Hagino, *Genji Monogatari, Nihon bungaku zensho*, 12: "Tenarai" 5 (*NKBZS* 6: 272; Tyler, *The Tale of Genji*, 1079). Note that the *NKBZS* uses nearly identical phrasing to annotate this passage, with the notable exception that "Ukifune's disappearance" (Ukifune *no shissō*) replaces "Ukifune's having thrown herself into the river to drown" (Ukifune *no jusui*).

25. Note that Motoori Norinaga's comment, which appears in the *Kogetsushō* here (Inokuma, *Zōchū Genji Monogatari Kogetsushō*, 3: 942), is almost the same as the note appearing in Hagino's *Genji Monogatari, Nihon bungaku zensho*, but Norinaga's language has been modified to more clearly emphasize that what is interesting about the text is its description of Ukifune's state of mind. It is revealing that Norinaga's interpretation is conveyed in this edition without reference to his authorship. This illustrates how deeply Norinaga's interpretation had become associated with the *kokubungaku* agenda at this point.

26. Hagino, *Genji monogatari, Nihon bungaku zensho*, 12: "Tenarai" 15 (*NKBZS* 6: 283–84; Tyler, *The Tale of Genji*, 1083–84).

27. The contrast is readily apparent when seen against the notes in the *Kogetsushō* that alternate between reminding readers that certain details are related to Ukifune's "disappearance" and her mental state when she went to throw herself into the Uji river.

28. Royall and Susan Tyler, "The Possession of Ukifune," *Asiatica Venetiana* 5 (2000): 177. This article inspired me to reformulate the basic premise for my argument in this chapter.

29. *SNKBT* 24: 385. Editing for the volume on *Sarashina Nikki* was supervised by Hasegawa Masaharu, Imanishi Ichirō, et al. Imanishi was also involved in editing of the volume on *Genji monogatari* in this series by Iwanami, which appeared in print in 1993.

30. Fujita Tokutarō, *Kokubungaku no sekai* (Kyoto: Jinbun shoin, 1939), 81.

31. Shigematsu Nobuhiro, *Genji monogatari kenkyūshi* (Tokyo: Tōei shoin, 1937), 333.

32. Shigematsu Nobuhiro, *Genji monogatari kenkyūshi,* 339.

33. Shigematsu Nobuhiro, *Genji monogatari kenkyūshi,* 345.

34. Sasaki Nobutsuna, "Hagiwara Hiromichi *no 'Mono no aware' setsu,*" *Kokugo to Kokubungaku* 16: 5 (1939), 1.

35. Ibid., 9.

36. Ibid., 14.

37. Ibid., 14. See chapter 2 for a discussion for Hiromichi's earlier treatise *Hongaku taigai.*

38. Noguchi Takehiko, "Hagiwara Hiromichi '*Genji monogatari hyōshaku*' no bungaku hihyō," 321. Noguchi notes that his 'second' reading of *Genji* was in graduate school under the famous *Genji* scholar Akiyama Ken.

39. Yoda Gakkai. *Gakkai nichiroku* (Tokyo: Iwanami shoten, 1990), 1: 96–97.

40. Yoda Gakkai. *Gakkai nichiroku,* 5: 236.

41. Yoda Gakkai. *Gakkai nichiroku,* 8: 18.

42. Yoda Gakkai. *Gakkai nichiroku,* 8: 114.

43. Yoda Gakkai. *Gakkai nichiroku,* 8: 116.

44. Kokumin Shinbunsha. *Kokumin shinbun.* (Tokyo: Kokumin Shinbunsha, 1890–1929) Meiji 23.9.15 (issue no. 227, 5).

45. Kokumin Shinbunsha. *Kokumin shinbun. Meiji* 23.9.15 (issue no. 227, 5).

46. Suematsu Kencho, *Genji monogatari.* (Rutland: Charles E. Tuttle, 1974). Kenchō's preface to the first edition is dated 1881.

47. Kokumin Shinbunsha. *Kokumin shinbun. Meiji* 23.9.18 (issue no. 230, 1).

48. Mori Ōgai. *Mori Ōgai Zenshū* (Tokyo: Chikumashobō, 1959), 1, 275.

49. See Akiyama, *Genji monogatari hihyōshūsei,* 3: 44–51.

50. See Kamei Hideo, *Shōsetsu ron* (Tokyo: Iwanami Shoten, 1999), 89–98.

51. Tsubouchi Shōyō, "Shōsetsu Shinzui" in *Tsubouchi Shōyō shū* (Tokyo: Chikuma Shobō, 1977) 16: 48.

52. As discussed in chapter 2, Hiromichi composed the final volume of Bakin's *Daring Adventures of Chivalrous Men* (*Kaikan kyōki kyōkakuden,* 1832–1835) in 1849 following Bakin's death the previous year.

53. To describe his relationship with Bakin, Shōyō uses a term associated with the practice of entering the Buddhist monastic community, *kechien suru.* This association of premodern religious practice with his interest in Bakin and Edo literature throughout the essay emphasizes the devotional quality of his association with the past versus the intellectual nature of his connection to modern culture.

54. Ihara Saikaku (1642–1693, poet and author of popular fiction) and Chikamatsu Monzaemon (1653–1724, playwright) were widely acknowledged as two of the greatest writers of the Edo period. Hachimonjiya was a publishing house famous for its comedies. Chapbooks (*kibyōshi*) were affordably priced illustrated novels. Pulp fiction (*konnyaku ban*) refers to literature produced using an inexpensive gelatin printing process.

55. Kusunoki Masashige is one of the heroes depicted in an early section of the classical text *Taiheiki* ("Chronicle of Great Peace"; ca. 1370). Kusunoki was a supporter of efforts to restore direct Imperial rule associated with the Kemmu Restoration (1333–1336). The text is noted for its emphasis on Confucian principles of governance and its frequent reference to legends from classical Chinese texts and Buddhist mythology. Bakin retold this popular tale in his *Daring Adventures of Chivalrous Men*.

56. In 1881, Shōyō was asked on an exam in an English literature course to write an essay "analyzing the character" of Queen Gertrude in *Hamlet* for a course taught by an American instructor, William Houghton. Shōyō received low marks for his essay due, he stresses, to his misunderstanding of the question. He evaluated Queen Gertrude's moral character in a way familiar to him from the commentary in Bakin's works rather than analyzing her personality or motivations. In a separate essay (pub. 1925) he suggests that it was the shock of receiving low marks for this essay that forced him to take Western literary criticism seriously for the first time and ultimately inspired him to write his treatise "*The Essence of the Novel.*" See *Shōyō senshū* (Tokyo: Daiichishobō, 1977), 12: 345–46.

57. Here Shōyō uses the term referring to the main object of worship in a Buddhist temple (*honzon*) to convey his long-standing veneration for the style of Bakin.

58. Tsubouchi Shōyō, *Shōyō senshū* (Tokyo: Daiichishobō), 295–303.

59. *GMH*, 84–85; *NKBZS* 1: 100; Tyler, *The Tale of Genji*, 5–6.

60. The *Kogetsushō* does not include a specific comment on this line. Modern editions of *Genji* provide annotation concerning grammatical structure. See *NKBZS* 1: 100. The *SNKBT* (19: 9) notes of this passage that Genji is described as gazing in "wonder" because he was too young to understand what was happening.

61. *GMH*, 84.

Appendix I

CHARACTER GLOSSARY OF PREMODERN NAMES, TITLES, AND TERMS IN CHINESE AND JAPANESE

---

amari no tokigoto 余釈
amayo monogatari 雨夜物語
An'na no hen 安和の変
Andō Tameakira 安藤為章 (1659–1716)
Ashi no ha wake あしの葉わけ (1845)
Ashikabi 蘆かび/葦芽 (1790)
baihua xiaoshuo 白話小説; J: *hakuwa shōsetsu*
Ban Gu 班固 (32–92)
binzhu 賓主; J: *hinshu*
Bizen 備前
bun 文
bungaku hihyō 文学批評
bungi 文義
bunsei 文勢
bunshō 文章
Bunshō kihan hyōrin chūshaku 文章軌範評林注釈 (1791)
Bunshō musō 文章無双
chengshi 程式; J: *teishiki*
chōhon 張本
chūhō 注法
Chunqiu 春秋 J: *Shunjū*
chūshaku 注釈
chuxue shifa 初学示法; J: *shogaku shihō*
Dai Nihonshi 大日本史 (late 17th century)
Daigo, Emperor 醍醐天皇 (897–930)
dajō tennō 太上天皇
dianjing 点睛; J: *tensei*
duncuo 頓挫; J: *tonza*
Emura Hokkai 江村北海 (1713–1788)
fadu 法度; J: *hatto*

fuan 伏案; J: *fukuan*
Fujiwara Koreyuki 藤原伊行 (fl. 1158–1180)
fūki onjun 富貴温潤
fukuan 伏案
Fūryū Genji monogatari 風流源氏物語 (1703)
fūyu 諷喩 allegory
gakumon 学問
Genchū shūi 源注拾遺 (1696)
Genchū yōteki 源注余滴 (1818)
Genji gaiden 源氏外伝 (ca. 1673)
Genji monogatari 源氏物語 (ca. 1010)
Genji monogatari chūshakushi 源氏物語注釈史
Genji monogatari goshaku 源氏物語語釈
Genji monogatari hyōshaku 源氏物語評釈 (1854–1861)
Genji monogatari tama no ogushi 源氏物語玉の小櫛 (1796)
Genji shaku 源氏釈 (late 12 c.)
gesaku 戯作
Gosenshū 後撰集 (ca. 955)
gūgen 寓言
Hagiwara Hiromichi 萩原広道 (1815–63)
Hakkenden 八犬傳 (1835)
Hanshu 漢書; J: *Kansho*
Han Yu 韓愈 (768–824)
hikaru Genji *no kimi* 光る源氏の君
hikaru kimi 光る君
hikiuta 引歌
Hiraga Motoyoshi 平賀元義(1800–1865)
hisetsu 秘説
hō 法
honbun 本文
honbun yaku · chū hanrei 本文訳注凡例
Hongaku taigai 本学大概
hon'i 本意
Hosokawa Yūsai 細川幽斎 (1534–1610)
hōsoku 法則
huqubu jieguo 戯曲部結構; J: *gikyoku kekkō*
Hyakunin isshu 百人一首 (ca. 1235–1241)
Hyakunin isshu shinshō 百人一首新抄 (1804)
hyō 評
hyōten 評点
ichibu daiji 一部大事
inga 因果
inishie no michi 古への道
Itō Tōgai 伊藤東涯 (1670–1736)
jianjia 間架; J: *kankaku*

jiegou 結構; J: *kekkō*
jiexue 結穴; J: *kekketsu*
Jimmu, Emperor 神武天皇 (660)–585 B.C.
jinjie 筋節; J: *kinsetsu*
Jin Shengtan 金聖歎 J: Kin Seitan (1608–1661)
joshi 助詞
juandian 圏点 J: *kenten*
Jugyōhen 授業編 (1781)
kagaku 歌学
kagayaku Fujitsubo no miya 輝く藤壺の宮
Kaikan kyōki kyōkaku den 開巻驚奇侠客伝 (1832–1835)
Kaitokudō 懐徳堂
Kakaishō, 河海抄 (1364)
kamigata 上方
kanbun 漢文
kan'in 姦淫
Kan-Ryū-Ou-Sō 韓柳欧蘇
kanshi 漢詩
kanzen chōaku 勧善懲悪
kaozhengxuepai 考證学派; J: *kōshōgakuha*
Keichū 契沖 (1640–1701)
kimyaku 気脈
Ki no Tsurayuki 紀貫之 (868?–945?)
Kin Seitan 金聖歎 (1608–1661)
kiri 段
kisha no go 記者の語
kochū 古注
kogaku 古学
Kogetsushō 湖月抄 (1673)
Kokinshū 古今集 (ca. 905)
kokoro naki hito 心なき人
kokoroshirai 用意
kokugaku 国学
kōshōgaku 考證学
kotoba 句
kudari 章
Kūkai 空海 (774–835)
Kyokutei Bakin 曲亭馬琴 (1767–1848)
kyūchū 旧注
lailong 来龍; J: *rairyū*
Liu Zong-yuan 柳宗元 (773–819)
Li Yu 李漁 (Li Li-weng 李笠翁); J: Ri Ryūō (1611–1680)
Lu Zhonglian 魯仲連 J: Ro Chūren (3rd century B.C.)
maki 巻
meimu 眉目; J: *bimoku*

Minamoto no Takaakira 源高明 (914–982)
Miyako no Nishiki 都の錦 (d. 1726)
mono no aware もののあはれ
mono no magire 物のまぎれ
moto no uta 本歌
Motoori Norinaga 本居宣長 (1730–1801)
mukui 報
narabi 並
Nihongi 日本記 (720)
ninjō 人情
nori 法則
norito 祝詞
ōdan 大段
Ogata Kōan 緒方洪庵 (1810–1863)
Okuiri 奥入 (ca. 1227)
ōmune 大むね
Ou Yang-xiu 欧陽脩 (1007–1070)
Ozawa Roan 小沢蘆庵 (1723–1801)
pingdian 評点 J: *hyōten*
polan 波瀾; J: *haran*
qifu 起伏; J: *kifuku*
Saga, Emperor 嵯峨天皇 (786–842)
Sagoromo monogatari 狭衣物語 (ca. 1070)
saibara 催馬楽
saigoku 西国
saitoku kenbi no kenpu nari 才徳兼備の賢婦なり
San'yōdō meisho 山陽道名所 (1850)
Seijū on'yakujiron 西戎音訳字論 (1845)
senmyōgaki 宣命書き
setchū gakuha 折衷学派
shi 氏
Shibun yōryō 紫文要領 (1763)
Shiji 史記; J: *Shiki*
Shijing 詩経; J: *Shikyō*
Shikashichiron 紫家七論 (1703)
Shiki-Sō-Kan-Ryū-Ou-Sō 史記荘韓柳欧蘇
shinchū 新注
shin'i 新意
Shinsen shōjiroku 新選姓氏録 (814)
shō 章
shōdan 小段
Shōsetsu shinzui 小説神髄 (1885–1886)
Shuihu zhuan 水滸傳; J: *Suikōden* (ca. 1644)
shukaku 主閣
Sima Qian 司馬遷 (b. 145 B.C.)

sōkō 総考
soku 則
sōron 総論
sōshiji 草子地
Sumiregusa 菫草 (1812)
Su Shi 蘇軾 (1037–1101)
Suematsu Kenchō 末松謙澄 (1855–1920)
Suzuki Kōrai 鈴木高鞆 (1812–1860)
tai 体
Tama arare 玉あられ (1792)
Tekijuku 適塾
Te-ni-o-ha keijiben てにを波係辞辨
Te-ni-wo-ha ryakuzukai てにをは略図解
Tianhao 添毫; J: *tengō*
tōgoku 東国
Tokugawa Mitsukuni 徳川光圀 (1628–1700)
Tominaga Nakamoto 富永仲基 (1715–1746)
tonza 頓挫
Tōsei shosei katagi 当世書生気質 (1885–86)
tōsho hyōshaku hanrei 頭書評釈凡例
Tsubouchi Shōyō 坪内逍遥 (1859–1935)
utsushikotoba 訳語
utsutsu 現
waka 和歌
Wenshitongyi 文史通義
Wenzhuang guifan 文章軌範; J: *Bunshō kihan* (12th century)
wuhu 嗚呼
Xianqing ouji 閑情偶寄; J: *Kanjō gūki* (1671)
Xie Fang-de 謝枋得 (1226–1289)
yiyang 抑揚; J: *yokuyō*
yōi 用意
yomihon 読本
Yotsutsuji Yoshinari 四辻義成 (1326–1402)
Yuan 源; J: *Minamoto*
Zhang Xue-cheng 章学誠 (1738–1801)
zhang-fa 章法; J: *shōhō*
zhaoying 照応; J: *shōō*
Zhuang Zi 荘子 (4th century B.C.)
zhuanhuan 転換; J: *tenkan*
zhunao 主脳; J: *shunō*

Appendix II

LIST OF MAJOR COMMENTARIES ON *GENJI*

The following is a translation of the introduction and list of major commentaries on *Genji* appended to the "General Remarks" in Hiromichi's *Appraisal of Genji*. This translation serves as a useful summary of premodern *Genji* commentaries and also illustrates Hiromichi's integration of these works into his own interpretation of *Genji*.

Remarks, whether from old or new commentaries, are indicated by their abbreviated titles printed inside small squares. My own remarks are indicated by the characters "*hyō*" or "*shaku*" printed inside small circles. The *hyō* remarks indicate interpretation of the text where it is noteworthy in some way. The *shaku* remarks explain parts of the text that are difficult to understand. Therefore, this commentary is called the *Hyōshaku*.

A list of the abbreviations that I use to denote titles of previous commentaries follows. Please refer to this list to find the complete title of the commentary.[1]

OLD COMMENTARIES (*KYŪCHŪ* 旧注)

奥 *Genji okuiri* 源氏奥入 (ca. 1227; 1 fasc.) by Fujiwara Teika.[2]

水 *Suigenshō* 水原抄 (ca. 1240; 54 fasc.) compiled by Minamoto. Mitsuyuki 源光行 and Minamoto Chikayuki 源親行. Holograph of this commentary not extant.

紫 *Shimeishō* 紫明抄 (ca. 1289) compiled by Sojaku 素寂.

1. Hiromichi only provides an abbreviation, a title, and an author in his list. Additional annotation is primarily taken from Ikeda Kikan's *Genji monogatari jiten*, NKBGJ, and *Kokusho sōmokuroku*.

2. This list also includes a minor work that appears to consist of additional material to Teika's *Okuiri*: 奥入の追注加 *Okuiri no tsuichūka*.

最 *Genchū saihishō* 源中最秘抄 (first preface dated 1313; 2 fasc.) attributed to Minamoto Chikayuki 源親行. The title is derived from the fact that it was believed to contain a record of the most secret annotation on the *Genji*.

河 *Kakaishō* 河海抄 (1364) by Minamoto no Yoshinari.

花 *Kachō yōjō* 花鳥余情 (1472) by Ichijō Kaneyoshi (1402–1481), poet, composer of *renga*, and scholar of Japanese studies (*wagaku*).

秘 *Gengo hiketsu* 源語秘訣 (1477) compiled by Ichijō Kaneyoshi. Contents are not particularly valuable. This work is noteworthy for its compilation of esoteric commentary from the late Muromachi period that had been preserved by certain aristocratic lineages.

和 *Genji wahishō* 源氏和秘抄 (ca. 1449; 1 fasc.) by Ichijō Kaneyoshi.

不 [*Genji*] *fushinshō shutsu* [源氏]不審抄出 (ca. 1490) by Sōgi (d. 1503); *Genji fushinshō* is an alternate title for this work.

衹注 *Hahakigi no betchū* 帚木の別注 (1485) by Sōgi. *Amayo danshō* 雨夜談抄 is an alternate title for this work.

弄 *Rōkashō* 哢花抄 (1476) by Sanjōnishi Sanetaka (d. 1537).

葉 *Ichiyōshō* 一葉抄 (1494) by Fujiwara 藤原正存.

細 *Sairyūshō* 細流抄 (1528) by Sanjōnishi Kin'eda 三条西公条 (1487–1563).

明 *Myōjōshō* 明星抄 (ca. 1539; 20 fasc.) by Sanjōnishi Kin'eda.

孟 *Mōshinshō* 孟津抄 (1575; 20 fasc.) by Kūjō Tanemichi 九条稙通.

岷 *Mingō nisso* 岷江入楚 (1598) by Nakanoin Michikatsu 中院通勝.[3]

巴 *Johashō* 紹巴抄 (1565) by Satomura Jōha 里村紹巴.

万 *Bansui ichiro* 萬水一露 (1575) by 熊登永閑.

湖 *Kogetsushō* 湖月抄 (1673) by Kitamura Kigin.

湖師 *Kogetsushō no shisetsu* 湖月抄の師説.

抄 *Kogetsushō chū no issetsu* 湖月抄中の一説.

NEW COMMENTARIES (*SHINCHŪ* 新注)

拾 *Genchū shūi* 源注拾遺 (1696; 8 vols.) by Keichū.

新 *Genji* (*monogatari*) *shinshaku* 源氏[物語]新釈 (1758) by Kamo no Mabuchi.

3. List includes a minor commentary based on the *Mingō nisso*: *Mingō nisso chū no issetsu* 岷江入楚中の一説.

玉　*Tama no ogushi* 玉の小櫛 (1796) by Motoori Norinaga.

玉補　*Tama no ogushi hoi* 玉の小櫛補遺 (1821) by Suzuki Akira 鈴木朖 (d. 1837).

餘　*Genchū yoteki* 源注余滴 (1818) by Ishikawa Masamochi 石川雅望 (1753–1830), poet and nativist scholar who specialized in the study of *Genji*. This commentary was noted for its correction of errors from the *Kogetsushō*. A reliable source for identifying poetic allusion in *Genji*.

雅集　*Gagen shūran* 雅言集覧 (1826–1849) by Ishikawa Masamochi. *Genji* dictionary in 21 volumes.

雅譯　*Gago yakkai* 雅語訳解 (1821) by Suzuki Akira 鈴木朖. *Genji* dictionary in one volume.

Other commentaries exist, but I do not refer to them often. Others I have not seen and thus do not list here. Two items in the previous list are not commentaries but rather dictionaries. I include them because they explain classical language. For those texts I refer to that are not included in the previous list, I provide the author's name along with the commentary. There are places where I quote from works by Motoori Norinaga where he has quoted other commentaries for which the sources are unknown. I have included the same references as Norinaga did in his *Tama no ogushi*.

From among the previous works listed, I omit quotations from the old commentaries except where there is something important said. I have mainly relied on the new commentaries, *Tama no ogushi* in particular. I have explained my reasons for this practice earlier in the text.

Comments from the *Kakaishō* and *Kachoyōjō* appear as they are in the *Rōkashō* and the *Sairyushō*. However, in the *Kogetsushō*, the later texts are cited, which is a practice criticized in *Tama no ogushi*. I agree with the principle that the earliest citation should be given when possible. However, there are many cases in which the later commentaries improve upon the earlier commentaries, in which case we can ignore which commentary came first and rely upon the text with the most reasonable commentary. Where both the former and the latter commentary are the same, I quote from the former. When the latter commentary is more detailed, one cannot help but refer to it.

In cases where the meaning is clear but the language of the older commentary is confusing, I include my own version under the mark for "*shaku*." However, I do not always explain why I have made the change. This is an unfortunate omission, but it is for the sake of making the main text easy to understand. However, in those cases where I can explain my criticism of previous commentary, I include a detailed explanation in the "Supplementary Annotation" ("*Amari no tokigoto*").

In the case where the same explanation appears in several commentaries, I have relied upon the shorter, easier to understand one, because comments appear as headnotes, and long notes would not be useful.

In cases where a long explanation is necessary, I do not leave this explanation for the "Supplementary Annotation" but rather include the entire explanation in a headnote. And in cases where the explanation concerns another text, a ritual, practice, or item that does not directly affect the meaning of the main text, I include an explanation in the "Supplementary Annotation."

For words where I include a colloquial explanation to the side of the main text, I do not refer to this explanation in the headnotes but rather explain it in the "Supplementary Annotation." I include notes from previous commentaries with my own thoughts where they add to the explanation.

For long explanations, I take the essence and include it in the headnotes from both old and new commentaries. The remaining explanations can be found in the "Supplementary Annotation."

BIBLIOGRAPHY

ABBREVIATIONS

GMH: See Muromatsu Iwao, ed., *Genji monogatari hyōshaku*.
KMZS: See Akiyama Ken, ed., *Kamo no Mabuchi zenshū*.
MNZS: See Ōno Susumu, ed., *Motoori Norinaga zenshū*.
Shikashichiron: See Taira Shigemichi and Abe Akio, eds., *Shikashichiron*.
NKBDJ: See Iwanami Shoten, *Nihon koten bungaku daijiten*.
NKBZS: See Abe Akio, et al., eds., *Nihon koten bungaku zenshū*.
SNKBT: See Yanai Shigeshi, et al., eds., *Shin Nihon koten bungaku taikei*.

Abe Akio, et al. "Genji monogatari." 4 vols. *Shinpen Nihon koten bungaku zenshū*. Vols. 20–23. Tokyo: Shōgakkan, 1994–1996.

Abe Akio, et al. "Genji monogatari." 6 vols. *Nihon koten bungaku zenshū*. Vols. 12–17. Tokyo: Shōgakkan, 1970–1976.

Abe Toshiko. "*Shukuse to mono no ke*." *Kokubungaku: Kaishaku to kanshō* 45:5 (1980): 5–15.

Akimoto Anmin. *Ise no hamaogi* manuscript from Osaka Municipal University Library, Mori Collection, 1854. Microfilm of manuscript from Kokubungaku kenkyū shiryōkan.

Akiyama Ken, et al. *Genji Monogatari handobukku*. Tokyo: Shinshokan, 1996.

Akiyama Ken. *Genji Monogatari jiten. Bessatsu Kokubungaku*. Tokyo: Gakutōsha, 1989.

Akiyama Ken, et al., eds. *Hihyō shūsei Genji monogatari*. Tokyo: Yumani Shobō, 1999.

Akiyama Ken, Kimura Masanari, and Shimizu Yoshiko, eds. *Kōza Genji monogatari no sekai*. 9 vols. Tokyo: Yūhikaku, 1980–1984.

Akiyama Ken, ed. *Kamo no Mabuchi zenshū*. Vol. 13. Tokyo: Zokugun Shorui Shōkansei, 1979.

Anderson, Benedict. *Imagined Communities: Reflections on the Origin and Spread of Nationalism*. London: Verso, 1983.

Anderson, Joseph L., and Donald Richie. *The Japanese Film: Art and Industry*. Princeton, N.J.: Princeton University Press, 1982.

Asō Isoji. *Edo bungaku to Chūgoku bungaku*. Tokyo: Sanseidō, 1957.

Bal, Mieke. *Narratology: Introduction to the Theory of Narrative* (*De theorie van vertellen en verhalen*). Translated by Christine van Boheemen. Toronto: University of Toronto Press, 1985.

Banfield, Ann. "Narrative Style and the Grammar of Direct and Indirect Speech." *Foundations of Language* 10 (1973): 1–39.

Bargen, Doris. *A Woman's Weapon: Spirit Possession in The Tale of Genji*. Honolulu: University of Hawaii Press, 1997.

Barthes, Roland. *Image, Music, Text*. Translated by Stephen Heath. New York: Hill and Wang, 1977.

Bell, David Avrom. *The Cult of the Nation in France: Inventing Nationalism, 1680–1800*. Cambridge, MA: Harvard University Press, 2001.

Benjamin, Walter. *Illuminations* (*Illuminationen*). Translated by Harry Zohn. New York: Harcourt Brace & World, 1968.

Bowring, Richard. *Murasaki Shikibu: The Tale of Genji* (Landmarks of World Literature series). Cambridge: Cambridge University Press, 1988.

Brower, Robert H., and Earl Miner. *Japanese Court Poetry*. Stanford, CA: Stanford University Press, 1961.

Brownstein, Michael C. "From Kokugaku to Kokubungaku: Canon Formation in the Meiji Period." *Harvard Journal of Asiatic Studies* 47:2 (1987): 435–60.

Burns, Susan L. *Before the Nation: Kokugaku and the Imagining of Community in Early Modern Japan, Asia–Pacific*. Durham, NC: Duke University Press, 2003.

Caddeau, Patrick. "Hagiwara Hiromichi's *Genji Monogatari Hyōshaku*: Criticism and Commentary on the *Tale of Genji*." Ph.D. dissertation, Yale University, 1998.

Caddeau, Patrick. "Hagiwara Hiromichi's Theory of the Principles of Composition and Its Application to *The Tale of Genji*, including an Index of Critical Terms" (*Hagiwara Hiromichi no bunshō hōsoku ron to sono Genji monogatari e no tekiyō: tsuki hōsoku no sakuin*), *Shirin* (Osaka Daigaku, Kokubungakubu) 21:4 (1997): 48–63.

Chatman, Seymour. "Characters and Narrators: Filter, Center, Slant, and Interest–Focus." *Poetics Today* 7:2 (1986): 189–204.

Clarke, Simon. *The Foundations of Structuralism: A Critique of Lévi–Strauss and the Structuralist Movement*. Sussex, England: The Harvester Press, 1981.

Clayton, Jay, and Eric Rothstein, eds. *Influence and Intertextuality in Literary History*. Madison: University of Wisconsin Press, 1991.

Cohn, Dorrit. "Narrated Monologue: Definition of a Fictional Style." *Comparative Literature* 18:2 (Spring 1966): 97–112.

Connor, Walker. *Ethnonationalism: The Quest for Understanding*. Princeton, NJ: Princeton University Press, 1994.

Copeland, Rita. *Rhetoric, Hermeneutics, and Translation in the Middle Ages: Academic Traditions and Vernacular Texts*. New York: Cambridge University Press, 1991.

Culler, Jonathan. "Fabula and Sjuzhet in the Analysis of Narrative." *Poetics Today* 1:3 (1980): 27–37.

Doak, Kevin M. "What Is a Nation and Who Belongs? National Narratives and the Ethnic Imagination in Twentieth-Century Japan." *The American Historical Review*, Vol. 102, no. 2. (April, 1997): 283–309.

Dolezel, Lubomír. "Mimesis and Possible Worlds." *Poetics Today* 9:3 (1988): 475–95.

Elman, Benjamin A. *From Philosophy to Philology: Intellectual and Social Aspects of Change in Late Imperial China*. Cambridge, MA: Harvard University Press, 1984.

Emura Hokkai. *Jugyōhen* (Preface dated 1781). *Nihon kyōiku bunko: Gakkōhen*. Vol. 8. Tokyo: Dōkubunkan, 1911.

Enomoto Masazumi. *Genji monogatari no sōshiji: Shochū to kenkyū*. Tokyo: Chikuma shoin, 1982.

Field, Norma. *The Splendor of Longing in The Tale of Genji*. Princeton, NJ: Princeton University Press, 1987.

Forster, E. M. *Aspects of the Novel*. New York: Harcourt, Brace and Company, 1954. (First ed., 1927.)

Frye, Northrop. *Anatomy of Criticism: Four Essays by Northrop Frye*. New York: Antheneum, 1970.

Fujii Sadakazu. *Genji monogatari: Iwanami seminā bukkusu*. Vol. 110. Tokyo: Iwanami Shoten, 1993.

Fujii Manabu. *Okayama-ken no rekishi*. Tokyo: Yamakawa Shuppansha, 2000.

Fujioka Tadaharu, et al. *Fukurozōshi: Shin Nihon koten bungaku taikei*. Vol. 29. Tokyo: Iwanami shoten, 1995.

Fujioka Tadaharu, et al. *Izumi Shikibu nikki, Murasaki Shikibu nikki, Sarashina nikki, Sanuki nosuke nikki. Shinpen Nihon koten bungaku zenshū*. Vol. 26. Tokyo: Shōgakkan, 1994.

Fujita Masayuki. *Eiga no naka no nihonshi*. Shohan. ed. Tokyo: Chirekisha, 1997.

Fujita Tokutarō. *Genji monogatari kenkyū shomoku yōran*. Tokyo: Rikubunkan, 1932.

Fujita Tokutarō. *Kokubungaku no sekai*. Kyoto: Jinbun Shoin, 1939.

Fukuda K. *Enshoku Genjie*. Tokyo, KK Besuto Seriazu, 1991.

Fukumoto Kazuo. *Nihon no runessansu shiron: 1661 nen yori 1850 nen ni itaru Nihon runessansu no hikaku*. Tokyo: Hōsei Daigaku Shuppankyoku, 1985.

Gatten, Aileen. "The Order of the Early Chapters in the *Genji monogatari*." *Harvard Journal of Asiatic Studies* 41:1 (1981): 5–46.

Genette, Gérard. *Narrative Discourse: An Essay in Method* (*Discours du récit*). Translated by Jane E. Lewin. Ithaca, NY: Cornell University Press, 1980.

Genette, Gérard. *Narrative Discourse Revisited* (*Nouveau discours du récit*). Translated by Jane E. Lewin. Ithaca, NY: Cornell University Press, 1983.

Genji monogatari kenkyūkai. *Genji monogatari no tankyū*. Vol. 15. Tokyo: Kazama shobō, 1990.

Gerstle, C. Andrew, ed. *Eighteenth-Century Japan: Culture and Society*. Sydney: Allen & Unwin, 1989.

Goff, Janet Emily. *Noh Drama and* The Tale of *Genji*: *The Art of Allusion in Fifteen Classical Plays, Princeton Library of Asian Translations*. Princeton, N.J.: Princeton University Press, 1991.

Hagino Yoshiyuki, et al. *Genji monogatari, Nihon bungaku zensho*. Tokyo: Hakubunkan, 1890.

Hagiwara Hiromichi. *Ashi no ha wake* (Collection of Comic Prose). Manuscript for publication, preface dated 1863. Manuscript from the collection of the Naka no Shima Osaka Prefectural Library.

Hagiwara Hiromichi. *Genji monogatari hyōshaku: kōsei yakuchū*. 13 vols. Osaka: Maekawa Zenbē. 1861. Woodblock print in calligraphy format (*hampon*). Contains prefaces not included in later moveable type (*katsuji*) reprints. See edition edited by Muromatsu Iwao for most references in this book.

Hagiwara Hiromichi. *Honkyō tei* (Presentation of the Main Teachings). Preface by Akimoto Anmin, dated 1846. Manuscript from the collection of the Naka no Shima Osaka Prefectural Library. The title of the work was changed to *Hongaku taigai* and appears as such in the *Kokusho sōmokuroku*.

Hagiwara Hiromichi. *Kogen yakkai* (Dictionary of Terms from Classical Texts). Preface dated 1848. Manuscript from the collection of the Naka no Shima Osaka Prefectural Library.

Hagiwara Hiromichi. *Kogen yakkai*. Osaka: Goshodō, 1851.

Hagiwara Hiromichi. *San'yōdō meisho* (*Guide to the San'yō Region*, ca. 1848). Manuscript from the collection of the National Diet Library. Copy of manuscript courtesy of Mr. Yamazaki Katsuaki.

Hagiwara Hiromichi. *Seijū on'yakujiron* (Essay on the Transliteration of Western Weaponry Texts). Opening paragraph by Hiromichi, dated 1845. Manuscript from the collection of the library of the department of the faculty of letters, Kyoto University.

Hagiwara Hiromichi. *Tamazasa* (Collection of Miscellaneous Writings). Preface dated 1844 from the collection of the Naka no Shima Osaka Prefectural Library. Hiromichi gives his name as Taira Hiromichi in this manuscript.

Hagiwara Hiromichi. *Te–ni–o–ha keijiben* (A Discourse on Grammar). Preface dated 1846. Manuscript from the collection of the Naka no Shima Osaka Prefectural Library.

Hagiwara Hiromichi. *Te–ni–o–ha keijiben* (1846). Photographic reprint. Tokyo: Bensei Sha, 1981.

Hall, John W., ed. *Cambridge History of Japan: Volume 4, Early Modern Japan (1550–1800)*. Cambridge: Cambridge University Press, 1991.

Hamada Keisuke. "*Bakin no iwayuru haishi shichi hōsoku ni tsuite*." *Kokugo kokubun* 28:8 (1959): 31–43.

Harootunian, H. D. *Things Seen and Unseen: Discourse and Ideology in Tokugawa Nativism*. Chicago: University of Chicago Press, 1988.

Harper, Thomas J. "Motoori Norinaga's Criticism of the 'Genji Monogatari': A Study of the Background and Critical Content of His *Genji Monogatari Tama no Ogushi*." Ph.D. dissertation, University of Michigan, 1971.

Harper, Thomas J. "The Tale of Genji in the Eighteenth-Century: Keichū, Mabuchi and Norinaga." In *Eighteenth Century Japan: Culture and Society*, ed. C. Andrew Gerstle, 106–28. Sydney: Allen & Unwin, 1989.

Hayashi Tsutomu. "*Mabuchi no Genji monogatari kenkyū*." In *Genji monogatari kōza*, Vol. 8 (*Genji monogatari no honbun to juyō*), ed. Imai Takuji et al., 209–29. Tokyo: Benseisha, 1992.

Hayashida Takakazu. *Genji monogatari jiten*. Tokyo: Daiwa Shobō, 2002.

Hisamatsu Sen'ichi, ed. *Genchūshūi Keichū zenshū*. Vol. 9. Tokyo: Iwanami shoten, 1974.

Hobsbawm, E. J., and T. O. Ranger. *The Invention of Tradition*. Canto ed. Cambridge and New York: Cambridge University Press, 1992.

Huang, Chin-shing. *Philosophy, Philology, and Politics in Eighteenth-Century China: Li Fu and Lu-Wang School under the Ch'ing*. Cambridge: Cambridge University Press, 1995.

Huters, Theodore. "From Writing to Literature: The Development of Late Qing Theories of Prose." *Harvard Journal of Asiatic Studies* 47:1 (June 1987): 51–96.

Ichinichi kai, ed. *Hagiwara Hiromichi shokan*. Osaka: Nakao Shosendō. 2000.

Ii Haruki. *Genji monogatari ronkō*. Tokyo: Kazama shobō. 1981.

Ii Haruki, ed. *Kachōyosei*. Vol. 1. Tokyo: Ōfūsha, 1973.

Ii Haruki, ed. *Sairyūshō*. Comp. Sanjōnishi Kin'eda (1528). *Genji monogatari kochūshūsei*. Vol. 7. Tokyo: Ōfūsha, 1975.

Ii Haruki. *Genji monogatari chūshakusho kyōjushi jiten*. Tokyo: Tōkyōdō Shuppan, 2001.

Ikeda Kikan. *Genji monogatari jiten*. 3rd ed. 2 vols. Tokyo: Tōkyōdō Shuppan, 1965.

Imai Takuji. "Genji monogatari hihyōshi." In *Genji monogatari kōza*. Vol. 8 (*Genji monogatari no honbun to juyō*), ed. Imai Takuji et al., 255–65. Tokyo: Benseisha, 1992.

Inoguchi Takashi. *Keichūgaku no keisei*. Tokyo: Izumi shoin, 1996.

Inokuma Natsuki, ed. *Zōchū (teisei) Genji Monogatari Kogetsushō*: Kitamura Kigin shō. 3 Vols. Osaka: Kōbunsha, 1927. (Reprint of 1891 edition.)

Irokawa, Daikichi. *The Culture of the Meiji Period*. Princeton, NJ: Princeton University Press, 1985.

Itasaka Noriko. "*Haishi shichi hōsoku' no happyō o megutte*." *Kokugo to kokubungaku* 55:11 (November 1978 special edition): 77–93.

Ito, Setsuko. *An Anthology of Traditional Japanese Poetry Competitions: Uta-Awase (913–1815)*. Chinathemen; Bd. 57. Bochum: Brockmeyer, 1991.

Iwanami Shoten. *Kokusho sōmokuroku*. Tokyo: Iwanami Shoten, 1963.

Iwanami Shoten. *Nihon koten bungaku daijiten*. Kan'yakuban. ed. Tokyo: Iwanami Shoten, 1986.

James, Henry. *The Art of the Novel: Critical Prefaces with an Introduction by R. P. Blackmur*. New York: Charles Scribner's Sons, 1934.

James, Henry. *Selected Criticism of Henry James*. New York: McGraw-Hill, 1965.

Kagawa Kageki, Toshikinu Ōtsubo, and Yasutaka Okamoto. *Hyakushu iken*; *Hyakushu Yōkai, Hyakunin isshu chūshakusho sōkan*; 19. Osaka: Izumi Shoin, 1999.

Kamei Hideo. *Shōsetsuron: shōsetsu shinzui to kindai*. Tokyo: Iwanami Shoten, 1999.

Kamens, Edward, ed. *Approaches to Teaching Murasaki Shikibu's The Tale of Genji*. New York: Modern Language Association of America, 1993.

Katō Shūichi. *A History of Japanese Literature: The Years of Isolation*. Translated by Don Sanderson. New York: Kodansha International, 1983.

Katō Shūichi. "Tominaga Nakamoto: A Tokugawa Iconoclast." *Monumenta Nipponica* 22 (1967): 1–2.

Keene, Donald. *World within Walls: Japanese Literature of the Pre-Modern Era, 1600–1867*. New York: Holt Rinehart and Winston, 1976.

Kobayashi Hideo. *Motoori Norinaga*. 2 vols. Tokyo: Shinchōsha, 1977.

Kōda Rohan. *Rohan zenshū*. 44 vols. Tokyo: Iwanami Shoten, 1978.

Kōdansha. *Kodansha Encyclopedia of Japan*. 1st ed. Tokyo; New York, N.Y.: Kodansha, 1983.

Kokumin Shinbunsha. *Kokumin shinbun*. Tokyo: Kokumin Shinbunsha, 1890–1929.

Konishi Jin'ichi. *Shinkō roppyakuban utaawase*. Tokyo: Yūseidō Shuppan, 1976.

Kudō Shinjirō. *Fujii Takanao to Matsuya-ha*. Tokyo: Kazama Shobō, 1986.

Kumakura, Chiyuki. "The Narrative Time of Genji monogatari." Ph.D. in Oriental Languages, U.C. Berkeley, 1980.

Kuwayama Ryūhei. "Hagiwara Hiromichi to *Kyōkakuden* no hon'yaku" (Hagiwara Hiromichi and His Translation of *Kyōkakuden*, a famous Chinese Novel of the Ch'ing Dynasty). *Biblia: Bulletin of the Tenri Central Library* 69 (June 1978): 22–31.

Kyūko Shoin. *Genji monogatari to Kanbungaku/Wa–Kan hikaku bungakkai hen*. Tokyo: Kyūko Shoin, 1993.

Lanser, Susan Sniader. *The Narrative Act: Point of View in Prose Fiction*. Princeton, NJ: Princeton University Press, 1981.

Lentricchia, Frank, and Thomas McLauglin, eds. *Critical Terms for Literary Study*. Chicago: University of Chicago Press, 1990.

Leutner, Robert W. *Shikitei Sanba and the Comic Tradition in Edo Fiction*. Cambridge, MA: Harvard University Press, 1985.

Liu, James J. Y. *Chinese Theories of Literature*. Chicago: University of Chicago Press, 1975.

Lodge, David. *Consciousness & the Novel: Connected Essays*. Cambridge, MA: Harvard University Press, 2002.

Maclean, Marie. *Narrative as Performance: The Baudelairean Experiment*. London: Routledge, 1988.

Mao, Nathan, and Liu Ts'un-yan. *Li Yü*. Boston: Twayne, 1977.

Mao Tsung–kang, ed. *Ch'üan–t'u shiu–hsiang San–kuo yen–i* (fully illustrated *San–kuo yen–i*: typeset reprint of 1679 edition). Huhehot: Nei–meng–ku jen–min, 1981.

Marceau, Lawrence. "The Emperor's Old Clothes: Classical Narratives in Early Modern Japan." *Proceedings of the Midwest Association for Japanese Literary Studies* 3 (1997): 182–203.

Masamune Atsuo. "Hagiwara Hiromichi rireki." *Bungaku* 3:9 (1935): 95–101.

Matsumoto Shigeru. *Motoori Norinaga: 1730–1801*. Cambridge, MA: Harvard University Press, 1970.

Matsumura Hiroji, et al. *Eiga monogatari: Nihon koten bungaku taikei*. Vol. 75. Tokyo: Iwanami shoten, 1964.

McClain, James L., and Osamu Wakita. *Osaka, the Merchant's Capital of Early Modern Japan*. Ithaca, N.Y.: Cornell University Press, 1999.

McMullen, James. *Genji Gaiden: The Origins of Kumazawa Banzan's Commentary on The Tale of Genji*. Oxford Oriental Institute Monographs; 13, Reading, England: Ithaca Press, 1991.

McNally, Mark. "Phantom History: Hirata Atsutane and Tokugawa Nativism." Ph.D. dissertation, University of California Los Angeles, 1998.

Mehl, Margaret. "Scholarship and Ideology in Conflict: The Kume Affair, 1892." *Monumenta Nipponica*, 48:3 (Autumn, 1993) 337–357.

Minamoto Ryōen, ed. *Edo kōki no hikaku bunka kenkyū*. Tokyo: Perikan sha, 1990.

Miner, Earl, ed. *Principles of Classical Japanese Literature*. Princeton, NJ: Princeton University Press, 1985.

Minnis, A. J., and A. B. Scott, eds. *Medieval Literary Theory and Criticism, c. 1100–1375: The Commentary Tradition*. New York: Oxford University Press, 1988.

Mizuno Kōgen, and Hajime Nakamura. *Butten kaidai jiten*. Dai 2-han. ed. Tokyo: Shunjūsha, 1977.

Mizuno Minoru. *Edo shōsetsu ronso*. Tokyo: Chuo Koron Sha, 1974.

Mori Ōgai. *Mori Ōgai zenshū*. 8 Vols. Tokyo: Chikumashobō, 1959.

Mori Ōgai, ed. *Shigarami–zōshi: bungaku hyōron*. Tokyo: Shinseisha, 1889–94.

Morikawa Akira. "*Genji monogatari hyōshaku no shuppan*." *Konton* 5 (1978): 33–39.

Morikawa Akira. "Hagiwara Hiromichi *no jijōden*." *Konton* 8 (1982): 11–23.

Morikawa Akira. "Hagiwara Hiromichi *no jōhan*." *Konton* 6 (1980): 38–43.

Morikawa Akira. "Hagiwara Hiromichi *shokan*." *Konton* 3 (1976): 32–34; 4 (1978): 18–24.

Morikawa Akira. "'Hagiwara Hiromichi *shosoku*' *ni tsuite*." *Konton* 12 (1988): 17–20.

Morikawa Akira. "*Honkyō teikō: Sono shoshi*." *Konton* 10 (1986): 59–71.

Morita, James. "*Shigarami–zōshi*." *Monumenta Nipponica* 29 (1969): 47–59.

Morohashi Tetsuji. *Taishūkan shin Kan-Wa jiten*. Kaitei dai 2-han. ed. Tokyo: Taishūkan Shoten, 1988.

Mostow, Joshua S. *Pictures of the Heart: The Hyakunin Isshu in Word and Image*. Honolulu: University of Hawaii Press, 1996.

Muneyuki Shūzo. "Hagiwara Hiromichi *no Genji monogatari tekusutoron*." In *Shin Monogatari–kenkyū 2: Monogatari–sono tensei to saisei*, ed. Abe Yoshitomi et al. 175–86. Tokyo: Yūseidō, 1994.

Muromatsu Iwao. *Genji monogatari hyōshaku*: Hagiwara Hiromichi chō (Reproduction of *Kokubun chūshaku zensho* edition [1909] *Nihon bungaku kochūshaku taisei*). Vol. 4. Tokyo: Nihon Tosho Sentâ, 1978.

Najita Tetsuo. *Visions of Virtue in Tokugawa Japan*. Chicago: University of Chicago Press, 1987.

Najita Tetsuo, and Irwin Scheiner, eds. *Japanese Thought in the Tokugawa Period, 1600–1868: Methods and Metaphors*. Chicago: University of Chicago Press, 1978.

Nakamura, Mitsuo. *Japanese Fiction in the Meiji Era, Series on Japanese Life and Culture*; Vol. 13. Tokyo: Kokusai Bunka Shinkokai, 1966.

Nakano Kōichi. "*Genji monogatari no sōshiji to monogatari ondokuron*." Genji Monogatari: *Nihon Bungaku Kenkyū Shiryō Sōsho*. Vol. 1. Tokyo: Yūseidō, 1971.

Niehoff, M. "Do Biblical Characters Talk to Themselves? Narrative Modes of Representing Inner Speech in Early Biblical Fiction." *Journal of Biblical Literature* 111:4 (1992): 577–95.

Nihon Daijiten Kankōkai. *Nihon kokugo daijiten*. Dai 1-han. ed. Tokyo: Shōgakkan, 1972.

Nishiyama Matsunosuke. *Edo Culture: Daily Life and Diversions in Urban Japan, 1600–1868*. Translated and edited by Gerald Groemer. Honolulu: University of Hawaii Press, 1997.

Nishiyama Matsunosuke, ed. *Edo chōnin no kenkyū*. Tokyo: Yoshikawa Kōbunkan, 1974.

Noguchi Motohiro. *Kodai monogatari no kōzō*. Tokyo: Yūseidō, 1969.

Noguchi Takehiko. *Genji monogatari o Edo kara yomu*. Tokyo: Kōdansha, 1985.

Noguchi Takehiko. "Hagiwara Hiromichi '*Genji monogatari hyōshaku*' no bungaku hihyō." In *Kōza Genji monogatari no sekai*. Akiyama Ken, et al. 7: 321–22. Tokyo: Yūhikaku, 1980.

Noguchi Takehiko. "The Substratum Constituting Monogatari: Prose Structure and Narrative in Genji Monogatari." Translated by Bob Tadashi Wakabayashi, In *Principles of Classical Japanese Literature*, ed. Earl Miner. 130–50. Princeton, NJ: Princeton University Press, 1985.

Nosco, P. *Confucianism and Tokugawa Culture*. Princeton, NJ, Princeton University Press, 1984.

Nosco, Peter. *Remembering Paradise: Nativism and Nostalgia in Eighteenth-Century Japan*. Cambridge, MA: Harvard University Press, 1990.

Oka Kazuo. *Genji monogatari jiten*. Tokyo: Shunjūsha, 1964.

Oka Masahiko, et al. *Edo Printed Books at Berkeley*. Berkeley: East Asiatic Library, University of California Press, 1990.

Okada, H. Richard. *Figures of Resistance: Language, Poetry and Narrating in The Tale of Genji and Other Mid–Heian Texts*. Durham, NC: Duke University Press, 1991.

Okawa Shigeo, et al., eds. *Kokugakusha denki shūsei*. 3 vols. Tokyo: Kunimoto Shuppan Sha, 1934.

Ōno Susumu, ed. *Motoori Norinaga zenshū*. 22 vols. Tokyo: Chikuma Shobō, 1968–1977.

Ooms, Herman. *Tokugawa Ideology*. Princeton, NJ: Princeton University Press, 1985.

Ōura Yasusuke. "*Kōzō bunseki*." *Kokubungaku: kaishaku* 36:7 (June 1991): 58–59.

Pollack, David. *The Fracture of Meaning: Japan's Synthesis of China from the Eighth through the Eighteenth Centuries*. Princeton, NJ: Princeton University Press, 1986.

Preminger, Alex, et al., eds. *The New Princeton Encyclopedia of Poetry and Poetics*. Princeton, NJ: Princeton University Press. 1993.

Prince, Gerald. *Dictionary of Narratology*. Lincoln: University of Nebraska Press, 1987.

Pyle, Kenneth B. *The New Generation in Meiji Japan: Problems of Cultural Identity, 1885–1895*. Stanford, CA: Stanford University Press, 1969.

Ricoeur, Paul. *Time and Narrative* (*Temps et Récit*). Translated by Kathleen McLaughlin and David Pellauer. Chicago: University of Chicago Press, 1984.

Rimmon–Kenan, Shlomith. *Narrative Fiction: Contemporary Poetics*. London: Routledge, 1983.

Robertson, Jennifer Ellen. *Takarazuka: Sexual Politics and Popular Culture in Modern Japan*. Berkeley: University of California Press, 1998.

Rolston, David L. *Traditional Chinese Fiction and Fiction Commentary: Reading and Writing between the Lines*. Stanford, CA: Stanford University Press, 1997.

Rolston, David L., ed. *How to Read the Chinese Novel*. Princeton, NJ: Princeton University Press, 1990.

Ronen, Ruth. "Completing the Incompleteness of Fictional Entities." *Poetics Today* 9:3 (1988): 497–514.

Rowley, G. G.,"Literary Canon and National Identity: *The Tale of Genji* in Meiji Japan." *Japan Forum* 9:1 (1997): 1–15.

Rowley, G. G., "Textual Malfeasance in Yosano Akiko's *Shin'yaku Genji monogatari*." *Harvard Journal of Asiatic Studies* 58:1 (1998): 201–19.

Rowley, G. Gaye. *Yosano Akiko and the Tale of Genji, Michigan Monograph Series in Japanese Studies No. 28*. Ann Arbor, MI: Center for Japanese Studies University of Michigan, 2000.

Sano Masami. *Kokugaku to Rangaku*. Tokyo: Yūzankaku, 1973.

San'yō Shinbunsha. *Okayama-ken rekishi jinbutsu jiten*. Okayama-shi: San'yō Shinbunsha, 1994.

Sasaida Shirō, and Wada Katsushi, eds., *Nihon setsuwa bungaku sakuin*. Osaka: Seibundō, 1976.

Sasaki Nobutsuna. "Hagiwara Hiromichi *no 'mono no aware' setsu*." *Kokugo to Kokubungaku* 16:5 (1939): 1–14.

Seidensticker, Edward G., trans. *The Tale of Genji*. New York: Alfred A. Knopf, 1983.

Shigematsu Nobuhiro. *Genji monogatari kenkyūshi*. Tokyo: Tōei shoin, 1937.

Shirane, Haruo. *The Bridge of Dreams: A Poetics of The Tale of Genji*. Stanford, CA: Stanford University Press, 1987.

Stinchecum, Amanda Mayer. "Narrative Voice in the 'Genji Monogatari'." Ph.D. thesis, Columbia University, 1980.

Stinchecum, Amanda Mayer. "Who Tells the Tale? 'Ukifune': A Study of Narrative Voice." *Monumenta Nipponica* 35:4 (Winter 1980): 375–403.

Suematsu Kenchō, tr. *Genji Monogatari*. Rutland: Charles E. Tuttle, 1974.

Suga Shūji. *Kyō Osaka no bunjin: Bakumatsu Meiji* (Famous Literary Figures of Kyōto and Osaka from the Bakumatsu and Meiji Eras). *Kamigata bunko series*. Vol. 11. Osaka: Izumi shoin, 1991.

Sugawara no Takasue no, Musume. Ivan Morris, tr. *As I Crossed a Bridge of Dreams: Recollections of a Woman in Eleventh-Century Japan*. London, New York: Oxford University Press; Dial Press, 1971.

Suwa Haruo, and Tatsuo Hino. *Edo bungaku to Chūgoku, Edo shirîzu; 4.* Tokyo: Mainichi Shinbunsha, 1977.

Suzuki Hideo. "*Shōwa no Genji monogatari kenkyū.*" *Kokugo to kokubungaku* 67 (May 1990): 64–75.

Taira Shigemichi, and Abe Akio, eds. *Shikashichiron by Andō Tameakira. Kinsei Shinto ron zenki kokugaku. Nihon shisō taikei.* Vol. 39. Tokyo: Iwanami Shoten, 1972.

Takahashi Tōru. *Genji monogatari no taihō.* Tokyo: Tokyo Daigaku Shuppankai, 1982.

Takahashi Tōru. "*Genji monogatari tekisuto no 'bunpō' josetsu.*" *Genji monogatari no tankyū* 12 Kazama shobō, 1987.

Takahashi Tōru, Naoko Kojima, and Yōichi Hijikata. *Monogatari no sennen:* Genji monogatari *to Nihon Bunka.* Shohan. ed. Tokyo: Shinwasha, 1999.

Takayanagi Mitsutoshi, et al. *Kadokawa Nihonshi jiten.* Tokyo: Kadokawa Shoten, 1966.

Takegasa Yoshio. *Genji monogatari shoshi.* Tokyo: Heigensha, 1934.

Takeuchi Michiko. "Genji monogatari *no bunsho: Heian–chō bunshoshi kijutsu no hitotsu no kokoromi.*" *Kokkugo to kokubungaku* 69:11 (1992): 77–86.

Takizawa Bakin, Hiromichi Hagiwara, and Rohan Kōda. *Kaikan kyōki kyōkakuden. 5-Shū: 25-Kan.* Tokyo: Tōadō Shōbō, 1911.

Takizawa Bakin. *Nansō Satomi hakkenden.* Vol. 6. *Iwanami Bunko.* Tokyo: Iwanami Shoten, 1990.

Tamagami Takuya, ed. *Genji monogatari hyōshaku.* 12 vols. Tokyo: Kadokawa shoten, 1964–1968.

Tamagami Takuya, et al., eds. *Shimeishō Kakaishō.* Tokyo: Kadokawa shoten, 1968.

Tanaka, Stefan. *Japan's Orient: Rendering Pasts into History.* Berkeley: University of California Press, 1993.

Todorov, Tzvetan. *The Poetics of Prose* (*La Poétique de la prose*). Translated by Richard Howard. Ithaca, NY: Cornell University Press, 1977.

Tokuda Takeshi. "*Bakin no haishi shichi hōsoku to Mō Seizan no 'Doku "Sankoku shi" hō'.*" *Bungaku* 48:6 (1980): 14–29; 48:7 (1980): 64–76.

Tokumaru Satoko. "*Hakkenden no 'koshikata no hōkoku' o megutte.*" *Kokugo kokubun* 58:8 (1989): 21–37.

Tokumaru Satoko. "*Hakkenden to Heiyōden.*" *Kokugo kokubun* 60:10 (1991): 1–18.

Tokumaru Satoko. "*Hiromichi no Genji monogatari hyōshaku.*" *In Genji monogatari kōza Vol. 8 Genji monogatari no honbun to juyō*, ed. Imai Takuji et al., 242–52. Tokyo: Benseisha, 1992.

Tokumaru Satoko. "*Hiromichi no Genji monogatari ron: Norinaga to Bakin no setten toshite.*" *Kokugokokubun* 56:11 (1987): 1–21.

Tominaga Nakamoto. Michael Pye, trans. *Emerging from Meditation.* Honolulu: University of Hawaii Press, 1990.

Totman, Conrad. *Early Modern Japan*. Berkeley: University of California Press, 1993.

Tsubouchi, Shōyō, and Shōyō Kyōkai. *Shōyō senshū*. Vol. 12 Tokyo: Daiichishobō, 1977.

Tsubouchi Shōyō, and Tatsurō Inagaki. *Tsubouchi Shōyō shū, Meiji bungaku zenshū; 16*. Tokyo: Chikuma Shobō, 1977.

Tsunoda Bunei, et al. *Heian jidai shi jiten*. Tokyo: Kadokawa shoten, 1993.

Tsutsumi Yasuo. "*Genji monogatari chūshakushijō ni okeru 'chūsei' to 'kinsei': Yūgao kaishi jiken wo megutte*." *Kokugo to kokubungaku* 67:1 (1990): 15–28.

Tsutsumi Yasuo. *Genji monogatari chūshakushi no kisoteki kenkyū*. Tokyo: Ōfūsha, 1994.

Tucker, M. E. *Moral and Spiritual Cultivation in Japanese Neo–Confucianism: The Thought of Kaibara Ekken, 1630–1714*. Albany: State University of New York Press, 1989.

Tyler, Royall, trans. *The Tale of Genji*. New York: Viking, 2001.

Tyler, Royall, and Susan Tyler. "The Possession of Ukifune." *Asiatica Venetiana* 5 (2000): 177–209.

Ueno Eiji. "*Genji monogatari no kyōju to honbun*." *Kokugo kokubun* 53:1 (1984): 1–21.

Umesao, Tadao. *Nihongo daijiten*. Dai 2-han. ed. Tokyo: Kōdansha, 1995.

Uno Shun'ichi. *Nihon zenshi = Japan Chronik: Japan Kuronikku*. Tokyo: Kōdansha, 1991.

White, Hayden. "Foucault Decoded: Notes from Underground." *History and Theory* 12:1 (1973): 32–54.

Williams, Linda Ruth. *Critical Desire: Psychoanalysis and the Literary Subject*. New York: St. Martin's Press (London: Edward Arnold), 1995.

Yamaoka Toshiaki, ed. *Ruijū meibutsukō*. Vol. 1. Tokyo: Kondō katsubansho, 1903.

Yamazaki Fusako. "*Genji monogatari hyōshaku no hōhō: Chūgoku bungaku no eikyō to kokugaku*." *Kokugo kokubun* 51:3 (1982): 38–50.

Yamazaki Fusako. "*Kinsei kōki no Genji chūshaku: Amayo monogatari to kyōkaisetsu*." *Kokugo kokubun* 50:6 (1981): 16–37.

Yamazaki Katsuaki. *Ashi*. Vols. 1–9, Osaka: Yunbunsha Co. Ltd, 1996–2003.

Yamazaki Katsuaki. "*Genji monogatari hyōshaku no issokumen*." *Nihon bungaku* 41:2 (1992): 56–67.

Yamazaki Katsuaki. "Hagiwara Hiromichi *no waka*." *Kokubunronsō* 18 (March 1991): 66–78.

Yamazaki Katsuaki. "Hagiwara Hiromichi *ryakunenpukō*." *Kokubunronsō* 17 (March 1990): 66–90.

Yamazaki Katsuaki. "Naoyō to Hiromichi: *Aru bakumatsu kokugakushatachi no kōryū*." *Nihon bungaku* 40:9 (1991): 4–63.

Yamazaki Katsuaki. "Okoreru Ise musha: Hagiwara Hiromichi *joron*." *Dōjinshi "Klaverina"* 5 (September 1989): 76–97.

Yamazaki Katsuaki. "Ōkuni Ryūmasa to Hagiwara Hiromichi: *Hitotsu no tadashigaki*." *Kokubunronsō* 20:3 (1993): 52–66.

Yamazaki Katsuaki. "*Sechi ni omou kokoro*: Hagiwara Hiromichi *no karon*." *Nihon bungaku* 41:12 (1992): 24–34.

Yamazaki Katsuaki. "Hagiwara Hiromichi to *Kyōkakuden* no daigoshū." *Konton* 24 (2000): 6–10.

Yanagida Izumi. *Shōsetsu shinzui kenkyū.* Tokyo: Shunjūsha, 1966.

Yanai Shigeshi, et al., eds. *Shin Nihon koten bungaku taikei.* Tokyo: Iwanami shoten, 1993–97.

Yasunaga, T., and S. Yasunaga. *Ando Shoeki: Social and Ecological Philosopher of Eighteenth-Century Japan.* New York: Weatherhill, 1992.

Yoda Gakkai, and Gakkai Nichiroku Kenkyukai. *Gakkai nichiroku.* Tokyo: Iwanami shoten, 1990.

Yoda, Tomiko. "Fractured Dialogues: Mono no aware and Poetic Communication in The Tale of Genji." *Harvard Journal of Asiatic Studies* 59:2 (December, 1999): 523–557.

Yosano Akiko. *Shin'yaku Genji monogatari.* 4 vols. Tokyo: Kanao Bun'endō, 1912–1913.

Yoshikawa, Kōjirō. *Jinsai, Sorai, Norinaga: Three Classical Philologists of Mid-Tokugawa Japan.* Translated by Yuji Kikuchi. Tokyo: Tōhō Gakkai, 1983.

Zeami. *On the Art of the Nō Drama: The Major Treatises of Zeami.* Translated by J. Thomas Rimer, Yamazaki Masakazu. Princeton, N.J.: Princeton University Press, 1984.

Zolbrod, Leon M. "Tigers, Boars, and Severed Heads: Parallel Series of Episodes in Eight 'Dogs' and Men of the Marshes." *The Chung Chi Journal* 7:1 (November 1967): 30–39.

INDEX